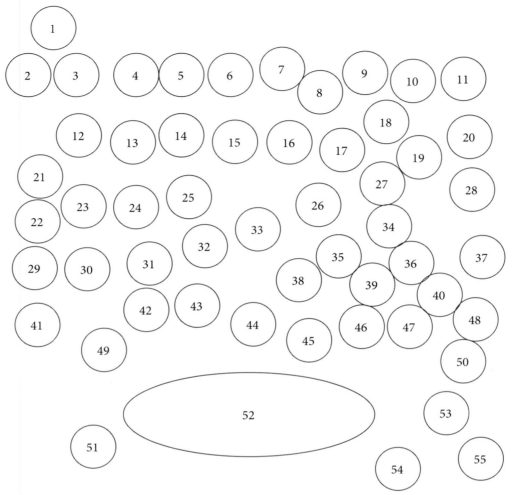

Legendary heads: 1. Indian runner ducks, *Hyden Farm Originals*; 2. Mike Smales, farmer & cheesemaker, *Lyburn Cheese*; 3. Jody Scheckter, farmer & producer, *Laverstoke Park Farm*; 4. Ramon Farthing, head chef & proprietor, *36 on the Quay*; 5. Gary Pearce, chef, *36 on the Quay*; 6. Pierre Chevillard, head chef, *Pebble Beech*; 7. David Wykes, chef & proprietor, *Verveine*; 8. Rob Cox, farm manager, *Dan Tanner's Sopley Farm*; 9. Wellington the sheep, *The Wellington Arms*; 10. Dan Maskell, chef & proprietor, *Dan's Kitchen*; 11. Cocky rooster, *Hyden Farm Originals*; 12. James Golding, executive chef, *The Pig*; 13. George Blogg, chef, *TerraVina**; 14. Gavin Barnes, head chef, *TerraVina*; 15. Luke Holder, head chef, *Lime Wood*; 16. Luke Matthews, executive head chef, *Chewton Glen*; 17. Jason King, chef & proprietor, *The Wellington Arms*; 18. Olly Rouse, head chef, *Lainston House*, an Exclusive Hotel; 19. *Natasha Edwards*, manager & cookery book author, *The Garlic Farm & Restaurant*; 20. Andrew MacKenzie, executive chef, *Exclusive Chefs Academy*; 21. Snuffling Hampshire Hog, New Forest; 22. Richard Jones, farmer, *Hyden Farm Originals*; 23. Alan Bartlett, butcher & sausage maker, *T Bartlett & Sons*; 24. Stuart Ayres, chef, *The Chestnut Horse & The Globe*; 25. Ben Cooke, head chef & owner, *The Little Gloster*; 26. Tanguy Martin, head sommelier, *TerraVina*; 27. Simon Page, proprietor & gardener, *The Wellington Arms*; 28. Andrew Johnson, fisherman & proprietor, *Johnson's Enterprises Ltd*; 29. Neil Reid, butcher, *The Farmer's Butcher at Swallowfields Farm*; 30. Jane Dick, proprietor, *Fundamentally Fungus*; 31. Sue Whiting, proprietor, *Fundamentally Fungus*; 32. Jaye Santiago, head chef, *The Little Gloster*; 33. Colin the very satisfied Jersey bull, *Meadow Cottage Farm*; 34. Vincent, happy dog & chief shepherd, *The Wellington Arms*; 35. John Fahey, *The Island Bakers*; 36. Spotty the Kune Kune at *The Pig*; 37. Chris Sole, butcher & proprietor, *Blackmoor Game*; 38. Fran Joyce, head chef, *The Thomas Lord*; 39. John Lightfoot, head chef, *The Oak Inn***; 40. Mark Haynes, farmer & cowherd, *Meadow Cottage Farm*; 41. Brian Ahearn, head chef, *The Rockingham Arms*; 42. Neil Beckett, head chef, *The Chestnut Horse & The Globe*; 43. Jennifer Williams, *Naked Jam*; 44. Damian Brown, head chef & stakeholder, *The Chesil Rectory*; 45. James Durrant, head chef & proprietor, *The Plough*; 46. Charlie Bartlett, head chef, *The Garlic Farm & Restaurant*; 47. Will Dobson, orchard grower, juice maker & owner, *Hill Farm Juice*; 48. Henrietta, a free range chicken; 49. Princess the Jersey cow (one of Colin's girlfriends), *Meadow Cottage Farm*; 50. Mike Curtis, fisherman & proprietor, *Captain Stan's Bembridge Fish Store*; 51. Sustainable organic exotic mushrooms, *Fundamentally Fungus*; 52. James Golding's 'piggy brew' at *The Pig*; 53. One of the morning's catch, *Johnson's Enterprises Ltd*; 54. Isle of Wight tomato, *The Tomato Stall*; 55. A bit of bread in the corner, *The Island Bakers*.

Just as this book went to print: *chef George Blogg left *TerraVina* and moved on to pastures new. We all wish him every success.

**chef John Lightfoot at *The Oak Inn* was awarded a new post at Fuller's newly re-furbished *The White Buck* in Burley.

Meats, Eats, Drinks & Leaves

around Hampshire & the Isle of Wight

Acknowledgements

Published by Repertoire Food & Design Ltd
www.meatseatsdrinksandleaves.com
www.repertoire.co

ISBN: 978-0-9565771-3-9

British Library Cataloguing-in-Publication Data:
A catalogue record for this book is available from the British Library.

© Repertoire Food & Design Ltd.
Text Penny Ericson.
Design and photographs Simon Firullo

Printed and bound in Malta

Managed and manufactured by Jellyfish Print Solutions, Swanmore, Hampshire UK

Stocks from sustainable sources

MIX
Paper from
responsible sources
FSC® C022612
FSC
www.fsc.org

Other photo credits: The Chesil Rectory - p46-47 - photos are released with permission from Paul Pascoe@Red Snapper and Milli McGregor; Blackmoor Game - p56 - Simon Hawkins; The Little Gloster - p60-61 - main image and bottom left; p72-73 - all images The Island Bakers; Lainston House - p140 - second, third and fourth in left column; The Garlic Farm - p184 - second, third and fourth in left column; Chewton Glen - p245 - main image; Laverstoke Park Farm - p255 - bottom 3 - courtesy of Laverstoke Park Farm; The Thomas Lord, Hyden Farm Originals p187 - main image - Penny Ericson; The Tomato Stall - p336-337 - courtesy the Tomato Stall

It's been a real pleasure writing this book. As always there are so many people to thank, a few of whom, without them, this project would never have got off the ground. To Simon Firullo, my collaborator, the photography is stunning. You've made this a truly beautiful book. To Simon Hawkins, my husband, for his untiring hard work behind the scenes, especially for doing the things Simon F and I either don't like to do or aren't very good at. Thanks also go to Yvonne, Ben & Cole and the Gabors; Zsa Zsa & Eva.

A million thanks to the chefs and proprietors for letting us into their kitchens and sharing their menus, recipes and food. And very special thanks for their generosity in helping me raise money for, *Live Well 4 Longer.*

Tanguy Martin, sommelier extraordinaire! I think the wine and tasting notes make the book complete. Thanks for being so generous with your expertise and time.

Peter Gentilli, thanks for your contribution on the wine and beer sections and Emma Caulton for yours on the Hampshire Larder section.

There are a few other people that deserve a very special thanks. Samantha Dewey at Jellyfish Print Solutions, you've been an absolute star from day one. Jane Johnston, Cressida Robson and Juliet Alexander for editing and proof reading, any errors are mine alone. Tracy Nash, for your enthusiasm and boundless energy. You helped me kick-off the project, gave me so much of your time and opened doors. Ben & Holly Cooke, thanks for your generous hospitality. For our readers, a stay at *The Little Gloster's B&B* on the Isle of Wight is highly recommended.

Cookery books are complicated things. In addition, this book features 22 chefs and their establishments, as well as the food producers they work with. That's a lot of stories to tell! I had a lot of help. In no particular order, thanks to: Ken Walker at Jellyfish, Antonio Lopez-Bustos and the team at Lainston House, Lindsey Steele, James Durrant, Andy MacKenzie, Joni Rhodes, Nina Basset, Victoria Townsend, Emma Cripwell, Lotti Eagles, Joy Peck, Derek Lowe, David Butcher, Andy Lazenby, Jen Hollick, Sarah Mills, Eleanor Dodd, Emma Tophill, Barbara Parry, Faye Payne, Colin Boswell, Mark & Penny Thornhill, Helen Fahy, Martin Sliva, Simon Page, Jane Dick and Sue Whiting, Janet Sole, Clare Winterbottom, Celia Haynes. The guys at TLR for testing recipes. Finally, a big thank-you to the chefs, kitchen and front of house teams at all the marvelous places featured in this book.

Meats, Eats, Drinks & Leaves

around Hampshire & the Isle of Wight

by **Penny Ericson**

photographs by **Simon Firullo**

foreword by **Angela Hartnett**

Foreword

Hampshire and the Isle of Wight are very special and it is no surprise that some of the UK's top chefs have found sanctuary here and their very own Garden of Eden. The warm southern limits of our temperate climate ensure that here, where sea meets land, we have some of the most abundant and varied ingredients for a chef's table.

I was once told that the only food Hampshire doesn't produce is crisps despite having potato growers in abundance. I've since learned that one of Britain's hallmark crisp brands uses Hampshire potatoes!

A cookery book that captures the essence of this part of the country is long overdue. It's a book that draws you into this fabulous part of England, where you can savour some of its sublime culinary experiences. This book does just that, it takes you on a voyage of discovery around some of Hampshire's most creative restaurants, introducing you to inventive chefs and authentic local produce.

The provenance of the food we eat is becoming more and more important. 'Field to fork' is a familiar and increasingly important principle. I believe it's here to stay. Today we want certainty about where our food comes from. Menus highlight local produce, sometimes even narrowing it down to a 15-mile or even a 5-mile radius of the restaurant. For rural chefs, provenance means, 'I serve this food because my neighbour produced it and my other neighbours produced the rest of the ingredients and their families have been doing this for centuries.' It means the chefs have watched the ingredients grow and mature before their eyes and trust in their integrity.

Our chefs are even stepping out into the countryside themselves to become their own producers. Foraged ingredients are increasingly popular on rural menus and chefs are embracing the opportunity to cameo the textures and flavours they find on their doorstep.

Relying on local produce can be a challenge taking real confidence, creativity and ingenuity. The availability of produce is never fully assured or predictable and menus have to be adaptable to what's available on the day. Often a well-planned dish might have to be postponed or scrapped altogether.

In 2012, when we opened *Hartnett Holder & Co at Lime Wood* in the New Forest, I found out first hand why the region draws so many top chefs.

Now Penny has persuaded more than twenty of the region's top chefs to share the secrets of their signature dishes, and introduce you to their local producers and the unique environment in which they work.

Samuel Johnson wrote, *'When a man is tired of London, he is tired of life; for there is in London all that life can afford.'* I venture that had he been alive today he'd have said the same of Hampshire. I hope if you haven't already visited the region, Penny's book will encourage you.

Best wishes

Angela

Contents

Notes

- The dishes presented here vary in complexity. Some are straightforward; some will challenge the accomplished amateur, while others simply cannot be achieved at home. These menus showcase how the chef's work, it's a peek over their shoulders so to speak. Take inspiration from their knowledge and skill and when you dine at their tables, appreciate their devotion.

- Whilst the recipes have been tested in home kitchens, there are some that we simply couldn't do. Olly Rouse's, *Lemon, basil chocolate & kiffir* is a good example. There may be instances where a process seems unclear or is missing. For this, I apologise, and then I blame the chefs. They think in culinary shorthand and each has his or her jargon. If I've missed something, it might be that they didn't tell me. (Extracting accurate recipes out of more than 20 chefs took some doing!)

- The recipe styles vary from chef to chef. I've done this intentionally. The measurements and quantities are harmonised and I've tried to be consistent but chefs simply don't work that way. Some are precise to the extreme, while others are a bit more 'freestyle.' There are some rules that they all follow though. For example, they all taste their food as they work, constantly balancing flavours and seasoning, hence you will see quite a few generic descriptions such as 'a knob of butter', which is about a tablespoon and 'season to taste', means salt and pepper unless otherwise specified. Finally, if a temperature control calls for something out of the ordinary like 121°C, it's not a typo, the chef meant it (and yes they do put cling film in ovens!)

- Oven temperatures are conventional ovens in °C. If you are using a fan-assisted oven, decrease the temperature by 15°C. Individual ovens can vary by as much as 10°C and possibly more when transferring from a commercial to domestic kitchen. Get to know your oven. The best gauge is a thermometer.

- Timings are given as a guideline and in most cases with a description of the finished article. I rely on you, the cook, to use your judgment.

- A word on eggs. Use large, free range and organic if there isn't a specific instruction. Egg yolks are measured in 2 ways, by quantity (ie 3 yolks) and also in grams. 1 large free range yolk = 25 g on average. The reason for the two styles is that many chefs use liquid pasteurised yolks. The measurements are accurate and they are safer from a health and safety perspective. If you are pregnant or in a vulnerable health group, avoid raw or partially cooked eggs.

- Salt is sea salt, unless specified (I use Maldon or Murray River Pink that I get from Jason & Simon at *The Wellington Arms*.) Pepper is freshly cracked black, unless specified.

- For cross-referencing weights & measures there is a full conversion chart at the back of the book.

Introduction

I've had the time of my life writing this book. It's been an absolute privilege to meet and work with so many wonderful and talented people. This is their book, not mine.

Meats, Eats, Drinks & Leaves reflects the taste and skill of twenty-two of Hampshire and the Isle of Wight's finest chefs. Their food is modern and traditional at the same time. All of them tell a story about how they interpret provenance and what using, and in many cases producing, local produce means to them. The dishes vary, some are elegantly simple, whilst others are just too difficult to replicate.

Great chefs don't complicate things without good reason. They get the very best out of every ingredient because they have skill, knowledge and imagination. I've given you their recipes as they've given them to me.

Many of these dishes can't be perfectly replicated at home. For example, most people don't have the time, patience, skill or equipment to spend two days making a wafer thin biscuit from a pig's ear or making the equivalent of the inside of a chocolate aerobar. Why would we? That's what these fabulous chefs are here for. Dine in their restaurants!

It's not just the chefs I wanted to celebrate, Hampshire & the Isle of Wight's diversity is wondrous. The farmers, fishermen, butchers, bakers, brewers, vintners, gardeners, beekeepers, jam makers, candlestick makers et al are second to none. It's been such an honour and education to meet them all and learn about what's made them and their industries what they are today. The region is so diverse; I've really only just scratched the surface.

I hope you enjoy this book as much as I have creating it. Take inspiration from the beautiful concoctions the chefs have created, then go to their restaurants, sit back and enjoy the hospitality of the folks that welcome you in. The producers are also an essential ingredient to what makes enjoying food a great pleasure. Visit their farm shops and buy their lovingly crafted goods. I promise, you won't be disappointed.

I must apologise to those I have missed this time around. There just wasn't a book large enough to do justice to all the wonderful chefs, cooks, hotels, restaurants, food

producers and professionals that serve the hospitality and food industry in the region. I feel another book coming on!

One last word, for the first edition of this book, all of the chefs and establishments have helped me raise much needed money for my fundraising campaign, *Live Well 4 Longer,* that has been set up to raise funds directly dedicated to buying desperately needed equipment in cancer wards and training for NHS medical professionals for the treatment and prevention of cancer. To all of them I am so very grateful. Thank-you.

Bon appetite!

Penny

LIME WOOD

Near Lyndhurst

*L*ime Wood has had a few identities over the centuries. It was once a sequestered hunting area for William the Conqueror's short-sighted son, William II. Apparently, he wasn't a terribly good shot so had the deer rounded up and brought to him by beaters through the 'pale' that still exists today. Then known as *Pondhead*, the hunting lodge underwent a succession of owners, each placing their personal stamp.

In 1740, the lodge was rebuilt by the Duke of Clarence. He significantly enlarged and renamed it, *Parkhill*. Then, in 1880, under the ownership of Mr. Willingham Rawnsley Esq, it became a preparatory school for 'the sons of gentlemen'. T.S. Elliott was one of its masters and Rawnsley's brother became founder of *The National Trust*. *Parkhill* eventually became a hotel and restaurant only to change roles one more time. During WW2 it became command central for the D-Day landings.

In 2004, this lovely Regency house saw the beginning of its meticulous transformation into what is now *Lime Wood*. Its present custodians have enjoyed every minute of bringing it new life and guests are invited to soak in it's luxurious present and past.

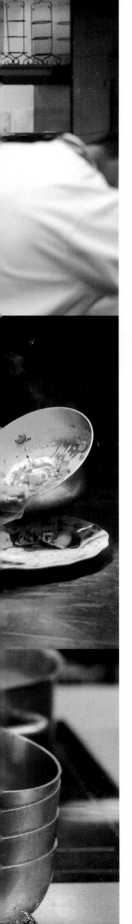

"For me, creating great dishes isn't about complexity, it's about how I perceive the ingredients and treat them appropriately to get the very best from them."

Luke Holder, head chef

The Menu

Coda uova affumicato & pickled fennel

Squid ink garganelli

Double agnolotti

Halibut

Milk & honey

Strawberry cream puff

Luke has worked in some of London's busiest and most exclusive restaurants including *Orrery*, *The Sloane Club*, and *Oxo Tower*. He then spent a year cooking in the Italian kitchen of 3 Michelin-starred, *Enoteca Pinchiorri*, in Florence. His time there changed his philosophy of food and firmly placed his focus on cooking locally, seasonally and at the highest level.

Lime Wood's restaurant, *Hartnett Holder & Co* has a relaxed style that is comfortable and upscale at the same time. Along with his partner in the kitchen, co-head chef, Angela Hartnett, and their team, they create locally sourced English dishes with flair that salutes their joint Italian culinary backgrounds. His approach is informal, fresh and pays homage to his New Forest produce and local producers.

When Luke escapes his kitchen he loves nothing more than to relax with his wife and children.

Tanguy's tips

Coda uova affumicato: *Ouzo of Plomari, Isidoros Arvanitis, Greece*
Squid ink garganelli: *Puro Malto (beer), Milan, Italy*
Double agnolotti: *Dolcetto d'alba Monte, Piedmont, Italy*
Halibut: *Bandol Rose, Provence, France*
Milk & honey: *Sauternes, Bordeaux, France*
Strawberry cream puff: *Vidal, (grape variety), Icewine, Peller Estate, Niagara Peninsula, Ontario, Canada, 2010*

Full tasting notes are on page 318

Coda uova affumicato & pickled fennel *with radish, crackling & rye*

Serves 8 as a canapé

Equipment: food processor, Japanese mandolin, pasta machine

200 g smoked cod roe
100 ml water
1½ litres vegetable oil
200 g crème fraiche
juice of 2 lemons
1 radish, very finely sliced
50 g pickled fennel
chives, chopped

Pork crackling
100 g pork skin

Pickled fennel
1 bulb fennel, finely shaved
50 ml white wine vinegar
50 ml water
50 g sugar

Rye lavosh
800 g rye flour
20 g salt
2 eggs
200 g milk
100 g butter
130 g water
black sesame seeds
Maldon salt

For the cod roe mousse, separate the roe from the skin and place in a food processor with the whisk attachment. Whip the roe and water on a medium speed while drizzling in the vegetable oil at a slow steady pace. Once all the oil has been added, finish by whisking in the crème fraiche and add lemon juice to taste.

For the crispy pork crackling, preheat oven to 180°C. Bake the pork skins for 15 minutes until blistered and firm. Allow to cool then crush the crispy crackling into small crumbs.

For the pickled fennel, bring the vinegar, water and sugar to the boil and whilst warm, pour over the shaved fennel and allow to cool in the liquor.

For the rye lavosh, preheat oven to 140°C. Mix all the ingredients together, except the salt, and knead like a bread dough until smooth. Rest for 1 hour then roll in a pasta machine to 2 mm thick. Cut into squares and place on a baking tray, spritz with some water and sprinkle with Maldon salt and bake for 15 to 20 minutes.

Shave raw radishes as thinly as possible and use to garnish the finished dish. (A Japanese mandolin is recommended.)

Squid ink garganelli *with crab & parsley*

Serves 4 as a starter

Equipment: pasta machine, garganelli board and rolling pin

2 Lymington crab, white meat only
(reserve the rest for other things)
1 red chilli, very finely chopped
a small bunch of parsley, finely chopped
a knob of butter
a splash of olive oil
a few chives, chopped
salt & pepper

Garganelli
200 g pasta flour (tipo '00')
7 egg yolks
50 ml squid ink

Garganelli is typical of the Emilia-Romagna region of Italy. It's an egg-pasta with an open-rolled flap and is usually ridged horizontally for texture and, of course, Northern Italian style.

For the pasta, blend the flour, egg yolks and squid ink together in a food processor until a dough is formed. Leave to rest in a refrigerator for 1 hour before use. Roll through a pasta machine to medium thickness (3 on a pasta machine). Lay the sheets on a garganelli board and gently roll to create ridges. Once rolled blanch for 20 seconds in boiling, salted, oiled water and refresh in ice water. You can then cook them in boiling water as you need them or warm them and serve al dente.

For the crab, heat the oil and butter in a pan, add the crab and chilli and when nicely cooked add some parsley and chives. Season to taste.

To serve, place the pasta in a deep dish, dress with hot crab and drizzle the residual liquor from the pan. Sprinkle with chives and serve hot.

Double agnolotti

with chicken, polenta, peas & broad beans

Serves 6 as a starter

Equipment: pasta machine, pasta cutter, robot coupe, piping bag

Pasta
200 g pasta flour (tipo '00')
9 egg yolks
5 ml olive oil

Chicken filling
500 g chicken thighs
2 onions, chopped
200 g lardo di colonnata (see page 354)
light chicken stock
a small bunch of sage
100 g aged Parmesan
1 egg yolk

Polenta filling
polenta
100 g Parmesan, grated
a splash of olive oil
a knob of butter

Broad beans & peas
200 g broad beans, blanched and shelled
100 g peas, blanched (frozen are fine)
1 garlic clove, crushed
a small bunch of parsley, chopped
a knob of butter
a splash of olive oil
salt & pepper

For the pasta, blend the flour, egg yolks and oil together in a food processor until a dough is formed. Separate into hands-sized portions, wrap in cling film and refrigerate for 1 hour. Using a pasta machine, roll into 3 ml thickness then trim into 30 cm x 8 cm sheets.

For the chicken filling, sear the chicken thighs on all sides then, in the same pan cook the onions without colour, add the stock and sage then return the thighs and braise until the meat falls from the bone. Drain on kitchen paper then pull the meat from the bones, skin and sinews. Reduce the liquor by $^2/_3$. Blend the meat, reduced stock, lardo di colonnata, Parmesan and egg yolk in a robot coupe until smooth, season to taste and spoon into a piping bag while still warm then chill until ready to use. The filling should be firm enough to pipe in a solid line.

For the polenta filling, mix together the polenta, oil and butter until it thickens. Reduce the heat to low, add the cheese and continue to stir every few minutes until the mixture is a nice thick consistency. Season to taste, spoon into a piping bag and chill until firm enough to pipe in a solid line.

Pipe straight lines of filling lengthwise down the pasta sheets, leaving enough pasta on one side to fold over the filling then fold the pasta over the top and press firmly to seal. Moisten the seam a bit if it needs help sticking together. Use a wheeled pasta cutter to cut the filled tubes of pasta away making sure to keep the sealed strip intact. Using the tips of your fingers, pinch the tube of pasta into equal sized portions, sealing between the pockets each time then cut with the pasta wheel. Use the wheeled pasta cutter or a sharp knife to separate the sections. Cook in a large pot of salted boiling water for 2 minutes or until tender.

For the broad beans and peas, blanch both in boiling water for 1 minute then plunge into ice water. When ready to serve, add the garlic, and enough butter and oil in a pan to make an emulsion, warm the beans, peas and parsley and season to taste. To serve, toss in the cooked pasta so they are evenly coated with the emulsion, spoon onto plates and serve immediately.

Halibut *with sweet peas & heritage tomatoes*

Serves 4

Equipment: thermometer, hand blender, fine sieve

4 140 g halibut fillets
1 litre olive oil
100 g fresh peas, blanched
a knob of butter
pea shoots
salt & pepper

Pea purée
100 g peas
30 g sugar
30 g salt
ice

Candied heritage tomatoes
200 g small heritage tomatoes
150 g sugar
zest of 1 lemon
1 cardamom seed, husk removed
　& ground

Prepare all the components of this dish before cooking the fish.

For the pea purée, blanch the peas in seasoned, boiling water then refresh in ice water. Blend with a hand blender, pass through a fine sieve and season to taste.

For the tomatoes, preheat oven to 80°C and combine the sugar, lemon zest and cardamom powder. Roll the tomatoes in the sugar and place on a tray in the oven for 8 hours.

For the halibut, heat the oil in a deep pan to 52°C. Poach the fillets for 9 minutes. Remove from the oil and serve immediately.

To serve, spoon purée onto plates and scatter with a few warm peas, top with the halibut and tomatoes and garnish with pea shoots.

Milk & honey

Serves 8 as a pre-dessert

Equipment: 8 small glass bowls

Goat's milk panna cotta

350 ml goat's milk

1 tbsp milk powder

60 g caster sugar

3 gelatine leaves, softened in cold water

150 ml whipping cream

2 tbsp natural yogurt

ice

Honey jelly

100 ml honey

100 ml water

2 gelatine leaves, softened in cold water

fresh almonds, finely sliced

Greek basil leaves

For the panna cotta, bring the milk to the boil, whisk in the milk powder and add sugar. Remove from the heat and add the soaked gelatine and place the bowl in iced water to cool. Whip the cream to soft peaks and when the milk is completely cold and just starting to set, whisk in the yogurt, then fold in the whipped cream. Pour the mixture into glass bowls cover with cling film and refrigerate for 2 hours until set.

For the honey jelly, bring the honey and water just to the boil, add the softened gelatine and stir until completely dissolved. When the panna cottas are completely set, pour a fine layer of the honey mixture over the top and return to the fridge to set. When ready to serve, sprinkle with a few almond shavings and fine Greek basil sprigs.

Strawberry cream puff

Luke only makes this dish from June through the summer, as the strawberries cannot be refrigerated

Serves 4, each cream puff is a sharing plate for 2 people

Equipment: greaseproof paper, silpat mat, bain marie

250 g freshly picked strawberries, trimmed and sliced
puff pastry, ready made is fine
1 egg, beaten for wash
a sprinkling of sugar
100 g white chocolate
Greek basil sprigs

White chocolate mousse
375 g white chocolate
150 ml double cream
1½ leaves gelatine, softened in cold water
500 ml whipping cream
2 egg whites

For the pastry cases, preheat oven to 170°C. Lay the pastry flat and cut into 20 cm x 12 cm rectangles and carefully score a rectangle 3 cm from the edge. Place on a baking tray lined with greaseproof paper, lightly brush with egg wash and sprinkle with sugar. Bake until puffy and golden. Remove from the oven and very carefully run a sharp knife around the scoring and lift off the 'lid'.

For the white chocolate mousse, bring the cream to the boil over a bain marie and melt the chocolate over another bain marie. Whisk the double cream to soft peaks and whisk the egg whites to soft peaks as well. Dissolve the softened gelatine into the hot cream then emulsify the chocolate into the cream by very slowly pouring in the chocolate and continuing to whisk. Fold in the whipped cream and then fold in the whisked egg whites. Spoon some of the mousse into the pastry baskets, place them in the fridge and refrigerate the rest until set.

Make a caramelised white chocolate powder by preheating oven to 160°C. Place the chocolate in the oven on a silpat mat for 20 minutes. The chocolate will melt and caramelise but not fall apart. Remove from the oven and cool then chop up into powdery crumbs.

When ready to serve, fill the baskets with strawberries then top with four rocher of mousse, sprinkle with caramelised chocolate and garnish with a couple Greek basil sprigs.

HARTNETT HOLDER & CO

Lime Wood's Hampshire hog smokehouse

When Luke is not in the kitchen he can be found down in what was once a children's playhouse. Aptly, it's now his smokehouse where, for the past four and a half years he's been playing with processes to perfect his Hampshire hog 'smoke house board'. The original hearth is now a smoking chamber surrounded by Luke's seven varieties of dry-cured pork sausages, sweet-cured beef brisket and Scotland's *Loch Duart* salmon. The unique arrangement of the meats hanging in the same place as the smoker gives the meats a subtle smokey perfume.

Luke is one of the founding chefs re-instating the original slow-growing Hampshire hog, known for its distinctive black and white stripes and floppy ears. *Laverstoke Park Farm* exclusively rears his hogs and then he patiently uses traditional methods he's learned in Italy, Spain and Hungary to create a truly exquisite variety of charcuterie.

Luke insists on using natural ingredients. The meats are cured only with salt and chef's choice of seasonings. When Luke joined *Lime Wood*, he was introduced to an accomplished team of kitchen porters some of whom were Hungarians. To his delight, he found that their families back home supplied sumptuous and sweet paprika that was hand-dried in small amounts. The porters are still in the kitchen and their families' paprika still proudly features in Luke's Hungarian-style chorizo.

It's also profoundly important to Luke that the Scottish salmon he uses is completely sustainable. *Loch Duart*'s fish swim in open water, so have bright colour and a firm texture. There are no additives used in the curing process, they are simply 'presented' to the smoke and are from loch to table in seven days but the rest of his produce takes significantly longer, sometimes up to four patient years.

The art of the smoke house board

Luke's philosophy and techniques are pure, use the finest possible meat and a bit of salt & seasoning to bring out the best of a good product.

A sharing board of dry-cured meats, sausages and salmon

Dry-cured ham

From *Laverstoke Park Farm* reared Hampshire hogs. This is cured in a traditional Parma style that can take up to four years.

Fennel salami

Cured with fennel and pink peppercorns this salami has a sweet piquancy.

Hungarian chorizo

This is made in the traditional way. The recipes were rarely written rather handed down through the generations. The slightly smokey sweet paprika comes from the families of Lime Wood's Hungarian members of the kitchen porter team.

Coppa

In Northern Italian tradition, this is made from the ribeye and seasoned with allspice, juniper berries and brown sugar.

Loch Duart salmon

This is fish with the firm, lean muscle that comes from fish that swim actively. It's cured with a pinch of salt and sugar for four days. Its high moisture content comes from its freshness so requires a little less salt. The excellence is unmistakable.

Tanguy's tip

Fish: *Arbois Chardonnay, Jura, France*
Meat: *Arbois Poulsard, Les Bruyeres, France*
Full tasting notes are on page 318

The Plough at Longparish

Longparish
James & Louise Durrant, chef/proprietor

Longparish, in the heart of the Test Valley, remains an agricultural and fishing village. A stroll from the pub to the pretty pre-16thC church lets you peel back layers of history whispering memories of pre-Roman communities, Saxon prosperity, 10thC royal passion, intrigue and murder and the dissolution of its abbey by King Henry VIII.

The Plough's early 18th century charm is the perfect setting to enjoy James' simple and elegant food. After 16 years serving some of the UK's finest eateries, award-winning chef James Durrant, along with his wife Louise and children decided the beautiful Test Valley was the perfect place to call home. Their approach is straightforward, provide excellent cask-aged ale, use fine local ingredients, serve wines as interesting as the food, make sure guests always feel welcome and add generous lashings of hospitality. For added fun son Charlie helps dad come up with original kids dishes such as *Baked hedgehog Alaska* and the rest of the family join in for quality control.

James's experience shines and his relaxed approach fits perfectly in this lovely village pub.

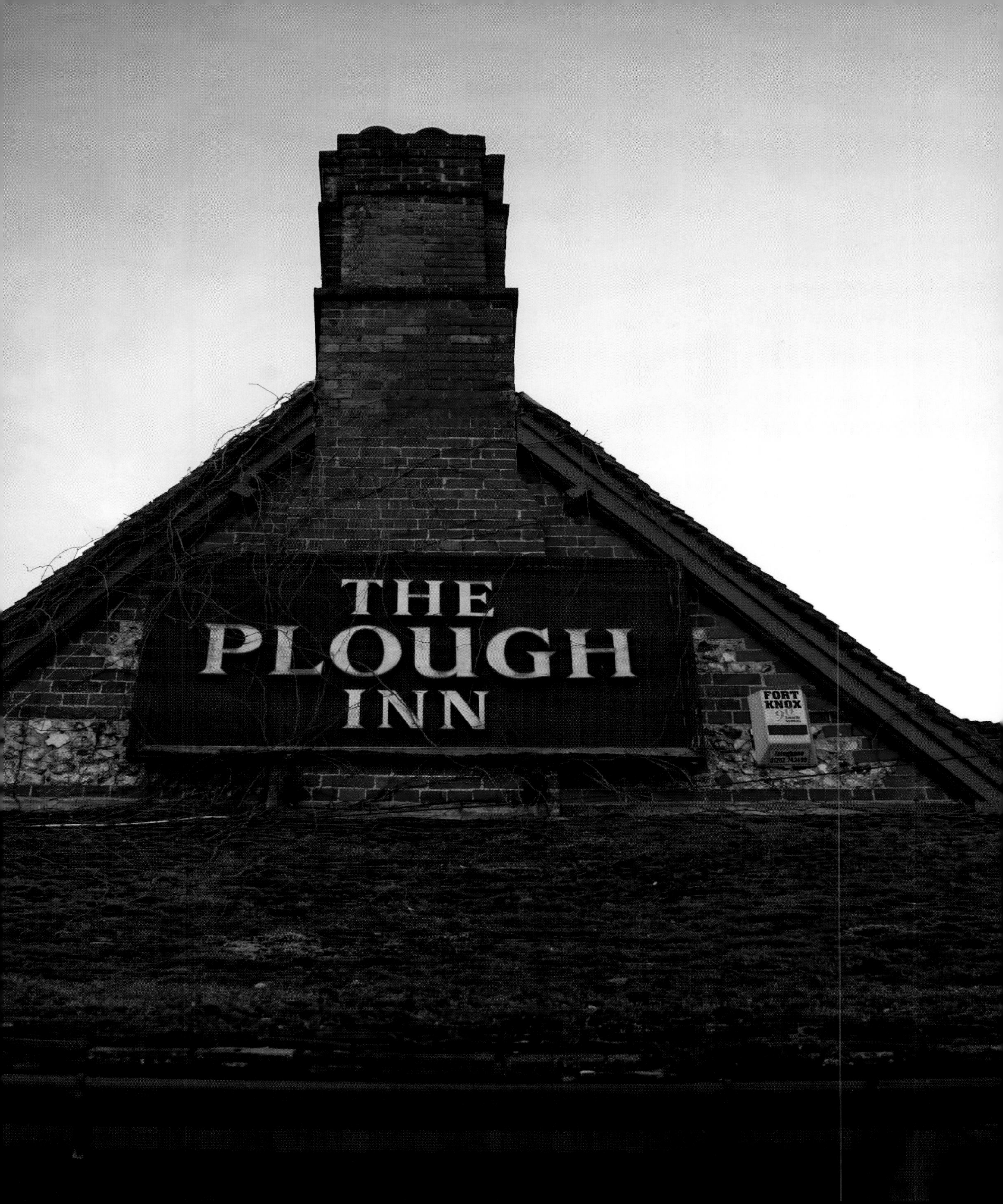
THE
PLOUGH
INN
FORT
KNOX

> *"For me, family comes first but in my kitchen flavour and quality rule above all."*

James Durrant

The Menu

Trout tartare & Scotch egg

Surf & turf: braised pork belly, cockles & sausages

Chocolate mousse

The Kid's Menu

Mama mia pizza

Sliders & brioche buns

Honeycomb & fudge clusters

Baked hedgehog Alaska

James has over 16 years experience in London's Michelin-starred restaurants.

He started cooking in his hometown of Chester and after 3 years moved to London to join the 3 Michelin-starred team at *Gordon Ramsay* in Chelsea. Soon he was senior sous chef responsible for *Ramsay's Restaurant* at *Claridge's* and if that wasn't enough of a challenge, after two years James joined Jason Atherton over the road to open *Maze* and *Maze Grill*, winning, amongst other awards, a Michelin star in its first year. He went on to become executive chef.

Now his own boss, James knows how to put quality and flavour first and he delights in serving up his brand of local authenticity.

Tanguy's tips

Trout tartare: *Sancerre, Loire Valley*
Surf & turf: *Barolo, Piedmont, Italy*
Chocolate mousse: *Sweet Madeira*
The kids menu: *Mocktails, New Forest Mist & Monkey Boy's Cosmonaut*

Full tasting notes are on page 318

Trout tartare & Scotch egg

with beach greens & avocado purée

Serves 4

**Equipment: 'hob-top smoker',
food processor, large scone cutter,
deep fryer, piping bag**

1 whole sea-reared trout (approx 700 g)
100 g samphire, blanched
a handful of purslane, fresh dill tops &
    micro-coriander
50 g crème fraiche
sea salt
1½ litres sunflower or rapeseed oil
    for deep frying

Trout marinade
500 g coarse sea salt
425 g sugar
100 g mixed white & black peppercorns
10 coriander seeds
8 cloves
juice & zest of 1 lemon & lime
2 bunches of fresh dill, chopped

Scotch egg
50 g cream cheese
50 g crème fraiche
2 handfuls of oak woodchips
8 quail eggs
Panko breadcrumbs
flour
2 eggs, beaten

Garnishes (see page 348)
avocado purée
tartar sauce
cucumber ribbons

To make the Scotch eggs, fillet, trim and slice the fish into 2 sides, skin on and set 1 piece aside for the tartare. Prepare the marinade by combining the ingredients and blitzing in a food processor. Lay out a sheet of cling film and sprinkle with a coating of the marinade, lay the trout fillet across it then sprinkle the remainder of the rub over the fish. Wrap the fish tightly and refrigerate for 6 to 8 hours. When the trout is cured, rinse the marinade off thoroughly under cold water.

Set up the 'hob-top' smoker by spreading a layer of wood chips in a roasting tin and place a wire rack on top. Cover and place on medium-high heat until the chips start to smoulder. Place the trout skin-side down on top of the smoking wood chips, cover tightly and smoke for 8 to 10 minutes on medium-high heat. The meat should remain pink and firm. Remove from the heat, clean the meat from the skin and combine the trout meat with dill, cream cheese and crème fraiche. Season to taste with salt and lemon juice and refrigerate for 1 hour.

To prepare the quail eggs, place in boiling water for 2½ minutes then plunge into ice water and refrigerate for 1 hour. Carefully peel the eggs.

Next spread the trout mixture 5mm thick onto parchment and cut into rounds with a large scone cutter. Place an egg in the centre and gently wrap. Roll the Scotch egg in flour followed by beaten egg and breadcrumbs. Place in refrigerator until ready to deep fry and serve.

When ready to serve, preheat a deep fryer to 180°C. Fry the Scotch eggs for 2 minutes until lightly golden. Drain on kitchen roll and serve.

To serve press about 2 cm of the tartare into a scone cutter on the centre of a plate and cover with a thin layer of crème fraiche. Dot the plate with avocado purée and arrange the samphire, purslane, cucumber ribbons, dill tops and micro-coriander in a ring around the tartare and top with warm Scotch eggs.

Surf & turf: braised pork belly, cockles & sausages *with white beans*

Serves 4

Equipment: hand blender, deep fryer, fine chinois

Cockles

500 g fresh cockles

100 ml white wine

a small bunch parsley, chopped

Pork belly & crackling

1½ kg pork belly & skin for crackling

mirpoix (2 onions & 2 carrots, chopped; 6 garlic cloves, smashed)

30 cloves

1 star anise

a few sprigs of thyme

1 bay leaf

1 tbsp tomato purée

300 ml honey

150 ml red wine vinegar

3 litres veal stock

1 litre chicken stock

250 g duck fat

1½ litres sunflower or rapeseed oil for deep frying

Bean cassoulet

300 g white beans, soaked overnight

100 g chorizo, diced

75 g black pudding, diced

4 sausage links, poached & shredded

4 rashers smoked bacon, diced

1 onion, finely chopped

2 garlic cloves, finely chopped

a few sprigs of thyme & 1 bay leaf

Garnish

100 g samphire, blanched

a handful of purslane

Avruga caviar for garnish (1 small jar)

1 large shallot, sliced

For the cockles, place a pan with a lid on high heat. When the pan is hot add the cockles and wine and cover immediately. Steam for 1 minute then drain. Discard any unopened cockles and pick the meat from the shells. Saving a few for garnish.

Preheat oven to 150°C. Skin, de-bone, roll and tie the pork belly and reserve the skin for crackling. Heat a pan and seal the pork on all sides then place in a heavy ovenproof casserole. Using the same pan caramelise the mirpoix then add the cloves, star anise, thyme and bay leaf. Cook for another 3 minutes to allow the spices to open then add the tomato purée and honey. Add this mixture to the pork, deglaze the pan with the vinegar until reduced to virtually nothing then add to the pot and cover with the stocks. Seal the casserole with foil, cover with its lid and roast for 6 hours. Remove the belly from the casserole, cut away the strings and wrap tightly in cling film and refrigerate overnight.

Next, pass the casserole liquor through a fine chinois into a clean pan and reduce by half on medium heat. Set aside a small amount to use as a glaze later and use the rest in the bean cassoulet.

For the crackling, preheat oven to 95°C and confit the pigskin in the duck fat for 12 hours then remove from the fat and cut into 2.5 cm strips. Stretch out on a tray and return to the oven for another 12 hours. When ready to serve heat a deep fryer to 180°C and fry the strips until puffy and crisp. Drain on kitchen paper and season to taste.

For the bean cassoulet, after the beans have been soaked, cook them with the thyme sprigs and bay leaf for 30 minutes until soft through. Remove ¾ of them and continue to cook the rest until very mushy then drain, add a splash of cream and blitz with a hand blender. Spoon into a piping bag and keep warm until ready to serve.

Next, in a casserole, sweat the onion and garlic without colour then add the chorizo, bacon and sausage. When cooked, add the black pudding and beans then stir in the pork sauce. Keep warm. Just before serving add the cockles and parsley.

For the shallot garnish, fry the shallot rings in butter until well caramelised to bring out the bitter onion flavour. Drain on kitchen paper.

To serve, re-heat the pork belly in the sauce that's been set aside allowing the sauce to reduce to a glaze. Cut into medallions and present with dots of bean purée and caviar sprinkled with crackling, caramelised shallots, a few cockles, samphire and purslane. Serve the cassoulet on the side.

Chocolate mousse

with praline, hot chocolate sauce, hazelnuts & sea salt & hazelnut ice cream

Serves 6

Equipment: small round pastry cutter, sugar thermometer, moulds, blowtorch (if using metal moulds), fine chinois and ice cream maker

Base
150 g white chocolate
190 g praline paste
75 g cocoa butter
250 g éclat d'or

Mousse
400 g dark chocolate, melted to 40°C
160 g egg yolks (8)
190 g caster sugar
700 ml double cream
100 ml whole milk

Chocolate sauce
350 ml double cream
100 g dark chocolate
75 g caster sugar

Salt & hazelnut ice cream
1 litre plain Anglaise ice cream*
150 g hazelnuts
12 g fleur du sel

For the base, melt the chocolate and cocoa butter over a bain marie then add the praline paste and make smooth. Add the éclat d'or and mix well. Roll the mix between two pieces of parchment to approximately 5 mm thick. Set in the fridge. When set, cut into small rounds a little smaller than the main size of the dessert.

For the mousse, if using plastic moulds, line with greaseproof paper. Begin by making a sabayon by whisking together the yolks and sugar in a bain marie to 121°C. Add in the cream and milk in small portions whisking continually to the ribbon stage*. Fold the sabayon into the melted chocolate ⅓ at a time until completely mixed. Fill moulds to half full, then chill.

For the chocolate sauce, melt all the ingredients together do not boil!

For the ice cream, prepare Anglaise cream* then preheat oven to 180°C. Roast together the hazelnuts and fleur du sel until golden then put the hot nuts into the Anglaise and blitz with a hand blender until nearly smooth, then infuse for 1 hour. Pass through a fine chinois and churn in an ice cream maker to manufacturer's instructions.

To serve, place the mousse in a shallow bowl, top with praline and a boule of ice cream. Serve with lashings of chocolate sauce.

* See *The basics*, page 356

Charlie Durrant & the kid's menu

At *The Plough* the kid's menu isn't an afterthought, it changes with the main menus and uses the same fresh & local produce. Charlie, helped by his sisters, Poppy and Tilly-May, along with cousins and friends make sure fun is a main ingredient. You don't have to be a kid to love pizza and the sliders are perfect for dainty hands.

The Kid's Menu

Mama mia pizza

Sliders & brioche buns

Honeycomb & fudge clusters

Baked hedgehog Alaska

Tanguy's tip

Kid's menu: *mocktails: New Forest Mist & Monkeyboy Cosmonaut*
Full tasting notes are on page 318

Mama mia pizza
Yield 4 to 6 pizza bases
Equipment: pizza stones

Dough
400 g strong flour & a bit more for dusting
250 g warm water
25 g yeast
1 tsp salt

Sauce & toppings
2 tsp olive oil
2 large cloves garlic, crushed
dash of chilli paste or 1 jalapeno pepper, finely chopped
1 medium onion, finely chopped
1 tin of tomatoes or 4 to 6 Italian tomatoes, chopped
1 tbsp tomato purée
a small handful of herbs de Provençe
250 ml red wine
salt & pepper
vegetables & meats of choice
mozzarella, Emmenthal, Parmesan cheeses, grated

For the dough, dissolve the yeast in the warm water then mix into the flour. Turn out onto a floured surface and knead for 10 minutes until smooth and elastic. Place in a floured bowl, cover

Brioche buns
45 ml milk
235 ml water
35 g butter
600 g strong bread flour
25 g yeast
35 g sugar
2 eggs, beaten
1½ tsp salt
1 egg yolk, beaten
100 g sesame seeds

For the burgers, mix all the ingredients together and divide into large meatballs then pat into small burgers. Fry over medium heat or BBQ.

For the buns, warm the milk, water and butter to blood temperature (37°C) then in a food processor mix together 400 g flour, yeast, sugar and salt. Add the beaten eggs then slowly mix in all the liquid and continue to mix for 1 to 2 minutes. (It will be a wet batter). Add the remaining flour and mix for a further 5 minutes. Place the dough into a clean bowl, cover with cling film and leave in a warm place for 30 minutes until doubled in size. Remove from the bowl and on a floured surface knead the dough back and form into a rough sausage shape. Cut into 16 evenly sized pieces and roll into balls. Preheat oven to 180°C. Place the balls on a greased baking tray and allow to prove for a further 20 minutes glaze the balls with the egg yolk and sprinkle with sesame seeds. Bake for 10 minutes until golden.

with cling film and leave for 5 hours. Section the dough into 70 g pieces, roll to the shape required, dust with flour and layer up between sheets of parchment.

Warm the garlic and chilli in a pan lightly coated with olive oil. Add the onion and cook without colour. Add the tomatoes, purée, herbs, salt and pepper and a generous amount of red wine. Leave to simmer and reduce for an hour, stirring regularly. As the sauce thickens, add more wine. Once the sauce has achieved a nice rich consistency, set aside to cool.

To make the pizzas, preheat oven to 220°C and heat the stones for at least 30 minutes. Place a base on a hot stone and let stand for a minute. Brush with a thin layer of oil then a thin layer of sauce, toppings and cheese. Bake on high heat until cheese is golden and bubbling.

Sliders & brioche buns
Yield 6 full-sized burgers & 18 to 20 sliders

1 kg beef, minced
100 g shallot, rosemary & thyme cooked
60 g breadcrumbs
60 g egg white
10 g salt
10 g Worcestershire sauce
50 g Dijon mustard
50 g tomato ketchup

Honeycomb, chocolate & rice crispy clusters

Yield 20 each dark & light 3 cm clusters

200 g dark chocolate
50 g rice crispies
200 g fudge, small chunks
100 g honeycomb, coarse crumbs
100 g white chocolate buttons
35 g cocoa butter
95 g praline paste
125 g éclat d'or (or corn flakes)

Melt the chocolate over a bain marie in a large mixing bowl. Add the rice crispies, fudge and honeycomb mixing with a rubber spatula so as not to crush the ingredients. Spoon the mix out onto a parchment lined tray and chill. Next melt 75 g of the chocolate and cocoa butter over a bain marie. Add the praline paste and make smooth. Now add the éclat d'or, mix well then allow to cool. Mix in the remaining chocolate buttons then spoon onto a parchment lined tray covered and chill.

White chocolate fudge

Yield 20

Equipment: sugar thermometer

550 g sugar
250 ml double cream
187 g glucose syrup
350 g white chocolate
62 g butter

Line a tray with parchment. In a heavy bottom pan bring the sugar, cream and glucose to 120°C. In a separate pan, over a bain marie, melt the butter and chocolate together. Pour the sugar mixture into the chocolate mixing thoroughly then pour onto the tray and refrigerate. When chilled cut it into a small dice ready to mix into the clusters.

Honeycomb

Yield 20

Equipment: sugar thermometer

120 g golden syrup
320 g sugar
360 g glucose syrup
80 g water
8 g bicarbonate of soda

Grease a baking tray. Mix the sugar, glucose, golden syrup and water together in a heavy bottomed pan and bring up to 148°C then whisk in the bicarbonate of soda and remove from the heat immediately and pour onto the tray and cool. Carefully cut the honeycomb into small pieces ready to add to the clusters.

Baked hedgehog Alaska

Serves 8

Equipment: sugar thermometer, hand mixer, piping bags, fine chinois, ice cream maker, hand blender, small pastry cutter, blow torch

Italian meringue
500 g egg whites
1 kg caster sugar
water, to saturate sugar

Place sugar in a pan and add just enough water to saturate. Cook the sugar to 118°C and no hotter. Whip the egg whites to soft peaks then heat the sugar to 121°C. Pour the sugar carefully down the inside of the bowl onto the whites and whisk until cold stiff peaks. Spoon into a piping bag.

Vanilla ice cream
500 g double cream
500 g whole milk

100 g egg yolks

175 g caster sugar

100 g dextrose

2 vanilla pods, split & scraped

ice

Boil together the cream and milk with the vanilla pod and seeds and whisk the yolks, sugar and dextrose together. Pour half the liquid onto the yolks and whisk together. Re-boil the other half then add the yolk mixture to the pan reducing to low heat and cook to 86°C until creamy. Pass through a fine chinois into a bowl over ice and whisk until completely cool. Churn in an ice cream maker as per manufacturer's instructions then freeze.

Cherry jam

500 cherry purée

120 g sugar

8 g pectin X58

Mix the pectin and sugar together. Bring the cherry purée to the boil then gradually whisk in the sugar mixture. Boil for 10 minutes stirring occasionally. Pass through a fine sieve to cool. When set blitz with a hand blender and spoon into a piping bag.

Bara brith

Yield 1 loaf

450 g dried mixed fruit

250 g brown sugar

300 ml warm black tea

2 tsp mixed spice (cinnamon, nutmeg, ginger & cloves or allspice)

450 self-raising flour

1 egg, beaten

Put the fruit, sugar and tea in a large bowl soak overnight. Next day preheat the oven to 170°C and line loaf tin with baking greaseproof paper. Mix the remaining ingredients with the fruit mixture and beat well. Pour the mixture into the loaf tin and bake for 1½ hours until a toothpick comes out clean. When cool slice into 1 cm thick slices and cut out into discs with a small pastry cutter.

To assemble the hedgehogs squeeze a dot of cherry jam on a plate and stick down disc of cake then squeeze another dot on top and place a large ball of ice cream. Carefully pipe the meringue around the ice cream starting with the nose then going the other way with the rest of the hog pulling the bag away to create peaks. Finish by blow torching the hedgehogs and using a dot of cherry jam to make eyes and a nose.

THE CHESIL RECTORY

EST. 1450

Great British Dining

Winchester
A group of friends: Mark Dodd,
Iain Longhorn & Damian Brown

In view of Saxon King Alfred's statue, the Chesil Rectory is one of Winchester's finest medieval buildings. Built in the early 15thC, it came into the ownership of King Henry VIII during the dissolution of the monasteries and he subsequently made a gift of it to his daughter, Mary Tudor. Walking through the original door you can almost feel Tudor lords brushing past as they prepared for Princess Mary's marriage to King Philip of Spain which was held at the cathedral in 1554. The wedding was so lavish that it nearly bankrupted the city so Queen Mary gave the building to the city as partial payment.

Since then this lovely building has housed many enterprises. Once known as '*Cheese House*', it's been a merchant's house, Winchester's first Sunday school, tannery, antiques shop, Bishop's residence and now one of Hampshire's finest eateries.

In 2008, restaurateur, Mark Dodd pulled together a team of like-minded, experienced friends to create what is now one of Hampshire's most delightful and delicious dining rooms. In times when high street dining is dominated by big chains the Chesil Rectory remains singular for its style, cuisine and personal touch.

This really is a family run restaurant: the three couples, Mark & Eleanor, Damian & Katie and Iain & Samantha work side-by-side. It's no wonder that the Chesil Rectory was voted one of the most romantic restaurants in the UK. It holds a sense of place that is as unique as the group of friends who created it.

> *"I create dishes using ingredients from some of the county's finest producers. I enjoy every moment."*

Damian Brown, head chef, stakeholder

The Menu

Blackmoor Game wood pigeon

Hampshire Dexter beef fillet, rump & bone marrow bon bon

Poached rhubarb & crème vanille

In 2008, Damian joined Mark Dodd to create their vision of a perfect Hampshire restaurant. Since then, they have acquired *The Three Tuns* pub in Romsey, where Damian also acts as executive chef. His experience and skill have resulted in a string of accolades including: *A Superior Quality & Local Produce Award,* in the Hampshire Hospitality Award Scheme; Hampshire Life's, *Best Local Food Menu*; Winchester BID *Member of the Year for Outstanding Contribution to the City of Winchester; Grade 4* in the *Which? Good Food Guide. The Three Tuns* has also been awarded Michelin *Bib Gourmand.*

Damian trained at Runshaw College and Northcote Manor under the wing of Michelin-starred chef Billy Reid, then went on to work in some of Britain's best kitchens including Marco Pierre White's, *L'Escargot* as well as the Michelin-starred *Vineyard* at Stockcross followed by stints in fine kitchens in Australia and California's wine region.

An excellent all-rounder in the kitchen, Damian specialises in modern British cuisine inspired by Hampshire's abundant produce. He loves having Hampshire as his supermarket.

Tanguy's tips

Blackmoor Game wood pigeon: *Beaujolais, France*
Hampshire Dexter beef fillet: *Barossa, South Australia*
Poached rhubarb & crème vanille: *Chenin Blanc, Stellenbosch, South Africa*

Full tasting notes are on page 318

Blackmoor Game *wood pigeon*

with caramelised walnuts, chicory, pickled Stockbridge mushrooms & Secretts beetroot dressing

Serves 4

(all components of this dish should be prepared in advance of searing the pigeon)

8 pigeon breasts

micro red-veined sorrel (or watercress)

several sprigs of thyme

a few knobs of butter

2 white chicory

salt & pepper

Caramelised walnuts

200 g walnuts

simple syrup*

300 g caster sugar

300 water

Pickled Stockbridge mushrooms

200 g exotic mixture mushrooms (from *Fundamentally Fungus*)

50 g caster sugar

45 ml white wine vinegar

45 ml water

1 bay leaf

a sprig of thyme

Secretts beetroot dressing

4 large *Secretts* beetroot

300 ml *Pratt's* rapeseed oil

For the caramelised walnuts, preheat oven to 100°C. Bring the simple syrup to the boil, add the walnuts and simmer until golden then remove with a slotted spoon onto a parchment lined baking tray and place in the oven for 30 minutes. Set aside.

For the Stockbridge mushrooms, trim so they are all the same size for even pickling and place in a clean jar large enough to be completely covered with liquid. Bring the rest of the ingredients to the boil, remove from the heat then pour onto prepared mushrooms. Set aside to cool. Seal and refrigerate if preparing in advance (can be made up to 24 hours in advance).

For the beetroot dressing, peel and grate beetroot & cover with oil then gently simmer until tender, season to taste and set aside.

For the pigeon, brush the breasts with oil then sear in a hot pan for no more than one minute on each side. Melt in the butter and thyme and allow the butter to bubble. Ladle the butter over the breasts for no more than a minute then rest on a cooling rack. Using the same pan toss in the chicory leaves and warm until wilted. Season to taste and serve immediately.

To assemble, slice pigeon breasts in half and arrange with the chicory and mushrooms through the centre of the plate. Crush the walnuts and sprinkle then dress with beetroot and finish with micro sorrel.

* See *The basics*, page 356

Hampshire Dexter beef fillet, rump & bone marrow bon bon

with Secretts *parsnip purée, potatoes dauphinoise, shallot crisps & red wine jus*

Serves 4

Equipment: deep fryer (optional), meat thermometer

1 kg feather blade beef
800 g locally reared Dexter beef fillet
400 g bone marrow
100 g beef suet
breadcrumbs
1 egg, beaten
flour
mirpoix: 2 onions; 2 celery sticks;
    2 carrots, chopped
1½ litres sunflower or rapeseed oil
    for frying
ice
salt & pepper

Side dishes & condiments

3 kg potatoes
1 litre double cream
1 head of garlic
4 parsnips, roasted
400 g *Secretts* leaf spinach, washed
1 large banana shallot, finely sliced
    in rings

Garnishes (see page 348)

potatoes dauphinoise
spinach
parsnip purée
red wine jus

For the feather blade preheat oven to 200°C and slice the meat into 4 portions. Sear each piece on all sides in a hot pan, transfer to an oven proof casserole or roasting tin, add the mirpoix, season and cover with water. Seal with foil and cover with a tight fitting lid and braise for 5 hours until tender. Before serving remove from the casserole, keep covered and allow to rest. Strain and reserve the liquor for glazing.

For the bone marrow bon bons, blanche the bone marrow in boiling water for 30 seconds then transfer to a bowl of ice water to chill. Scoop the marrow into a bowl and mix in enough beef suet to make a consistency that will roll into 1 inch diameter balls. Roll in flour, egg and coat in crumbs and refrigerate.

For the fillets, preheat oven to 200°C. In a hot frying pan sear the medallions on all sides and season to taste. Place them in the oven for 3 minutes, turn and roast for another 3 minutes then turn and repeat for a final 3 minutes, 9 minutes total. Place the thermometer into the centre of one of the fillets for cooking accuracy. It should be warm, not hot or cold (120-130°C for rare to medium). Allow to rest for 2 to 3 minutes.

When ready to serve, reduce the beef liquor by ¾ until shiny and season to taste. Place the blade pieces back into the liquor, coat and warm.

Heat the vegetable oil in a deep fryer or deep pan to 180°C. Remove marrow bon bons from fridge and roll in a few more breadcrumbs. Fry until golden, transfer with a slotted spoon to kitchen paper to drain. Thinly slice the shallots and fry quickly until just golden.

Assemble the plates with vegetables and meat, pour over hot red wine jus and dress with crispy shallots.

Poached rhubarb & crème vanille

Serves 4

**Equipement: fine sieve,
4 dessert glasses, chilled**

*This dish should be prepared
well in advance*

Crème vanille

750 ml *Bere Dairy* double cream

1 vanilla pod

100 g caster sugar

3 gelatine leaves, soaked in cold
    water & squeezed

40 ml white rum

Rhubarb jelly

500 g *Secretts* rhubarb

300 g caster sugar

200 ml water

4 gelatine leaves, soaked in cold
    water & squeezed

30 ml grenadine

a thumb of fresh ginger, peeled & grated

Poached rhubarb

1 large rhubarb stick

100 g sugar

100 ml water

1 star anise

10 ml grenadine

To make the crème vanille place all ingredients in a pan except the gelatine and bring to a simmer. Remove from the heat, stir in the gelatine until completely dissolved and allow to cool.

To make the jelly, place the sugar and rhubarb in a bowl and gently simmer over pan of water for 1 hour. Remove from the heat and add 200 ml of water. Pass through a fine sieve then add the ginger and grenadine. Stir in the gelatine until completely dissolved and allow to cool.

To poach the rhubarb, preheat oven to 160°C. Slice the stick into 1 inch pieces and place in a single layer in a roasting tin. Dredge with sugar and add the star anise. Mix the water *a*nd grenadine together and pour evenly over the rhubarb. Cover and bake for 10 to 15 minutes and remove from the oven. Watch carefully as timing will vary according to the thickness of the stalk, the rhubarb should be slightly al dente. When cool, the rhubarb should be perfectly soft but hold its shape.

To prepare the dish, pour a small amount of jelly into each glass and refrigerate for 15 minutes until set. Then add a layer of the cream, again refrigerating until set. Continue alternating layers until the glasses are $^2/_3$ full. Garnish with chopped poached rhubarb and serve chilled.

Blackmoor Game Ltd

Upper Wield, near Alresford
Peter & Chris Sole
Tom Voice, game keeper

In the 1980's Peter Sole was working as a butcher for a successful game dealer in nearby Newton Valence and in 1988 his boss decided to retire giving Peter the opportunity of acquiring the business. His brother Chris, also a butcher, joined him, as did their wives. The two couples set out to establish one of the most successful enterprises specialising in the manufacture and production of wild game.

What started over 30 years ago, as a modest business supplying feather game to a select clientele in the UK and Europe is now a European Commission approved plant supplying oven ready birds and wild venison to wholesalers, butchers, hoteliers and chefs. In fact, over half a million pigeons, partridge, pheasant, grouse, woodcock and wild duck per year make their way from local and regional UK shoots and are prepared to grace the finest tables across the UK, France, Belgium, Germany, Italy and beyond.

In 2005, with extra land available, they expanded the business to include rearing their own pheasant chicks and poults that gave the business a unique opportunity to buy and sell their own produce. They now provide birds to local shoots then finish and prepare them for market thus giving them more confidence in the game's provenance. For Hampshire residents it also means that the birds have a carbon footprint of less than five miles.

The Sole families take quality so seriously and no one knows better how wild, free-range game can add nutritious and diverse alternatives to our daily menus.

In 2009, *Blackmoor Game* was awarded *The Hampshire Farmers Market's*, 'Best Product of the Year' and in 2010 and 2012 they were finalists for the prestigious *Hampshire Independent Food Producer of the Year* award from *County Magazine*.

Crown of Blackmoor Game *pheasant* *with parsnips & sweet & spicy red cabbage*

Serves 4

Equipment: hand blender, thermometer

2 oven-ready Blackmoor Game pheasant crowns (legless)

4 large parsnips, 1 for purée, 1 for crisps & 2 for roasting

125 ml milk

600 ml Pratt's rapeseed oil for frying

200 g butter for basting

salt & pepper

Sweet & spicy red cabbage

large head of red cabbage, shredded

300 g sultanas

200 g brown sugar

100 ml red wine

100 ml red wine vinegar

1 large dessert spoon of cumin seeds

a splash of *Pratt's* rapeseed oil

2 large Granny Smith apples, peeled, cored & grated

For the cabbage, in a heavy-based pan, heat the oil gently then add the cabbage and sweat until just soft. Add the rest of the ingredients, stir and season to taste. Turn up the heat for a minute, cover with tin foil then lower the heat and simmer for 45 minutes stirring occasionally. The cabbage should keep its body but also be soft and almost sticky. This can be made well in advance and heated when ready to serve.

For the parsnip purée, peel and chop the parsnip, just cover with milk in a small pan & simmer gently until tender. Purée with a hand blender until smooth.

For the parsnip crisps, peel the outer skin and discard then continue peeling into broad ribbons. In a deep pan heat the rapeseed oil to 160°C and deep fry the ribbons until golden. Season to taste.

For the roasted parsnips, pre-heat oven 200°C. Peel & quarter the remaining 2 parsnips, blanch in salted water for 4 minutes, season and coat with rapeseed oil & roast until golden brown.

To oven roast the pheasant, pre-heat oven to 200°C. In a hot pan, caramelise the breast on both sides then place the whole pan in the oven and roast for 6 minutes. Turn the crowns and roast for a further 6 minutes. Remove from the oven, add the butter and baste then allow to rest for 12 minutes. Reserve the juices.

To serve, remove the breast from the bone, add a spoon of cabbage and a spoon of purée in the centre of the plate and place breast on top. Add the roasted parsnip, drizzle with the reserved juices and sprinkle with crisps.

Tanguy's tip

Crown of Blackmoor Pheasant: *Cote Rotie, Rhone Valley, France*
Full tasting notes are on page 318

the little gloster
restaurant & bar

Gurnard, Isle of Wight
Ben & Holly Cooke, chef/proprietors

Light, land and sea, a breathtaking view

Gurnard is an idyllic seaside village nestled just west of Cowes on the Isle of Wight overlooking Gurnard Bay and the West Solent. It's an interesting place, on the move and full of character, young and old. There are only traces of the Roman villa and prominent medieval fortress that both stood at the mouth of the wonderfully named 'Luck River.' It's all been washed away. The village has moved with time and tide in continuous regeneration. What better place for Ben & Holly Cooke to pay homage to his grandparent's hotel, *The Gloster*, that proudly stood a few miles away and housed the Royal Yacht Squadron in the 1800's.

It was Mormor, as young Ben called his gran, that taught him the joy of simple and elegant Scandinavian cuisine. Like its namesake, *The Little Gloster* is a real family effort, Ben cooks, his wife Holly takes skillful care of front of house including their delightful B&B, mum Eileen works behind the scenes and importantly, maintains their charming seaside garden and Mormor Lilian is always on hand to supervise the vegetable beds and fill the restaurant with flowers and stories.

"We've been having fun working together for over a decade and we share the same approach to cooking. We finish each other's sentences like an old couple and we finish each other's dishes as well."

Ben Cooke & Jay Santiago, head chefs

The menu

The Little Gloster **breakfast**

House cured gravadlax

Gurnard in turmeric butter

Apple tarte tatin

In 2004, Ben met Jay Santiago working the ski season in St Anton. Two years later the friends were found working together again, this time in Greece. Wherever the two were in the world they always stayed in touch. Jay returned to the UK to train seriously and spent several years in Yorkshire while Ben continued to work around the globe from Sweden to New Zealand, even going through the Arctic's Northwest Passage on one of the world's most luxurious yachts. He picked up a trick or two circumnavigating the globe and brought them home to build *The Little Gloster* and who better to work alongside him than his buddy. Jay was keen, packed his bags and set off for Cowes, it wasn't until he was on the ferry that he discovered he'd bought a ticket to Ryde!

Ben & Jay's laid-back styles and experience of working with what's to hand lend themselves perfectly to how they work with local suppliers and artisans. If they like the look of the fish on the boat in the morning, it's on the menu that afternoon. It might seem impulsive but it's backed with experience and style.

Dining at *The Little Gloster* is a delight. Ben, Jay and their team effortlessly make you feel as if you're sitting at the table of one of those magnificent yachts. They make dining personal and special.

Tanguy's tips

The Little Gloster **breakfast:** *Bloody Mary: Reyka Vodka, Iceland*
Gravadlax & caviar: *chilled Aquavit or a dry vodka martini on ice, shaken not stirred*
Gurnard: *Chenin Blanc, Saumur, Loire Valley, France*
Apple tarte tatin: *God bless The Queen apple cocktail*

Full tasting notes are on page 318

The Little Gloster *breakfast*

Avocado poached eggs & crispy smoked bacon on sourdough with chilli & mint

Serves 2

6 rashers smoked streaky bacon, grilled

4 large free-range eggs

1 large ripe avocado, pitted, peeled & thinly sliced

½ jalapeno chilli, deseeded & finely diced

2 sprigs of garden mint, shredded

2 tbsp extra virgin rapeseed oil

2 slices of sourdough bread

2 tbsp of white wine vinegar

salt & pepper

Grill the bacon until crispy and keep warm and toast the sourdough then butter.

To poach the eggs, in medium pan heat the water to just simmering, swirl in the vinegar then poach the eggs to your liking. While the eggs are poaching assemble the dish by stacking the toast, bacon and avocado. Remove the eggs with a slotted spoon and drain on kitchen paper. Place on top of the stack and finish the dish by garnishing with the mint, chilli and extra virgin rapeseed oil. Season to taste.

House cured gravadlax
with buttered rye bread, crème fraiche & Danish caviar

Serves 10 to 12 starter-sized portions, yields 1 large round loaf of bread & 100 g butter

Equipment: fine needle-nose plyers, trays with weights (stones or bricks will do), 1 litre mason jar

2 kg side of salmon, descaled, pin boned and scaled (sushi grade recommended)

Marinade
2 kg sugar
2 kg salt
2 tbsp fennel seeds
2 star anise
juice & zest of 3 lemons
2 tbsp black mustard seeds
2 tbsp white mustard seeds
2 tbsp coriander seeds
1 tbsp caraway seeds

Honey & mustard glaze
3 tbsp runny honey
3 tbsp Dijon mustard
a large bunch fresh dill or fennel tops, chopped

1 jar of Danish lumpfish caviar
crème fraiche
fresh dill tops or herbs for garnish
cold pressed rapeseed oil

Garnishes (see page 348)
Scandinavian rye bread
freshly churned butter

For the gravadlax, combine all the marinade ingredients and cover the fillet half with the mixture. Wrap in cling film and let marinate at room temperature for 6 hours until the mixture is melted. Place the wrapped fillet on a tray and cover with another tray then add weights and refrigerate for a minimum of 2 days but no more than a week turning the fish every 12 hours. Remove the gravadlax from the refrigerator, scrape off most of the seasoning and pat dry with kitchen paper. Using a sharp knife cut the cured gravlax into paper-thin slices.

For the glaze, place the ingredients in a saucepan and warm.

To serve, arrange slices of the gravadlax on a plate, dress with generous dollops of crème fraiche and caviar, drizzle with a few drops of rapeseed oil, sprinkle with fresh dill or herb tops and serve with warm bread and fresh butter.

Gurnard in turmeric butter

with wild mussels & crevettes in coriander curry broth

Serves 4

4 gurnard fillets (ask your fishmonger
  to prepare)

16 wild mussels

12 tiger prawns, shelled & de-veined

2 large potatoes (Maris piper), peeled
  & cut into 1 inch pieces

a small bunch of spinach

Turmeric butter

2 tbsp butter

1 small shallot, very finely chopped

1 garlic clove, very finely chopped

zest of 1 lemon

½ tsp turmeric

1 tbsp coriander, finely chopped

Coriander curry broth

2 tsp yellow mustard seeds

vegetable oil

1 onion, chopped

4 garlic cloves, finely chopped

2½ cm piece ginger, julienned

20 curry leaves (or 2-3 tbsp garam
  masala)

1 tsp turmeric

1 tbsp tamarind sauce

500 g coconut milk

4 green chillies, finely sliced

200 ml chicken stock

2 tsp fish sauce

a bunch of coriander, chopped

1 red chilli, finely julienned

Prepare the broth in advance. Cook the mustard seeds in some hot oil until they start to pop. Add the onion, garlic, ginger and curry leaves, lower the heat and cook for 5 minutes. Next add the turmeric and chilli powder and cook for another 5 minutes. Add the tamarind sauce and cook for another 5 minutes, then add the coconut milk, chicken stock and fish sauce, stir well and simmer for 30 minutes. Add the potato cubes and let simmer until just soft through.

Prepare the butter in advance by mixing all the ingredients with semi-soft butter, roll it into logs in cling film and chill until ready to use.

For the gurnard, preheat oven to 180°C and prepare the turmeric butter in a saucepan. In a hot pan, sear the fillets in a bit of hot oil on both sides then bake until just cooked through. This will only take a minute or two. Place the pan back on the stovetop, add a knob of turmeric butter and baste for just a minute then set aside to rest.

Heat the curry broth to a rolling simmer, add the prawns and mussels and simmer until the prawns are pink and the mussels open.

In a separate pan wilt the spinach in a tablespoon of water. When soft remove and drain on kitchen paper.

To serve, ladle prawns, mussels and broth into large soup bowls, scatter with a few wilted spinach leaves and top with the gurnard fillets. Garnish with a sprinkle of fresh coriander and chilli julienne.

Apple tarte tatin
with vanilla ice cream & calvados caramel sauce

Serves 4

Equipment: melon baller, 18 cm round baking tin, ice cream maker (if making your own ice cream)

8 large Granny Smith apples, peeled, cored & quartered

2 tbsp cold water

130 g caster sugar

50 g unsalted butter, cold & diced

200 g puff pastry, ready rolled

flour for dusting

Calvados caramel sauce

110 g dark soft brown sugar

110 g butter

2 tbsp Calvados

175 ml double cream

500 g vanilla ice cream*
   (good quality store bought is fine)

For the tarte tatin, on a floured surface roll out the puff pastry to 2 mm thickness and prick all over with a fork. Cut the pastry in a 20 cm circle and refrigerate on a lightly floured tray. Next, using a melon baller, scoop out the apple cores.

Pre-heat the oven to 190°C. Pour 20 g of water in a heavy saucepan, add 100 g of sugar and cook on medium heat for 5 minutes to a golden brown caramel (do not stir). Add 30 g of butter, swirl in the pan and pour into a round baking tin and let the caramel start to set. Arrange the apple pieces upright around the edge then tightly pack the remaining apples into the caramel wedging as many in as possible. Melt the remaining 20 g of butter and brush over the apples. Sprinkle the remaining 30 g of caster sugar over the top and bake for 35 minutes. Place the puff pastry circle on top of the apples tucking the edge into the mould. Bake for a further 30 minutes. Cool for 1 hour until barely warm.

Slide the blade of a sharp knife full circle against the mould to release the tart. Place a large plate over the tart and turn upside down, shaking sideways to release.

For the calvados caramel sauce, place the sugar and butter in a saucepan and cook until well combined. Pour in the cream and calvados and simmer for three to five minutes until the mixture thickens slightly.

To serve, place slices of warm tart on plates, top with ice cream boules and slather with caramel sauce. Serve immediately with a snifter of Calvados on the side.

* See *The basics*, page 356

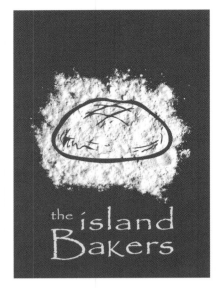

Isle of Wight
John & Helen Fahy

Bread and doughnuts fit for a king!

John and Helen's professional experience is a veritable who's who of the bread world. They met in 2003 at Buckingham Palace as part of the Royal Chefs team. Before that, Helen was a chef for Marcus Wareing at *The Savoy Hotel's, The Grill Room*. She went on to work as a private chef before teaching at Gordon Ramsey's school, *Tante Marie School of Cookery*.

Meanwhile, John was honing his skills and gaining a love of natural sourdough at one of California's most exclusive restaurants, *The French Laundry*, in the Napa Valley. He returned to the UK to take up residence as a chef at the even more exclusive *Waterside Inn* in Bray. Finally he too joined Gordon Ramsey's, *Tante Marie*. It was while teaching that his love for bread awoke.

In 2010 the couple decided to do things their way so headed for the Isle of Wight to create, *The Island Bakers*. They started modestly, renting another bakery and working nights, (as all great bakers should), but demand for their bread, brownies and doughnuts soon outgrew their accommodation.

John, Helen and their team still work through the nights making beautiful breads and goodies ready for delivery across the island and to their shop in Newport. Their doughnuts are so moreish it simply isn't possible to stop at one. They are truly fit for royalty!

The Little Gloster *celebration burger on* Island Bakers *brioche buns* *with Gallybagger cheese & pickled cucumbers*

Serves 4
(with 2 1 litre jars of pickled cucumbers)

Equipment: 2 1 litre kilner jars, sterilised (see page 354)

500 g coarse beef steak mince (20% fat content)

4 slices smoked bacon

2 tbsp olive oil

salt & pepper

4 *Island Bakers* brioche burger buns

Pickled cucumbers

750 g cucumbers (Kirby are crunchiest but English will do)

4 garlic cloves, smashed

2 tsp dill seeds

½ tsp red pepper flakes

250 ml cider vinegar

250 ml water

1½ tsp pickling or kosher salt

Garnish

1 beefsteak tomato, sliced

½ a head of round lettuce

200 g Gallybagger cheese, sliced

For the cheeseburger, put the mince in a large bowl and season with salt and pepper. Use your hands to shape the mince into four burger-shaped patties. Wrap the patties in cling film and place in the fridge for an hour.

Heat a large frying pan and cook the bacon until crisp then drain on kitchen paper. Once hot, sear the burgers and cook each side for 2 to 3 minutes. When cooked, set aside to rest.

For the pickled cucumbers, sterilise the jars in advance. Trim the ends of the cucumbers and slice into finger-sized batons or 2 mm slices, as you prefer. Divide the dry ingredients into 2 halves, add each to a jar and tightly pack the jars with cucumbers.

Put the cider vinegar, water and salt in a pan and bring to the boil. Pour into the jars filling to 2 mm from the top, gently tap the jars to remove any air bubbles then fill completely to the top and seal. Cool at room temperature then store in a cool place for at least 48 hours or longer. They will last after opening for several weeks in the fridge and up to a year with proper storage.

Build the burgers on toasted brioche buns stacked with preferred garnishes, hold together with a skewer and pop a few pickled cucumbers on the side.

Tanguy's tip

Burger: *The Nova Foresta, The Vibrant Forest Brewery, Hampshire*
Full tasting notes are on page 318

Baughurst, Nr Tadley
Jason King & Simon Page, chef/proprietors

Seemingly effortless to the finest detail.

Just a few miles North of Basingstoke lies Baughurst. Passing through, it seems a quiet spot where the locals casually greet each other and the postman is on a first name basis with everyone. The origin of its Anglo-Saxon name has two interpretations: 'the badger's wood' and 'the broom forest'. Both are fitting. The abundant birch forests still produce iconic 'besom brooms' and the surrounding forest has always been home to a healthy badger population.

During the Reformation and because of its central and neutral location, Baughurst became a thriving hotbed of religious debate housing healthy communities of Anglicans, Wesleyans and Quakers. Perhaps it was the Quaker influence that brought the besom broom its fame. In 1847, Baughurst came under the ownership of the Duke of Wellington and it remained with subsequent heirs until 1943.

In 2005 this tranquil village saw the beginning of its next quiet revolution. Australian-born chef Jason King and his partner Simon Page bought the run down pub and started building their special brand of stylish country inn, *The Wellington Arms*.

Soon after opening, the present day Duke of Wellington thought he should pay a visit to his newly refurbished namesake. As the Duke pondered a beautifully painted rendition of his coat of arms, Simon asked, "Your Grace, perhaps now would be a good time to ask your permission for us to display the Wellington coat of arms." The Duke said, "Yes it is," and he went on to enjoy his lunch.

Today, *The Welly*, as it's known by the locals and postman, takes pride of place. Simon and Jason have created a perfect fine dining pub with rooms as luscious as the food. They've lovingly created stunning ornamental and kitchen gardens and manage beehives, a selection of rarebreed livestock and a combination of rarebreed and rescue battery chickens.

"Having chooks, pigs, sheep, bees and veggies out back is what many chefs dream of. Luckily for Simon and me our dream came true."

Jason King, chef

The Menu

Twice baked cheese soufflé

Terrine of tiger prawns & leeks

Crying leg of lamb

Jelly of Wellington Arms elderflower cordial

Jason began his culinary career in his hometown of Melbourne, Australia. At just 18 he was awarded the Aussie equivalent of the UK's *Acorn Awards*, the *Australian Apprentice of the Year for Melbourne*, which landed him a place on the *1992 Australian Culinary Olympic Team*. They went on to win gold in Frankfurt in 1992.

Whilst working at Melbourne's famous, *Fanny's Restaurant*, Jason was spotted by chef Paul Bocuse. Under the French master he established his classic style and also whet his appetite to go abroad. He spent the next six years at Hong Kong's popular and lively Spanish eatery, *La Bodega*. Little did he know how much would change! For six years, ex-pat English musician Simon Page was a regular customer but the two never met. Simon was headed home so popped in for one last meal. The rest is history. Simon returned to the UK and Jason followed soon after. In 2005 they bought the clapped out old pub in Baughurst.

In 2011, *The Good Food Guide* named Jason, *Pub Chef of the Year*, and 2012 saw him named, *Best Gastropub Chef of the Year*, by *The Morning Advertiser* and *The Times* named the pub, "The second best place to eat in the countryside." Simon, *The Welly's* guests owe you a big 'thanks' for going back to *La Bodega* for a final farewell!

Tanguy's tips

Cheese soufflé: *Sauvignon Blanc, Waterkloof, Stellenbosch, South Africa*
Terrine of tiger prawns: *Albarino, Coopers Creek, Gisborne, New Zealand*
Crying leg of lamb: *Mourvedre, Yangarra Estate, McLaren Vale, South Australia*
Jelly: *Moscato d'Asti, Canelli, Cerutti, Cassinasco, Piedmont, Italy*

Full tasting notes are on page 318

Twice baked goat's cheese soufflé

Jason usually serves this on a bed of wilted spinach but will also look at what he has ready to pick in his garden.

Serves 8

Equipment: soufflé moulds, hand blender

90 g butter

65 g plain flour

400 ml warm milk

80 g Rosary goat's cheese

3 tbsp freshly grated Parmesan

½ bunch flat leaf parsley, chopped

3 Wellington free range egg yolks

Murray River pink salt flakes*

freshly ground black pepper

5 egg whites

a little double cream for second cooking

a handful of pine nuts, toasted

your choice of spinach, garden vegetables, grilled

fresh salad leaves and vinaigrette on the side to serve

For the soufflé, preheat oven to 180°C. Melt a little butter and grease 8 soufflé dishes.

Melt the remaining butter in a small heavy-based saucepan. Stir in the flour without overheating for 2 minutes. Gradually add milk, stirring all the while. Bring to the boil, then reduce heat and simmer for 5 minutes. Mash the goat's cheese until soft and add to the hot sauce, then add the Parmesan and parsley and allow the mixture to cool for a few minutes. Fold in the yolks thoroughly and taste for seasoning. Beat the egg whites until they form stiff peaks then fold into the cheese mixture. Divide the mixture between the prepared moulds and smooth the surface of each. Stand moulds in a baking dish lined with a tea towel and pour in boiling water to come ⅔ up their sides. Bake for 20 minutes until firm to the touch and well risen then remove from the oven. (They will deflate and look wrinkled.) Allow to rest for 10 minutes, and then gently ease them out of the moulds. Invert onto a plate covered with cling film and leave until needed.

To serve, preheat oven to 180°C. Place soufflés in a buttered ovenproof gratin dish, so that they are not touching. Pour over cream to moisten them thoroughly. Return to the oven for 15 minutes. The soufflés will look swollen and golden.

Serve with a little double cream, toasted pine nuts, shaved Parmesan and sautéed spinach, garden vegetables or a green salad. Have the garnish on the plate and serve immediately as the soufflés start to deflate as they leave the oven.

* Jason uses this unique Australian salt that's produced to help relieve the salinity problems of the Murray-Darling Basin caused primarily by the introduction of European farming and crops.

Terrine of tiger prawns & leeks
with Marie Rose sauce

Serves 12

Equipment: bamboo steamer, bamboo skewers, 2 terrine moulds and weights (bricks from the garden, wrapped in foil will do)

2 kg large tiger prawns, shelled
   & de-veined

salt & pepper

a pinch of sugar

juice of 1 lemon

2 kg baby leeks

2 leaves of gelatine, soaked in cold water

Marie Rose sauce

4 tbsp mayonnaise

2 tsp ketchup

1 tsp horseradish, finely grated

juice & zest of 1 lime

a dash of Tabasco sauce

a dash of Worcestershire sauce

20 ml vodka (for an extra kick)

Marco Pierre White's iconic book, White Heat, *was the first cookery book Jason ever owned. He, like so many, still pays homage.*

To prepare the prawns lightly season then skewer on short bamboo skewers and cook in a steamer for 2 minutes until just pink. Remove from the steamer, squeeze a little lemon juice over the prawns then leave to cool.

To prepare the leeks, trim the roots then wash in cold water to remove any grit and dirt. Bring a large saucepan of water to the boil, season with a handful of salt and sugar then add the leeks to the boiling water. Place a plate on top of the leeks to keep them submerged then place a lid on the saucepan. Cook for 15 minutes until very tender. Carefully remove from the saucepan then drain on kitchen paper. Retain the water.

Reduce the liquid until syrupy. Add 2 leaves of gelatine and set aside. This will take about 20 minutes.

Line a terrine mould with foil with an overhang of 10cm each side. This will help you to remove the terrine later. Arrange the leeks in the terrine mould alternating the leeks from top to tail and top with a little leek syrup in between each layer. Ensure the leeks are tightly packed in the base of the terrine then season with a little salt and pepper.

Remove the skewers from the prawns then arrange some prawns in a row on top of the leeks, along with a little more leek syrup. Repeat the process of alternating layers of leeks, prawns and syrup until the last layer of leeks is approximately 3cm higher than the top of the terrine mould. Cover the terrine with cling film then make 8 small incisions in the cling film to later allow excess fluid to drain. Place another terrine mould on top then place weights on top and refrigerate for at least 4 hours.

To prepare the Marie Rose sauce, stir together all the ingredients. Chill until ready to serve.

To serve, un-mould the terrine then, using a sharp knife, cut a slice approximately 2 cm thick. Arrange on a plate with some sauce and season with a few dill sprigs and season to taste.

Crying leg of lamb

Serves 8

Equipment: blender or food processor

1 whole leg of lamb, de-boned &
  butterflied
250 g yoghurt
100 g Dijon mustard
2 garlic cloves, finely chopped
10 sprigs thyme, rosemary or oregano

Vegetables
1 kg red onions, finely sliced
2 kg potatoes, finely sliced
½ bottle white wine
extra virgin olive oil
juice of 1 lemon

Green Sauce
a bunch of flat leaf parsley
a bunch of mint
10 sprigs of thyme, rosemary or oregano
100 g capers
2 garlic cloves, peeled
200 ml extra virgin olive oil

To marinate the lamb, mix the yoghurt, mustard, garlic and herbs into a paste and spread thickly over the meat, wrap in cling film and marinate for at least 3 days in the fridge. The longer it is left the more tender the lamb will be.

To prepare the vegetables, place the onions in a large shallow roasting pan with plenty of salt, pepper, lemon juice and extra virgin olive then neatly layer the potato slices on top. Pour over white wine and more olive oil. (This will help the potatoes crisp up.)

To roast the lamb, preheat oven to 250°C. Place the lamb directly on the top rack and carefully position the tray of vegetables on the rack beneath to catch all juices. Cook for approximately 45 minutes to 1 hour until cooked through but still pink, according to taste. Rest for 20 minutes, covered with foil to keep warm.

While the lamb is roasting, combine all green sauce ingredients in a blender and purée roughly.

Serve in shallow bowls by placing spoonfuls of vegetables, topped with slices of lamb and a drizzle of green sauce.

Jelly of Wellington Arms elderflower cordial & raspberry ripple ice cream

Serves 10

Equipment: fine sieve, muslin or J Cloth, jelly moulds, sugar thermometer, ice cream maker

Elderflower cordial

Without the tartaric acid the cordial will soon ferment, as Jason & Simon once discovered.

40 elderflower heads (picked in the morning before the bees get them)

1.4 kg granulated sugar

juice & zest of 3 lemons & 2 oranges

1 tsp tartaric acid (optional)

Jelly

1 litre elderflower cordial

8 gelatine leaves, soaked in cold water

1 litre filtered water

500 ml iced water

sunflower oil to wipe the moulds

350 g raspberries for garnish

Ice cream

Jason uses the pub's eggs, if using shop bought add an extra yolk for richness.

18 yolks or 9 whole eggs

3 vanilla pods, seeds removed

175 g caster sugar

2 bay leaves

1.25 litres milk

500 g double cream

450 g fresh or frozen raspberries

100 g sifted icing sugar

For the elderflower cordial, remove any bugs, leaves or brown bits, put them into a large bowl with the citrus zest and cover with boiling water. Cover and leave overnight in a cool spot (like Monaco or Cornwall). Next day, pass through a fine sieve and squeeze the pulp to extract all juice. Measure the amount of flower liquid and for every 550 ml add 375 g sugar, 60 ml lemon juice and tartaric acid if you are using it. Gently warm to dissolve the sugar then bring to the boil skimming off any scum. Allow the cordial to cool then strain through a muslin cloth. Store the cordial in sterilised bottles. It also freezes well.

To serve as a drink mix about 4 to 1 sparkling or freshly drawn water to cordial with a wedge of lime, sprig of mint and lots of ice or use as a delicious syrup over vanilla ice cream or red berries.

For the jelly lightly oil 10 jelly moulds. Bring 500 ml filtered water to the boil then whisk in the softened gelatine. Add this to the remaining 500 ml filtered water along with the elderflower cordial. Pour into the prepared moulds, cover and refrigerate for at least 12 hours.

For the ice cream, in a large saucepan add the milk, cream, vanilla pods and bay leaves and bring to the boil. Remove from the heat and cover with cling film. Leave to infuse for a minimum of 30 minutes. Next, in a large stainless steel bowl, rub the vanilla seeds into the caster sugar. Whisk in the eggs until light. Add the infused milk a ladle at a time then transfer to a saucepan and cook on low heat stirring constantly until it reaches 82°C (for sterilisation). Remove from the heat, continuing to stir as the pan cools. Pass through a fine sieve, wash the vanilla beans lightly and add back into the strained mixture then cover with cling film and refrigerate. When ice cream base is very cold churn in an ice cream machine following manufacturers instructions.

For the raspberry ripple, mash the raspberries with a little icing sugar. Cover a non-metallic container with a layer of ice cream then spread on a layer of the raspberry followed by the remainder of the ice cream.

To serve, invert the jelly onto cold plates. Mix raspberries gently with elderflower syrup and spoon over and around jelly with a scoop of raspberry ripple ice cream.

> *"The garden has taken nine years to get to this point. It was no easy task but it's a wonderful place for our guests to relax and for us to unwind after a busy day. Would we do it again?"*

For Jason and Simon, their labour of love and one of their best rewards has been building their garden, both kitchen and ornamental and adding to it their polytunnels, chickens, pigs, sheep and bees and the whole Wellington Team pitches in on daily maintenance. Everything has been carefully designed to support Jason's fresh and relaxed take on classic cuisine, using honey from their own bees, plucking eggs from their rescue chickens' nests and popping them straight into the daily menu.

They grow salad leaves, herbs and many of their vegetables all year-round and kitchen waste including meat, fish and dairy is safely composted in special containers to get the most out of re-generating nutrients.

Crispy fried homegrown pumpkin flowers stuffed *with ricotta & Parmesan on a salad of homegrown leaves*

Serves 5

Equipment: piping bag, deep fryer

Flowers

10 pumpkin or courgette flowers, stamens removed

250 g ricotta cheese

150 g Parmesan, grated

a pinch of nutmeg, grated

a pinch of cayenne pepper

zest of ½ a lemon

sea salt & pepper

1½ litres vegetable oil for frying

Note: the stamens are very bitter, and must be removed. No short cuts!

Batter

300g self-raising flour

150 to 200 ml real ale

sea salt

Lemon dressing

juice of 1 lemon

2 tbsp honey

250 ml extra virgin olive oil

sea salt & black pepper

Salad leaves & shaved Parmesan for garnish

For the cheese filling, combine both cheeses and spices together using a fork then spoon into a piping bag. Fill the flower cavity with the cheese mixture and twist the tips of the petals together to seal the flower and refrigerate until required.

For the batter, whisk the beer into the flour along with a pinch of salt. The batter should resemble thick double cream. Add more beer if required.

For the lemon dressing, combine all ingredients in a jam jar and shake vigorously. Season to taste.

To cook preheat a deep fryer to 180°C. With a pastry brush or your fingers, lightly smear each flower with batter so you can still see the flower. Deep fry in small batches until lightly golden then remove with a slotted spoon and drain on kitchen paper. Serve immediately with a fine leaf salad with lemon dressing and a little shaved Parmesan.

Tanguy's tip

Ricotta & Parmesan stuffed pumpkin flowers:

Madeleine Angevine, Danebury Vineyards, Hampshire

Full tasting notes are on page 318

HOTEL
TERRAVINA

Netley Marsh, New Forest
Gerard & Nina Basset, proprietors

Hotel TerraVina is the fresh and vibrant result of Gerard and Nina Basset's unparalleled skill and experience. Outside it's a comfortable Victorian country house nestled in the heart of the New Forest. Inside, Nina's fresh design has brought in all the colour, texture and light of the forest, showcasing the craftsmanship of local artists and artisans. Her love of their surroundings is reflected in every detail.

It's a wonderful setting to enjoy fine food. Chefs Gavin Barnes and George Blogg celebrate the New Forest's natural bounty and fine produce in their modern classic styles. George also presents a unique private dining experience of a foraged tasting menu prepared and served exclusively by him with wines matched and served by head sommelier Tanguy Martin.

All of this is the backdrop for something unique. The wine. Gerard Basset, OBE, alone holds all the titles of *Master Sommelier, Master of Wine, Wine MBA* and *Best Sommelier in the World*. TerraVina's wines and cellar are his and his wine team's passion and they delight in sharing them. Showcasing newly discovered wines, hosting special wine events and conducting regular wine courses are just a few ways Gerard and the team, headed up by his protégé, Tanguy, share their infectious enthusiasm.

At *Hotel TerraVina* meals are transformed into events and a visit is something to delight all the senses.

"We're completely spoiled in the New Forest. We have everything on a plate."

Gavin Barnes, head chef

"I love that the whole team here is so passionate about what we do."

George Blogg, executive chef

The Menu

Gavin's fine dining

Seared salmon confit & Swiss chard & pine nut galette

Roast loin, braised leg & faggot of fallow venison

Blackcurrant soufflé & apple ice cream

George's fine & foraged
Pork, wild leek & pear

Lobster, carrot & buttermilk

Acorn, chocolate & sugars

Gavin Barnes

Gavin brings more than twenty years of fine culinary expertise to *TerraVina* and he's in his natural environment. He trained under renowned Hampshire chef, Alex Aitken at *Le Poussin at Parkhill*, which was the only Michelin-starred restaurant in the New Forest. He then went on to complete a stint in London at *Gordon Ramsey* before returning home.

For Gavin, being a chef isn't about accolades and awards, its about customers. He loves everything about the New Forest and his real reward is serving his special version of it.

George Blogg

George began his culinary career in his home county of Dorset working at *The Riverside Restaurant* followed by two years under Philip Howard at double Michelin-starred restaurant *The Square* in Mayfair. He then moved to Cheltenham to join David Everitt-Matthias at two Michelin-starred *Le Champignon Sauvage*. In 2014 George was awarded the *Good Food Guide* Editor's Award as the 'Chef to Watch'.

Tanguy's tips

Seared salmon confit: *Rosé, Cotes de Provençe, France*
Local fallow venison: *Vinha pan, Beira, Portugal*
Blackcurrant soufflé: *Banyuls, Roussillon, France*

Pork, wild leek & pear: *Chambolle-Musigny, Burgandy, France*
Lobster, carrot & buttermilk: *Riesling, Stúrovo, Slovakia*
Acorn, chocolate & sugars: *Muscat, Victoria, Australia*

Full tasting notes are on page 318

Seared salmon confit & Swiss chard & pine nut galette

with sorrel sauce & Avruga caviar

Serves 4

Equipment: scone cutter, blender, fine sieve

4 100 g pieces of salmon fillet, skin removed

olive oil for frying

knob of butter

salt & pepper

1 jar Avruga caviar

Galette

250 g Swiss chard

50 g pine nuts, toasted (a few extra for garnish)

50 g oats

3 medium eggs, whisked

25 g dry breadcrumbs

ice for cooling

Sorrel sauce

200 ml double cream

50 ml white wine

100 g large leaf sorrel

juice of ½ lemon

50 g of butter

ice for cooling

For the galette, line a baking tray with parchment and pre-heat oven to 160°C. Blanch the Swiss chard in boiling water for 30 seconds and refresh in ice water then squeeze to remove excess moisture and mix with the other ingredients. Press the mixture into a scone cutter 1 inch deep onto the tray and bake for 5 minutes until set. Before serving lightly coat a non-stick frying pan with oil and lightly brown on both sides until warm through.

For the sorrel sauce, reduce the cream and wine by a third then place in a blender with the sorrel and butter and liquidise until smooth. Pass through a fine sieve and place in a bowl over ice water to cool quickly so it doesn't turn brown. Season carefully with salt and lemon juice.

For the salmon, lightly coat a frying pan with oil and when hot sear the salmon on both sides. When it has a nice even colour remove from the heat, add a knob of butter, lightly season to taste and baste. Finish cooking in the pan's residual heat. Serve slightly pink in the middle.

To serve, on a deep plate place the galette then top with the salmon and a dollop of caviar. Surround with a fine layer of sauce sprinkled with a few pine nuts.

Roast loin, braised leg & faggot of local fallow venison

with red cabbage & parsnip

Serves 4

Equipment: meat grinder, deep fat fryer, mandolin, terrine dish with tight fitting lid and weights, blender

800 g venison loin, reserve trim
500 g venison shoulder, reserve trim
a splash of pomace oil
salt & pepper

Faggot
100 g venison mince
50 g pork back fat
50 g pork liver or kidney
1 egg
1 tbsp whole grain mustard
50 g fresh breadcrumbs
small bunch of fresh thyme leaves
500 ml venison (or veal) stock

Venison sauce
spare trim of the venison
250 ml red wine
mirpoix: 1 shallot, peeled & chopped;
    1 carrot, chopped; 1 stalk of celery,
    chopped; 1 leek, chopped; 2 garlic
    cloves; 1 sprig of thyme
2 knobs of butter

Garnishes (see page 348)
Braised red cabbage
Parsnip purée & crisps

Prepare the faggot in advance by mincing together the venison, fat and offal to a fine consistency then mix with the breadcrumbs, egg, mustard and thyme so the mixture will hold together nicely when rolled into balls. Add a bit more breadcrumb or egg if needed. When ready to cook, preheat oven to 90°C, cover the faggots with stock and braise for 1½ - 2 hours. Pass the stock through a fine sieve into a pan and reduce by ⅔ to a sticky glaze. When ready to serve, baste the warm faggots with the glaze.

To confit the leg, preheat oven to 90°C and line a terrine with cling film. Braise the meat for several hours until the meat falls off the bone. Pull the meat into shreds removing any fat and press into the terrine, cover with cling film and press with a tight fitting lid, apply weight and chill. When ready to serve, slice the confit into 2.5 cm portions and pan fry in a bit of pomace oil until crispy on both sides.

For the loin, sear whole on all sides keeping the meat pink inside. Season to taste and rest for five minutes before slicing into medallions.

For the sauce, fry the venison trim and mirpoix in a large, heavy-based pan until nicely caramelised. Deglaze the pan with red wine, allow to reduce slightly, cover with water and slowly simmer for about 4 hours. Pass through a sieve and return to the heat in a clean pan to reduce to a velvety sauce consistency. Check seasoning and whisk in the butter just before serving.

Blackcurrant soufflé & apple ice cream

Serves 4

Equipment: 4 soufflé moulds, hand blender, fine sieve, piping bag, ice cream maker

Soufflé base
500 g blackcurrants
50 g caster sugar
150 ml cold water
25 g cornflour

Moulds
soft butter
pain d'epices crumbs, fine & dry
  (see page 348)

Soufflé mix
100 g egg white
2 drops of lemon juice
150 g caster sugar
100 g soufflé base

Apple ice cream
1 litre Anglaise cream*
2 cooking apples (Bramley), peeled,
  cored & sliced
2 tbsp sugar
1 tbsp water

The soufflé base is best prepared the night before. Mix the water with the cornflour then add it with the rest of the ingredients in a saucepan. Stir over a low heat for 10 to 15 minutes until the blackcurrants are soft then purée with a hand blender. Pass through a fine sieve and pour into an airtight container. Seal with cling film to prevent a crust forming, cover and refrigerate. (This makes several batches and will store in the fridge for three days or in freezer.)

To prepare the moulds, brush the inside of each soufflé mould with a thin, even layer of soft butter. Add a spoonful of very fine pain d'epices crumbs* and tap it around until the butter is completely coated. Pour out the excess crumb into the next butter-lined mould and continue. (Pain d'epices can be substituted with store bought ginger bread.)

For the soufflé preheat oven to 180°C. Add the egg white & lemon juice into a dry, clean bowl and whisk until the egg white starts to foam then slowly add the sugar continuing to whisk until the mix reaches soft peaks. Gently fold in half the mix to the soufflé base in a round-bottomed bowl to form an even colour then fold in the rest until even.

Spoon the mix into a piping bag and pipe into the prepared moulds to 2 mm below the rim. At this point the soufflé can be stored in the fridge for up to an hour or a bit longer if the mixture is firm and stable. Preheat oven to 180°C. From the fridge place the moulds on a tray and cook for approximately 8 minutes, turning 180° halfway through. Serve immediately with apple ice cream.

For the apple ice cream, make an apple purée by cooking the apples and sugar with a splash of water until very soft then purée with a hand blender. Add this to the Anglaise cream in an ice cream maker and churn to manufacturer's instructions.

* See *The basics*, page 356

Pork, wild leek & pear

Serves 4

Equipment: fine sieve, terrine moulds with weights, ice cream maker, vacuum packer, blowtorch, hand blender, piping bag

10 pig cheeks

mirpoix: 1 small carrot; ½ stick of celery; 2 garlic cloves; 1 shallot

4 peppercorns

2 cloves

1 star anise

100 ml red wine

50 g butter

6 wild leek plants, blanched

2 pigs ears

200 g pear purée

1 leaf gelatine, soaked in cold water

100 ml water

juice of ½ a lemon

30 g caster sugar

20 wild leek seeds

rapeseed oil

Maldon salt

For the pigs cheeks preheat oven to 90°C. Trim the pig cheeks and sear on high heat then add to a roasting pan with the mirpoix and aromats. Deglaze the pan with a splash of red wine and pour over the cheeks then cover with water and seal with foil or a lid. Braise for 6 to 8 hours until the cheeks are tender then allow to cool in the liquor. Place the cheeks in a bowl. Pass the stock through a fine sieve into a clean pan and reduce on high heat to a sauce consistency then whisk in the butter. Pour the sauce over the cheeks and fold the mixture through, season to taste and divide into 3 portions. Line a terrine mould with cling film and push down the first third of pork to form a single layer. Cover with half the blanched leeks, and then add the second layer of pork meat, pushing down to form another even layer. Add the rest of the leeks, and then finally the rest of the pork meat. Wrap the sides of the cling film over the top, poke a few small holes to let any air escape and then compress with a snug fitting board or second terrine mould with a weight on top and refrigerate overnight.

For the crisp pig ears preheat oven to 90°C and line a terrine mould with cling film. Blanch the ears for 5 minutes then braise for 6 hours until soft. Remove them from the liquor and set in a terrine mould, cover with cling film, press with weights and freeze. When frozen, shave into very thin slices and place between sheets of greaseproof paper, drizzle with rapeseed oil and sprinkle with salt. Bake on a metal tray, with another well fitting tray on top for 6 minutes on each side at 180°C until crisp.

For the sorbet, heat the water, sugar and lemon juice until dissolved, stir in the gelatine sheet until dissolved, and then stir in the pear purée, churn following manufacturer's instructions.

Prepare the leek seeds as you would capers. Make a brine of 10% salt. Add the seeds then pour into a bag and vacuum pack to remove any air, and leave for at least 2 days before use.

To plate the dish, take a slice of the terrine, sprinkle some caster sugar onto the surface and blowtorch. Put this on the plate with the sorbet and wild leek seeds, and add a crispy pigs ear wafer.

To make pear purée peel, core and chop 2 ripe pears, steam for 3 to 5 minutes until very soft. Purée with a hand blender, pass through a fine sieve, spoon into a piping bag and chill.

Lobster, carrot & buttermilk

Serves 2 as a main

Equipment: thermometer, squeeze bottle, kitchen scissors, vacuum packer, blender, 120cm cake tin

1 600 g live native lobster, chilled in freezer for 30 minutes

2 large carrots, peeled & chopped

2 small knobs of butter

100 ml milk

4 g agar agar (see page 355)

100 ml buttermilk

a small amount lemon juice

1 bunch of baby mixed colour carrots with tops

1 piece of carrot cake, diced finely & dried

Maldon salt

extra virgin rapeseed oil

ice

Carrot cake

500 g granary flour

50 g baking powder

2 tsp cinnamon

2 tsp nutmeg

8 eggs

500 g Demerara sugar

370 g rapeseed oil

100 g carrots, grated

To prepare the lobster, take it out of the freezer, rip off the claws and head from the tail. Cook the tail in boiling salted water for 3 minutes and refresh in ice water until cold.

Take the water off the heat (it should be 80°C) and add the claws, cooking them in the hot, standing water for 6 minutes, then plunge into ice water to cool. To extract the meat from the shell cut the tail down the middle, remove the intestinal tract then pull out the half tails whole. Carefully cut the claws and elbow pieces and extract the meat in the same way making sure to remove any bones from the claws. Cut each half of the tail into two pieces, divide the claws and elbows into halves and place them each into a vacuum pack bag with a knob of butter and seal, removing all the air and store in the fridge. To reheat, put the bag in some water at 50°C for 8 to 10 minutes.

For the carrot purée, in a heavy-based saucepan sweat the carrot in butter without colour until they start to soften then add the milk and boil until soft. Place in a liquidiser and blend until very smooth. Season to taste and serve warm.

For the buttermilk purée, heat 100 ml of milk with the agar agar until dissolved, add to the buttermilk, season with salt and a little lemon juice and set in a container in the fridge. When set, purée in a blender, pass through a fine sieve and place in a plastic squeeze bottle.

To braise the baby carrots, blanch for 3 minutes then add to a hot pan with some rapeseed oil and salt to colour the outside.

To plate, add the carrot purée first with a spoon, followed by the hot lobster, pieces of braised carrot, thinly sliced raw carrots, buttermilk purée dots, dried carrot cake crumb, pieces of carrot tops & finish with a drizzle of rapeseed oil and a sprinkle of Maldon salt.

For the carrot cake, preheat oven to 170°C and grease and flour cake tin. Whisk the eggs, sugar and oil together until twice the volume. Sieve together the dry ingredients and fold into the egg mixture then fold in the carrots and raisins. Pour into a greased loaf tin and bake for 45 minutes until a toothpick comes out clean.

Acorn, chocolate & sugars

Serves 4

Equipment: fine sieve, metal rings, sugar thermometer, moulds, blowtorch (if using metal moulds), blender, leaf moulds, silpat mat, flat pastry brush

Acorn set crème
500 ml double cream
270 ml milk
40 g roasted crushed acorns
95 g caster sugar
180 g egg yolks

Dark chocolate mousse
400 g 70% dark chocolate, melted to 40°C
160 g egg yolks (8)
190 g caster sugar
700 ml double cream
100 ml whole milk

Leaves
100g isomalt
25g cocoa nibs

Walnut crumble
30 g icing sugar
60 g chopped walnuts
60 g chopped white bread
80 g Demerara sugar
20 g corn flour
3 g salt
1 vanilla pod, seeds only
1 egg
75 g melted butter
20 g walnut oil

For the acorn set crème preheat oven to 95°C and place metal rings lined on the outside with cling film and foil in a deep tray for a bain marie. Heat the milk, cream and acorns without boiling for 30 minutes to infuse the flavour of the acorns. Whisk together the caster sugar and yolks and pour into the cream, whisking all the time. Pass through a fine sieve and pour into the rings. Add hot water to the tray half way up the rings and bake for 1 hour until set. Remove and leave to cool, then refrigerate.

For the mousse, make a sabayon by whisking together the yolks and sugar on a bain marie to 120°C. Add in the cream and milk in small portions whisking continually to the ribbon stage*. Fold the sabayon into the melted chocolate $1/3$ at a time until completely mixed. Pour into a deep container and chill.

To make the leaves preheat oven to 160°C, heat the isomalt until it is just starting to colour. Pour this into a tray over the cocoa nibs and leave to set hard. Add to a blender and whizz to a powder. Sprinkle a little of the powder into a leaf mould on a silpat mat and bake until the sugar has dissolved. Remove from the oven and bend the mat into a curve and hold it in place until the leaves have set.

For the walnut crumble, preheat oven to 160°C and mix together all ingredients except the melted butter and walnut oil. Stir these together separately then slowly mix the liquid in to a crumbly consistency. Bake on a tray, stirring every few minutes until golden.

To plate melt a little chocolate mousse and brush a stroke onto the plate. Remove the cling film and foil from the moulds and lift the set crème with a spatula onto plates, and remove the ring. Add some walnut crumble, a rocher of mousse and the leaf tuilles.

* See *Glossary*, page 354

Karen Wells, *proprietor*

Arlesford is a prosperous market town on the river Itchen that has thrived on the sheep and cattle trade since the 12thC. It's split between the Old and the New. *Old Alresford* has existed since the Neolithic age since when there have been Bronze, Iron Age and Roman settlements. Located on the north side of the river seven miles upstream from Winchester, it thrived during medieval times as a wool-trading town and was also the first staging post of *'The Pilgrim's Way,'* which ran between the King's seat in Winchester and the Archbishop's in Canterbury.

NB For horse lovers, this is the origin of the word for the relaxed three beat gait of a horse allowing it to go faster than a trot whilst reserving the energy required to maintain a gallop; the Canterbury trot, or canter.

In comparison, New Alresford, on the south bank of the Itchen, is a young whippersnapper. The brainchild of Henri de Blois, brother of King Stephen, Bishop of Winchester in the 12thC, New Alresford is one of six *'Novum Forum'*, 'T'-shaped towns Henri built based on Roman Republic market towns. Henri's programme was masterminded from his nearby palace, *Bishop's Sutton*. During one of the expansions he built a stone bridge and weir connecting the two settlements creating one of the oldest canal systems in England and the 'pond' beside which *The Globe* has been prettily perched since the 17thC.

Four miles downstream is the picture perfect village of Easton. In 1872, *The Imperial Gazetteer of England & Wales* listed it as…*'a parish in Winchester district on the river Itchen…small and uninteresting.'* The locals like it that way and in the heart of this 'small and uninteresting' village is the picture perfect 16th century pub and farm shop, *The Chestnut Horse* but there's nothing small and uninteresting about Karen Wells, proprietress of these sister pubs that sit at the heart of the Itchen Valley community.

Karen is synonymous with hospitality and her support of all things local. Her pubs are so famous for their local produce she doesn't always publicise it. The locals laugh and say, 'Of course our names aren't always on Kazza's menu, we don't need to be told she's serving our produce.'

At *The Globe* and *The Horse* the open fires are always lit when there's a chill, the beer is always good, the food is pub perfect, dogs are always looked after and Karen and her team are always welcoming.

"Great pub food should be wholesome, simple and authentic. Local pubs are at their best when showing off their own patrons' produce."

Stuart Ayres & Neil Beckett, chefs

The Menu

Terrine of wild rabbit & smoked bacon

Avington smoked trout mousse

Simon's pie

Lemon tart

Sometimes great food comes in the form of complete simplicity and reliability. In the UK, when we go to our local for fish & chips or Sunday roast, we expect nothing less than perfection. That's why we keep going back and why we affectionately call our 'favourite' pub our 'local', even when its miles from home!

The kitchen teams at *The Globe* & *The Chestnut Horse*, led by chefs Neil and Stuart, pride themselves in serving up their local farmers produce and Karen delights in serving the local farmers their favourite pint or tipple after a long day in the fields. It's a win win!

The menus might change regularly but the repertoire remains the same. It's an honest and open approach to dining and it's always delicious. But honest and simple doesn't necessarily mean lacking in imagination or creativity. Chef Stuart has a particular fondness for puddings. His tarts are something to look forward to and chef Neil's Yorkshire puddings and terrines are always just right. And that's the reason the dining rooms at *The Globe* and *The Horse* are jam-packed every day and night.

Tanguy's tips

Avington smoked trout mousse: *Côtes de Gascogne, South West, France*
Rabbit & game terrine: *Pinot Noir, Leyda Valley, Chile*
Simon's pie: *Petit Verdot, Casa Lapostolle, Rappel Valley, Chile*
Tarte Citron: *Lemontini cocktail, Langley's Gin, Hampshire*

Full tasting notes are on page 318

Wild rabbit & game terrine

Serves 10

500 g rabbit, saddle & hindquarters, boned

500 g pigeon or pheasant breast

500 g sausage meat

250 g game (or chicken) livers, finely chopped

2 handfuls breadcrumbs

1 egg

3 tbsp parsley, finely chopped

a few sprigs of thyme, leaves only, chopped

6 juniper berries, crushed

2 garlic cloves, finely chopped

a splash of brandy and red wine

300 g smoked streaky bacon, flattened & stretched with a knife

salt & pepper

To make the forcemeat, combine the sausage meat and chopped livers in a large bowl, mix in the breadcrumbs, egg, parsley, thyme, juniper berries and garlic, then add the brandy & wine and season to taste.

Cut the game into roughly 2 cm strips. Lightly coat a heavy-based frying pan with oil heat and fry the game for 2 minutes until nicely browned. Line a loaf tin or ceramic terrine dish with the stretched bacon then add a layer of sausage meat followed by a layer of game and continue to build the terrine by alternate layers finishing with sausage.

Fold the exposed bacon over the terrine and cover tightly with foil. Preheat oven to 160°C and place the terrine dish in a bain marie and cook for 1½ to 2 hours. When cooked a metal skewer comes out piping hot.

To cool, cover the terrine with a layer of cling film then another tin (so the whole surface is weighted equally then add weight such as a brick or two to the terrine will compress while cooling. Chill overnight.

Avington smoked trout mousse

Serves 4 as a starter

Equipment: food processor

125 g Itchen River smoked trout
100 g crème fraiche
2 tsp horseradish sauce
juice of ½ lemon
½ lemon, sliced
a few sprigs of flat-leaf parsley
salt & pepper
toast to serve

Place all the ingredients in a food processor and whiz until smooth. Season to taste. Divide between four small ramekins and garnish with a slice of lemon and flat-leaf parsley and serve with toast.

Simon's pie

Serves 6

Equipment: slow cooker

4 lamb shanks

2 tsp olive oil

½ bottle of red wine

6 garlic cloves

2 onions, chopped

a generous handful of mixed herbs

50 ml lamb stock

a dash of chilli paste

2 bay leaves

1.25 kg potatoes

2 tbsp plain flour

100 ml water

200 g shallots, finely chopped

800 g Puy lentils, cooked

a pinch of nutmeg

salt & pepper

Place the lamb shanks, olive oil, wine, garlic, onions, herbs, bay, chilli paste and stock in a slow cooker on medium for 8 to 10 hours. Set the meat aside to cool and strain jus through a fine sieve. Pull the meat from the bones ensuring to remove all fat.

Boil and mash potatoes and season with salt, pepper and nutmeg.

To make the gravy, Bring the jus to hard boil for 2 minutes then reduce heat to a gentle simmer. Using the flour and water, make a smooth paste then whisk into the jus avoiding lumps. Bring back to the boil and season to taste.

Finally, layer the lentils at the bottom of a casserole dish followed by shallots and lamb. Add sufficient gravy to completely cover the meat. Cover with a generous layer of potatoes. Take care to seal to the edges to prevent the sauce from boiling over. Rough up the surface using a fork. Bake in oven at 200°C until golden brown on top. Remove from heat and leave to rest for 10 minutes before serving.

Lemon tart

Yield 1 9inch tart

short pastry* (store bought is also fine)
5 eggs
150 g caster sugar
150 ml whipping cream
juice and zest of 2 lemons
juice of 1 orange
25 g icing sugar
fresh raspberries to garnish

Preheat oven to 160°C. To prepare the crust* or follow packet instructions, line a 9 inch tart tin with greaseproof paper, press in the pastry and blind bake then set aside to cool. In a chilled glass bowl, whisk the eggs and caster sugar together until mixed, then add the whipping cream, lemon zest, lemon and orange juice and beat until smooth but not frothy. Take care not to introduce too much air into the mixture. Place the crust on a baking sheet positioned near the oven and pour in the mixture. Bake for 30 minutes until just done. The centre should spring to the touch. Do not allow the filling to brown. When cool, dust with icing sugar and serve with a few fresh raspberries.

* See *The basics*, page 356

The Chestnut Horse's Village Shop
Easton
Karen & Diane Wells

Though Easton is just a few miles from Winchester, the nearest shop isn't any closer so, with a little help from her mum, Diane, Karen decided to build a shop that brought Hampshire to the village. She also created a few local jobs in the process.

In addition to the extensive list of local producers and suppliers, the shop provides dry cleaning and shoe repair drop-off & delivery, daily papers and meat and catering special orders. On frozen winter mornings and sunny bbq days alike, Easton residents are grateful they can just 'nip down the road for their bits 'n bobs'.

Here is a list of some of the local businesses Karen supports. It's not exhaustive and occasionally changes with the seasons:

Avington Fishery

Bay Tree Food (Somerset) closest for packaged sauces

Bookhams (Sussex) closest pasta company

Burley Fudge

Canndo Cakes

Char Teas

Clarkes Dairy

Chocolate Craft

Evans Butchers

Hampshire Chutney Co.

Hampshire Jam & Chutney Co.

Hen House Crafts

Hill Farm Juice

Jude's Ice Cream

Holybourne Candles

Longbarn - soaps and lotions

Lyburn Cheese

MooMix

Pipers Honey

Pratts Rapeseed Oil

Ready meals prepared by The Chestnut Horse

Soles Butchers

Summerdown Pure Mint Teas

The Naked Baker

The Veg Shack

Winchester City Mill

The Globe's *perfect ploughman's*

Wedges of Lyburn
Old Winchester **cheese**

A thick slice of
Hampshire ham

Piccalilli

Tomato chutney

Flowerpot brioche

Pickled onions

Butter

Piccalilli

Yield 2 litres

Equipment: 4 500 ml kilner
jars or equivalent

700 ml malt vinegar
2 tbsp coriander seeds
a pinch of salt
500 g cauliflower, very
    small florets
2 onions, chopped
3 tbsp dry mustard
3 tbsp plain flour
1 tbsp ground turmeric
2 tsp ground ginger
50 ml cider vinegar
100 g French beans, trimmed
    to 1cm pieces
2 garlic cloves, sliced
200 g granulated sugar

Tomato chutney
25 g butter
1 tbsp olive oil
½ onion, finely chopped
1 garlic clove, chopped
1 tbsp red wine vinegar
1 tsp caster sugar
1 tbsp tomato purée
1 beefsteak tomato, seeds
    removed & chopped
a small bunch of parsley,
    finely chopped
a few chives, chopped
salt & freshly ground black
    pepper

Flowerpot brioche (see page 348)

Before starting sterilise the jars.* Place the vinegar, coriander seeds and a pinch of salt in a large pan and bring to the boil then add the cauliflower and onion and simmer for five minutes, or until slightly softened but still crunchy then remove from the heat. Put the mustard, flour, turmeric and ginger in a small bowl and whisk in the cider vinegar until smooth. Set aside. Add the green beans, garlic and sugar to the cauliflower and return to medium heat for 2 minutes until the sugar has dissolved. Drain the vegetables, reserving the vinegar and return the liquid to the pan. Add the mustard mixture, bring back to the boil then reduce on low heat for 10 minutes until it coats the back of a spoon and season to taste. Return the vegetables to the sauce, add a bit of water if dry and balance the flavour with seasoning or a bit of sugar and spoon into sterilised jars. Seal immediately and cool. The piccalilli should cure for 2-3 months before eating but can be served fresh. Once opened use within 1 week.

For the tomato chutney, heat the butter and oil in a pan and cook the onion and garlic until soft and lightly coloured then stir in the vinegar, sugar, tomato purée and chopped tomato and season to taste. Simmer gently for a few minutes until the tomato just starts to break down. Stir in the chopped herbs, cool and store in an airtight container.

* See *Glossary*, page 354

Tanguy's tip

Traveller's ploughman's: *Bood Doggle,*
Ringwood Brewery, Hampshire
Full tasting notes are on page 318

VERVEINE
FISHMARKET RESTAURANT

verveine

Milford-on-Sea
David Wykes, chef & proprietor

Food as pleasure and laughter

It simply doesn't get better than spending an afternoon with David at *Verveine*. He approaches food like a painter and alchemist. Every morsel matters and every bite is like a sensation discovered for the first time.

Verveine celebrates the finest local produce of Milford-on-Sea and its surrounds. The village sits on the shores of the Solent tucked in the furthest western corner of Hampshire in view of the Isle of Wight and the crest of Dorset's spectacular Jurassic coastline. It has always been a fishing village, changing hands through the centuries from Saxon lords through medieval royalty, Knights Templar, bishops and abbesses from various nobility to modern times. It has always thrived.

From the street *Verveine* is fittingly a fishmongers. On entering you walk past a perfect array of the morning's catch. The mouth waters as you glide past. The open-air kitchen is part of the intimate and chic dining room. You're welcomed into David's imaginarium.

The relaxed and friendly atmosphere is matched by the attention to detail and everything is delivered with a smile. And this is a place where smiles are infectious. David's food is designed to delight all the senses.

"The idea of 'local' means more than sourcing produce. It's creating a feeling of nature."

David Wykes, head chef

The Menu

This is a tasting menu that pays homage to the versatility and heightened sensation of smoke. All of the dishes are served in small portions.

Smoked treacle wholemeal bread

Smoked kombu rice crackers

Home smoked sea bass

Brixham turbot & smoked pigs cheek

Scallops & pickled rhubarb

Seared tuna

Chamomile smoked wild sea trout

Langoustines & Granny Smiths

Pear tree

David started his professional career in Jersey at the illustrious *Grand Hotel*. He then moved to the Michelin-starred *Bath Place Hotel* in Oxford followed by several years in some of France's finest kitchens including the exclusive *Restaurant Chantecler* at the *Negresco* in Nice.

Accolades and awards have followed him including *Hampshire Life's* 'Chef of the Year' two years running, best restaurant, best menu, best customer service, and has also been recognised as 'Hampshire's Best Restaurant' by Trip Advisor.

David's concept of 'local' is much more than sourcing produce. It's actually piecing together a landscape, creating a sense of place and bringing it to the table.

Tanguy's tips

Smoked treacle wholemeal bread: *Cossack, Danebury Vineyards, Hampshire, UK*

Brixham turbot: *Les Muriers, Mas Bruguiere, Côteaux du Languedoc, Languedoc, France*

Scallops: *Picpoul de Pinet, Domaine de Font Mars, Languedoc, France*

Seared tuna: *Pinot Noir, Cotes D'Auxerre, Domaine Goisot, Burgundy, France*

Sea trout: *Riesling Kabinett, Wehlener Sonnenuhr, Joh Jos. Prüm, Mosel, Germany*

Langoustines: *Maria Gomes, Luis Pato, Beira, Portugal*

Pear tree: *AOC Calvados Domfrontais Reserve, Victor Gontier, Normandie, France*

Full tasting notes are on page 318

Smoked treacle wholemeal bread

with seaweed butter & roast chicken skin

Serves 8 as a side

Equipment: cold smoker*, mixer with whisk attachment

Bread

900 g smoked wholemeal flour (cold smoked with whisky oak chips for 15 hours)

600 g white flour

600 g water

290 g smoked black treacle (cold smoked at the same time as the flour)

86 g fresh yeast

42 g salt

1 egg, beaten for egg wash

Seaweed butter

1 litre whipping cream

35 g dried seaweed

10 g Maldon salt

Roast chicken skin

the skins of chicken breasts

tapioca maltodextrin (see page 355)

For the bread, dilute the yeast into warm water and add the treacle. In a separate bowl sift together the flours and salt with the rest of the ingredients. Turn onto a lightly floured surface and knead for 5 minutes until smooth and elastic. Leave in a warm place to prove for 1 hour, knock back, cut and shape into golf ball sized buns. Egg wash the tops and dust with a little of the smoked flour. Leave to prove again until nearly doubled in size (not doubled as this will be over-proved.) Preheat oven to 190°C and bake the buns until dark. (The treacle makes this bread dark but gives it an amazing bitter crust.)

For the butter, use a mixer with a whisk attachment to whip the cream stopping every few minutes to scrape the cream from the sides of the bowl, continue this until you have butter. Separate the whey, (in this case buttermilk, and use for another recipe. It's perfect for bread.) Rinse the butter solids under cold running water and drain. Add the seaweed and shape by rolling into a log in cling film and chill.

For the roast chicken skin, preheat oven to 140°C. Lay the pieces of chicken skin on a tray, lightly season with salt, cover with a piece of greaseproof paper then place another tray on top and bake until golden. Remove and drain on kitchen paper and tip the excess chicken fat into a bowl. Stir in enough maltodextrin to create a fine powder.

*See *Glossary*, page 354

Smoked kombu rice crackers
with Cajun salmon foam & young shoots

Serves 10-12 as a snack or hors d'oeuvres

Equipment: food processor, vacpac and water bath, fine sieve, deep fryer, espuma canister and 2 nitrous oxide capsules, hand-held smoker*, cloches

Rice crackers
200 g Arborio rice
800 g water
20 g dried kombu (see page 355)
15 g salt
1 ½ litres vegetable oil for deep frying

Salmon foam
300 g skinned salmon
30 g Cajun spice rub
300 g cream cheese
juice of two limes
150 g natural yogurt

bamboo tea, dried
a few micro-shoots, pea or otherwise

For the rice crackers, place all the ingredients in a pan bring to the boil and cook until the rice is extremely soft and most of the water has evaporated. Blend until smooth and spread very thinly onto trays. Preheat oven to 52°C and dehydrate for 24 hours until it's a transparent sheet. Break into medium-sized shards and store in an airtight container until ready to use.

For the salmon foam, rub the Cajun spice over the salmon, vacuum seal with the lime and poach in a water bath at 60°C for 30 minutes (as an alternative it can be roasted in a cool oven.). Remove from the bath and when cold transfer all the ingredients in the bag into a blender with the remaining ingredient, blend until smooth and pass through a fine sieve. Fill a 1 litre espuma canister and charge with 2 capsules and chill for at least 6 hours before use.

To serve, preheat a deep fryer to 180°C, fry a few of the dried rice crackers at a time until they triple in size and drain on kitchen paper. Dispense the Cajun salmon foam onto the crackers and garnish with small shoots. Prepare a hand-held smoker with some dried bamboo tea fill a glass cloche with smoke. Put cloche on plate and serve.

* See *Glossary*, page 354

Home-smoked sea bass in its natural surroundings
with beach herbs & laverbread emulsion

David serves this dish on frozen rocks that he finds on the same beach he forages his sea herbs. His bass is also caught just off the beach and eaten with your fingers as nature intended.

Serves 8

Equipment: needle nose pliers or tweezers, cold smoker*

1 3 kg sea bass, scaled, filleted & pin boned
200 g soft dark brown sugar
500 ml boiled then chilled seawater**
4 juniper berries crushed
zest of 1 lemon

Laverbread emulsion
35 g laverbread (tinned is fine)
50 g mayonnaise
juice of 1 lemon

a handful each of samphire, sea fennel, sea purslane, sea beet, sea aster

For the sea bass dissolve the brown sugar in seawater and add the zest and juniper. Place the sea bass in the water mix and chill for 6 hours. Wash the fish off and pat dry, leave uncovered for two hours on a tray in the fridge to dry a little. Set up a cold smoker with whisky oak or alder chips and cold smoke* the fish for 3 hours. Wrap the fish in parchment after smoking and leave in the fridge overnight for the flavours to settle.

As an alternative brush a fine layer of liquid smoke onto the fish and wrap with the parchment then chill overnight.

For the laverbread emulsion, mix together the laverbread and mayonnaise, adjust the seasoning and sharpness with the lemon juice and reserve in a plastic bottle.

To serve cut the fish into bite-sized strips and nip the beach herbs into delicate fronds. Drape and dot them on a plate in an open arrangement with dots of laverbread emulsion.

* See *Glossary*, page 354

**If you aren't by the sea, boil a generous handful of sea salt in fresh water then chill.

Brixham turbot & smoked pigs cheek *with burnt apple & salt baked celeriac*

Serves 8

Equipment: hot smoker*, blender, water bath & vacpac

8 100 g turbot fillets
a handful of dried seaweed
olive oil
1 whole pig's cheek
3 litres water
1kg salt
300 g treacle

Salt baked celeriac
1 small celeriac
100 g fine sea salt

Burnt apple purée
6 Granny Smiths

a handful of small sea beet leaves, blanched
some high quality balsamic

For the pig's cheek soak in the brine solution of water, salt and treacle for 3 days in a cool place and a sealed container then rinse, remove the skin and trim. Hot smoke the cheek with applewood chips at 77°C for 12 hours then chill until ready to use.

For the celeriac, preheat oven to 220°C run under cold water and roll in fine sea salt until completely covered. Bake on a tray until soft in the middle. Remove from the oven, crack off the salt and peel the celeriac, blend until smooth and check seasoning, keep warm.

For the burnt apple purée, preheat oven to 200°C. Bake the apples until very dark brown. Every 25 minutes remove from the oven and using a spatula mix the apples to mush. Continue baking until all the apple juices have caramelised (It might look terrible but will taste fantastic.) Blend until smooth, pass through a fine sieve and check seasoning adding a little sugar if too bitter.

For the turbot, set the water bath to 60°C. Lightly season the fillets with dried seaweed and olive oil, vacpac and cook in the water for 12 minutes.

To serve, line the plate with the fillets and very fine slices of pig's cheek. Dot with warm celeriac and apple purée then finish the plate with a few sea beet leaves and balsamic (David uses a vintage 35 year old Modena.)

* See *Glossary*, page 354

Verveine

Scallops & pickled rhubarb
with smoked blood orange

Serves 8

Equipment: cold smoker*, hickory chips, sterilised kilner jar, blender, squeeze bottle

16 scallops in their shell, cleaned
  (see *The basics*, page 356)
a splash of good quality olive oil
juice of 1 lemon
salt & pepper
fennel tops for garnish

Rhubarb pickle
500 g rhubarb, very thinly sliced
300 g caster sugar
400 ml white balsamic & white wine
  vinegar

Smoked blood orange purée
4 blood oranges
500 ml blood orange juice
150 g caster sugar (maybe a little more)
xanthan gum (a small amount)
  (see page 355)
ice

For the pickled rhubarb, place the sliced vegetables in a sterilised jar. In a pan mix together the vinegar and sugar and bring to the boil. Pour the liquor over the fruit and leave to cool. Top up the jar to the very top to create an airtight seal and chill. (This can be kept for months as with all pickles.)

For the blood orange purée, set up a cold smoker, then put the oranges in boiling water for 3 minutes, refresh in ice water and repeat 2 more times, cut in half and cold smoke for 8 hours with hickory chips. Bring the juice and sugar to the boil, reduce by a third, add the oranges and cook for a further 5 minutes then transfer to a blender. Blend until smooth, checking sweetness. (It should be on the side of bitter to counter the sweetness of the scallops). Thicken with a little xanthan gum, pass through a fine sieve, transfer to a squeeze bottle and chill until ready to serve.

Pan fry the scallops in good quality olive oil until golden one side, turn over and do the same, season to taste and finish with a little lemon juice.

To serve, place the scallops on plates and decorate with a few slices of rhubarb, a few drops of the pickling liquor and dots of orange purée and decorate with a few strands of fine fennel hair.

* See *Glossary*, page 354

Seared tuna *with wild mushroom tea smoked*
with blackcurrant leaves

Serves 8 for a tasting menu

Equipment: hand-held smoker, fine sieve

4 150 g pieces of sashimi grade tuna, seasoned with seaweed salt

100 g assorted wild mushrooms

a splash of good olive oil

1 lime, cut in half

1 head of baby bok choi

1 red pepper, charred with the skin left on

a few coriander shoots

soy sauce

Wild mushroom tea

100 g dried cepe mushrooms

500 g water

20 g piece of dried seaweed (kombu)

3 spring onions

a pinch of dried tarragon

15 g smoked Maldon salt

5 g dried blackcurrant leaves (for smoking)

For the tuna, heat a pan with good quality olive oil and sear the tuna for 15 seconds on each side and squeeze over the lime. Remove from the heat and drizzle with a little more olive oil.

To make the tea, place all the ingredients, in a pan and bring to a simmer, skim several times, leave to simmer for 40 minutes then remove from the heat. Leave to infuse for an hour and pass through a fine sieve. Reserve the spring onions and slice lengthwise for garnish.

Sauté the wild the mushrooms in the olive oil and keep warm. Blanch the bok choi leaves and keep warm. Slice the pepper and remove the seeds.

To serve, place the wild mushroom tea in the teapot and using a hand held smoker lightly smoke with the blackcurrant leaves, leave to infuse for two minutes before pouring. Slice the tuna and garnish with the vegetables, coriander shoots and a few drops of soy sauce.

Chamomile smoked wild sea trout
with broad beans & lemon balm

Serves 8

Equipment: blender, fine sieve, squeeze bottle, roasting pan with tight fitting lid, chef's blowtorch

1 wild sea trout, filleted and pin boned

100 g caster sugar

200 g salt

100 g fresh lemon balm, roughly chopped

1 small handful of hay

50 g dried chamomile

500 g broad beans, blanched & shelled

Spinach & lemon balm purée

300 g baby spinach

10 g lemon balm

xanthan gum (if required) (see page 355)

salt & pepper

ice

Dressing

100 ml olive oil

35 ml elderflower vinegar

a pinch of Maldon salt

a handful of micro-cress for decoration

This dish comes with a health warning, it requires burning hay over an open flame so needs to be done in a well-ventilated kitchen with careful supervision.

For the sea trout, rinse the fish and pat dry and place in a plastic tray skin-side down. Combine the sugar, salt and lemon balm, sprinkle over the fish and cure in the fridge for 1 hour. In a deep roasting pan with a tight fitting lid, lay out the hay and chamomile and place on a wire rack. Put the trout on and light the hay with a blowtorch. This will catch light very quickly so be very careful! Place on the lid to smother the flame and hold the smoke and leave for 15 minutes. When at room temperature, remove the trout and dress with a little olive oil and lemon juice.

For the spinach and lemon balm purée blanch for 10 seconds, shock in ice water and blend on high speed with fresh lemon balm, check seasoning, thicken slightly with the xanthan if required, pass through a fine sieve and chill until ready to use. Just before serving heat and transfer to a squeeze bottle.

To serve, lightly toss the broad beans in the dressing. Dress with pieces of the trout with a few beans, purée and micro-cress.

* See *Glossary*, page 354

Langoustines & Granny Smiths
with soft cheese, smoked raisins & verjus

Serves 8

Equipment: water bath and vacpac, cold smoker*, Japanese mandolin, thermometer, muslin cloth, cheese baskets

16 langoustines
1 litre water
750 g white wine vinegar
65 g salt
ice
soft goat's cheese
1 Granny Smith apple
2 candy beetroot

Smoked raisins
200 g golden raisins
400 g verjus (sour grape juice)

Verjus dressing
20 g smoked verjus
100 g olive oil
20 g white balsamic vinegar
5 g lime juice
a pinch of salt

Fresh soft goat's milk cheese
2 litres goat's milk (semi-skimmed)
100 g lemon juice
1 tsp dried tarragon

1 cucumber, peeled skins only

For the langoustines, bring all the ingredients to the boil, blanch the langoustines for 90 seconds and refresh in iced water. Peel and de-vein.

For the smoked raisins, combine the raisins and verjus in a vacpac bag, seal on the highest setting and cook in a water bath at 61°C for 8 hours. Empty the contents into a plastic container and cold smoke for 6 hours.

Cover the beetroot with cool water and bring to the boil with a pinch of salt. Simmer until tender to the point of a knife, anything from 20 to 40 minutes depending on age and size. Drain and cool. Remove the skins with your fingers. Cut into halves, quarters or dice, depending on size. Place in a pan with the sugar and vinegar and a sprig of mint. Bring to the boil and simmer, stirring occasionally, until the liquid forms a sticky glaze. Set aside.

For the cheese, place the goat's milk and tarragon in a medium-sized pan over moderate heat and using an accurate thermometer, bring the temp up to 90°C. Remove from the heat and lightly whisk in the lemon juice. Stir gently until curds form and then leave to rest for 35 minutes. Ladle the curds into a muslin-lined colander and leave to drain for 5 hours. Carefully lift the muslin into cheese baskets and allow to drain for 4 hours in a cool, dry place. The cheese must be stored in a sterilised airtight container for 3 days.

For the cucumber ash, preheat oven to grill. Place the cucumber skins under the grill until completely blackened. Reset oven to 52°C, lay out on greaseproof paper and dehydrate for 8 hours then grind into a powder.

To serve, combine all the ingredients for the dressing, balance the seasoning and dress very thin slices of apple and beetroot. Delicately arrange the langoustines on plates with the garnish, a few raisins and a drizzle of the dressing.

* See *Glossary*, page 354

Verveine

Pear tree

Serves 8

Equipment: water bath & vacpac, ice cream machine

10 baby pears, peeled
650 ml water
300 g caster sugar
4 pieces of cassia bark

Smoked wood ice cream
950 g whole milk
75 g pear wood shavings
100 g double cream
190 g egg yolks
145 g caster sugar

Celeriac bark
1 small celeriac, very thinly sliced
120 g local honey
110 ml water

Branches
1 bunch of chervil, stems only
30 g egg whites
100 g caster sugar
45 g Horlicks powder
45 g dark cocoa powder (80%)

Birch syrup powder
100 g birch syrup (or maple)
200 g dark chocolate, melted (84%)
80 g maltodextrin (approximately)
   (see page 355)

Valrhona marquise
150 g Valrhona 84% dark chocolate
275 g caster sugar
150 g egg yolks
60 g cocoa powder
550 g double cream, semi-whipped
330 g melted butter
a pinch of salt

To poach the pears, heat the water, sugar and bark and reduce by half to make syrup. Evenly distribute the syrup and pears in vacpac bags and cook in a water bath at 74°C until tender. (They can also be poached in the syrup.)

For the smoked wood ice cream, preheat oven to 220°C and roast the pear wood shavings for 15 minutes then reset the oven to 78°C. Add the wood shavings to the milk and infuse in the cool oven for 1 hour. Pass through a fine sieve then add the rest of the ingredients, vacpac and place in a water bath at 78°C for 20 minutes, pass through a fine sieve and churn in an ice cream machine as per manufacturer's instructions.

For the celeriac bark, caramelise the honey in a pan over medium-low heat. Remove from the heat and deglaze with water small amounts at a time. Be very careful, as the honey will spit. Vacpac and cook very thin slices of celeriac in a water bath at 78°C for 50 minutes then cool. Preheat oven to 52°C, submerge the celeriac in the cold honey mixture, lay out on a tray and dehydrate for 8 hours until crispy and 'bark-like'.

For the branches, remove all the leaves from the chervil and use for something else. Whisk together the egg whites and sugar in one bowl and the Horlicks and cocoa in another. Pass the branches through the egg white mixture and dust on the cocoa mix.

Preheat oven to 52°C, place the sticks on greaseproof paper and dehydrate for 6 hours until they are 'branch-like'.

For the birch syrup powder, whisk the two ingredients together and add enough maltodextrin to make a powder and store at room temperature.

Whisk together the yolks and the caster sugar until doubled in volume and in a separate bowl, whisk together the cocoa powder and the melted butter. Add the cocoa mixture to the yolk mixture. Melt the chocolate over a bain marie add to the chocolate, whisk in the cream and chill until set.

To serve, sprinkle powder over the plates, add rochers of ice cream and chocolate, top with a few pear halves and decorate with the bark and branches. Finish with a bit more powder.

LAINSTON HOUSE
AN EXCLUSIVE HOTEL

Sparsholt, near Winchester
Antonio Lopez-Bustos, general manager

The epitome of the word terroir. Nearly thirty years of something very special!

In 1683 Charles II commissioned Sir Christopher Wren to build a rural nest to snuggle up with his mistress Louise de Kérouaille, Duchess of Portsmouth. The palace was built on the foundations of an existing medieval site, fragments of which are still part of the complex and grounds.

Its stunning 63 acres boasts the longest and one of the oldest lime avenues in the UK, inspired by Sir John Evelyn's memories of his famous grandfather's landscape architecture. Many of the original trees planted in 1716 still grace the spectacular nearly mile long sweeping vista.

For nearly 28 years, chef Andrew MacKenzie has matched the beauty of his surroundings with equally elegant cuisine. He and his team have built and nurtured luscious kitchen gardens and hand-rear selected livestock. When not tending his own garden Andrew continues to be a driving force working with local farmers, agricultural colleges and specialist producers, helping them to set the highest standards in horticulture and farming bringing spectacular ingredients to his and our kitchens.

And the story continues. Andrew recently passed the reins of executive chef over to the talented Olly Rouse in order to build the *Exclusive Chefs Academy* for *Lainston House*'s owner, *Exclusive Hotels* to train up and coming chefs to the highest standards where no doubt he will pass on his culinary skill, love and care.

"Nature provides us with everything, in abundance. It's my starting point. As a chef I think we're the custodians of nature's larder. What better place to be than Hampshire."

Olly Rouse, head chef

The Menu

Herring

Lamb, sweetbreads & broad bean falafel

Lemon, basil chocolate & kiffir

Olly's career began in 1996 when he was 13 at *Les Bouviers* in Dorset. By 2002 he was in London at his first Michelin-starred restaurant *Petrus*. Over the next decade it was Olly's star that was shining. *The Vineyard* at Stockcross earned its second Michelin star when he was there as sous chef.

Olly opened *The Dorchester Collection*'s only country house hotel *Coworth Park*. He was the head chef of *Restaurant John Campbell* where he was awarded with a Michelin star in its first year. During his time at *Coworth Park* Olly received an *Acorn Award* and contributed to the *Hodder Education Books, Practical Cookery*.

Olly joined *Lainston House* in the winter of 2013. Everyday since he's been developing menus and dishes using unique combinations and techniques designed to please and delight. His commitment is to use perfect ingredients and bring out the very best of each in harmony. Nothing is wasted and all is used with extraordinary imagination and attention to detail in the extreme. Borrow from his imagination because some of it only he can create!

Tanguy's tips

Herring: *Muscadet Sèvre et Maine, Sur Lie, Clos des Allées, Loire, France*
Lamb, sweetbreads & broad bean falafel: *Vourla Urla, Ukuf Mevkii, Turkey*
Lemon, basil chocolate & kiffir: *Botrytis Riesling, Tamar Ridge, Tamar River, Tasmania*
Strawberries & cream: *Muscat de Beaumes de Venise, Rhone Valley, France*

Full tasting notes are on page 318

Herring *with purple carrot, mooli, shallots, bacon & apple*

Serves 4

Equipment: Japanese mandolin, vacpac, steamer, hand blender, fine chinois, 6 squeeze bottles, griddle screen, food processor, 1 litre Kilner jar

8 herring, filleted
4 baby purple carrots, trimmed
4 baby mooli (daikon)
2 medium-sized banana shallots, peeled
    fennel pollen*
sprouting broccoli seeds**
ice

Pickling liquor for the herring
3 shallots, finely chopped
2 garlic cloves, finely chopped
1 bay leaf
50 ml vegetable oil
150 ml white wine
900 ml white wine vinegar
400 ml water
20 black peppercorns
170 g sugar

Pickled Onions
300 ml white wine vinegar
90 g sugar
1 bay leaf
15 peppercorns
1 vanilla pod
1 red chilli, de-seeded & julienned
30 baby onions

Garnishes (see page 348)
Bacon vinaigrette
Bacon jus
Apple & vanilla purée
Parsley purée

For the pickling liquor for the herring, sauté the shallots, garlic and bay without colour add the rest of the ingredients except the fish, bring to the boil and leave to cool. Strain and pour into a vacpac add the herrings, seal airtight and refrigerate for at least 36 hours. (The marinade will dissolve the fine bones.)

For the baby purple carrots, vacpac with a pinch of salt and a generous splash of the vinaigrette and marinate for 2 hours. Boil for 10 minutes until soft then plunge into ice water then set aside until ready to serve.

For the baby mooli, remove and reserve the nice small leaves then gently remove the skin with a griddle screen under cold water leaving the root intact. Vacpac with a little olive oil and salt and boil for 12 to 15 minutes until tender then plunge into ice water until cold then set aside until ready to serve.

For the roasted shallots, preheat oven to 180°C. Wrap the shallots and thyme in foil and bake for 1 hour. Cool in the foil then cut off the skins with scissors and slice into disks and set aside until ready to serve.

For the pickled onions, in a saucepan, mix all the ingredients together and bring to the boil. Allow to cool slightly and place in a Kilner jar and allow to marinate for 24 hours. Cut the onions in half and flake the layers and set aside until ready to serve.

To serve, pan fry the carrots and mooli in a little olive oil and deglaze with some bacon vinaigrette. In a separate pan, sear the shallot disks on one side until blackened but not burned. Dress the plates with a bed of sprouting broccoli seeds and vegetables adding dots of apple and parsley purée and a few pickled onion flakes. Drizzle with a tablespoon of bacon jus top with the herring fillets and dust with fennel pollen.

*Fennel pollen can be obtained at the end of the flowering season. When the heads are just past their bloom, contain them in a plastic bag and shake the pollen. Store in an airtight container in a cool environment.

** Sprouting broccoli seeds are made by soaking the seeds under heat lamps until they sprout and served while very young and tender.

Lamb, sweetbreads & broad bean falafel *with mint emulsion & tomato*

Serves 4

Equipment: food processor, deep fryer, piping bag, fine sieve, thermomix jug, squeeze bottle

800 g lamb rump

400 g lamb sweetbreads

2 garlic cloves, crushed

a sprig of thyme

flour for dusting

a couple knobs of butter

ice

a handful of sugar snaps

Broad bean falafel

30 g dry chickpeas, soaked for 24 hours

200 g broad beans, blanched & pods removed

a generous pinch of ground cumin & coriander

1 tsp freshly cracked black pepper

small pinches of cinnamon & nutmeg

5 spring onions, finely sliced

4 garlic cloves, finely minced

10 g parsley, finely chopped

5 g coriander, finely chopped

½ tsp baking powder

salt & pepper

Garnishes (see page 348)

Hummus purée

Tomatoes & lemon verbena

Mint & spinach emulsion

Prepare all the components of the dish prior to pan-frying the rump steak and sweetbreads. When ready, preheat oven 200°C. Season and sear in a hot pan so the fat is nicely rendered and golden. Transfer to the oven for 5 minutes until rare to medium rare then rest for five minutes. Slice into medallions.

For the sweetbreads, blanch for one minute in boiling water then plunge into ice water and remove the skins and sinews. Marinate for four hours in vegetable oil, garlic and thyme. Just before serving, pat dry, lightly dust with flour and pan-fry until crispy then baste with a knob of butter. Season to taste and slice thinly to serve.

For the broad bean falafel, blitz the chickpeas in a food processor then add the beans and pulse until the mixture is the consistency of breadcrumbs. Mix the rest of the ingredients in a bowl then stir in the bean mixture and season to taste. Preheat deep fryer to 180°C. Roll the falafel mixture into ping pong-sized balls and deep fry until golden and drain on kitchen paper.

Lemon, basil chocolate & kiffir with honey jelly & yoghurt sorbet

This is a masterpiece from Olly and pastry chef Tyrone Hull. It's elegant and looks deceptively easy but there are several techniques that can't be replicated in a home kitchen so they have been described to take inspiration from.

Serves 4

Equipment: plastic sieve, muslin cloth, hand blender, 22 cm greaseproof tin, pacojet, vacpac, espuma canister and 1 capsule, gastro (or shallow) trays, squeeze bottles

Kiffir
1 tbsp kiffir grains (see page 354)
1 litre semi-skimmed milk

Honey jelly
300 g honey
200 ml water
4 gelatine leaves, soaked in cold water
ice

Frozen lemon jelly (see page 348)
250 ml lemon juice
250 ml simple syrup (see page 354)
400 ml water
20 ml limoncello
7 gelatine leaves, softened in cold water
zest of 2 lemons
ice

Yoghurt sorbet
500 g yoghurt
200 g icing sugar
30 ml cream
100 ml milk
25 g yoghurt powder (made from dehydrated Greek yoghurt)

Additional components (see page 348)
Lemon cake
Basil chocolate
Lemon curd

For the kiffir, place the grains and milk together and leave at room temperature for 24 hours. Once curdled, drain through a plastic sieve and hang in a muslin cloth, reserving the whey, which drips out. The white thick paste left in the muslin is the kiffir curd, similar to natural yoghurt. Refrigerate in a squeeze bottle until ready to use.

For the honey jelly, bring the honey and water to the boil, add the gelatine stir until dissolved then pour into a shallow tray and chill until set.

For the frozen lemon jelly, line a gastro (or shallow) tray with cling film. Boil all the ingredients adding the gelatine when the rest is at the boil. Place the mixture in a bowl on top of a bowl filled with ice and a bit of water and whisk until cooled. Spread into the tray and freeze until ready to use.

For the yoghurt sorbet, boil the cream and milk and add to the yoghurt, icing sugar and yoghurt powder then stir and freeze. When ready to serve, pacotise in a pacojet just prior to serving.

To serve, cut the cake, jelly and frozen jelly into 3 cm cubes and arrange in a checkerboard. Top with pieces of the basil chocolate and dollops of lemon curd. Add a small rocher of sorbet in the middle and decorate with kiffir dots and micro-basil leaves.

Meadow Cottage Farm
Headley near Bordon
The Haynes family

It's sunshine and clover. It's a cow's life at Meadow Cottage!

Producing unpasteurised or 'raw' milk is a careful business and its benefits are a continuing debate. Those in favour maintain that the products are richer in nutrients and taste better and the bacteria are human friendly when correctly managed, (they are found in most cheeses and yoghurts), while those against argue that transmitting bacterial disease is too risky. Until 1864 there was no method for pasteurising dairy. Today, excellent animal husbandry and scientific techniques are applied but it takes a special kind of farmer to do it.

Up in the northeastern tip of Hampshire is *Meadow Cottage Farm* where, in 1967 Peter and Celia Haynes, along with Celia's brother Hugh Blackburne, established their pedigree herd of 'Weydown' Jersey cows. Their vision was to produce the finest dairy products in the country. By 1969 they were selling their cream and unpasteurised milk and by 1984 ice cream and sorbets were added. Today daughter and chef Julie makes 22 flavours having won many *Great Taste Awards* over the years.

While Julie is busy making the ice cream, brother Mark and dad, Peter take care of every single detail of their herd and youngstock. They originally chose the Jersey breed for its longevity and ability to produce milk off grass. They painstakingly care for the pastures, making sure the grass is high quality and mixed with clover for maximum nutrition that results in well-feeding cows and excellent flavour. The cows are pasture-reared so they have time to smell the roses and enjoy producing their highly sought after milk and cream. It's no wonder top chefs covet their precious consignment!

Strawberries & cream

with whey sherbet & burnt cream & macadamia crumble

Serves 4

Equipment: sugar thermometer, fine sieve, dariole moulds, chef's blowtorch, pacojet, piping bag, silpat mat

Strawberries, red, white & green

Crème brûlée

500 ml *Meadow Cottage Farm* 'raw' Jersey cream

1 egg & 4 more yolks

125 g sugar

½ vanilla pod, seeds only

Vanilla whey sherbet

500 g whey, reserved from kiffir (see page 348)

250 g sorbet syrup, (see page 348)

juice of 1 lemon

1 vanilla pod, seeds only

Strawberry meringue

100 g sugar

100 g glucose

100 g egg whites

10 g freeze-dried strawberries

Strawberry & tarragon soup

500 g garden ripe strawberries, quartered

300 g sugar

200 ml water

1 large sprig of tarragon

Macadamia crumble

200 g whole macadamia nuts

50 g sugar

a pinch of salt

For the crème brûlée, bring the cream and vanilla to a simmer. Whisk together the sugar, egg and yolks then pour the scalded cream over the egg and sugar mixture and whisk well. Return all to a pan, and whilst whisking place on a medium heat until the mixture reaches 85°C. Pour through a fine sieve into lined moulds and leave to set in the fridge.

For the vanilla whey sherbet, mix all the ingredients together, pass through a fine sieve and freeze then run through a pacojet when ready to serve.

Pick a selection of varying ripened strawberries, ensuring they never go into a fridge. Slice, dice, quarter and leave some whole to give varying textures. When ready to serve, dress with a tiny amount of strawberry and tarragon soup.

For the strawberry meringue, make an Italian meringue*, soft whip the whites, boil sugar and glucose to 121°C then pour over eggs while continuing to whisk. Keep whipping until the meringue is full volume and cool. Spoon into a piping bag then pipe and evenly spread onto a silpat mat to dry. Once dry, crumble and mix with crushed freeze dried strawberries.

For the strawberry and tarragon soup, place the strawberries, water and sugar into a metal bowl over a bain marie for one hour to steep. Remove from the heat and cool for 30 minutes, then add the tarragon. Cool completely, then strain through a muslin cloth without squeezing and pour into a squeeze bottle.

For the macadamia crumble, heat the sugar to syrup with a dash of water and cook to 121°C then add the nuts and salt and stir constantly until they crystalise. Leave to cool then chop coarsely.

To serve, release the brûlées from their moulds, dust with sugar and torch. Arrange on plates with a scoop of sherbet and strawberries, drizzle with a bit of soup and top with macadamia crumble.

* See *Glossary*, page 354

Tanguy's tip

Strawberries & cream: *Muscat de Beaume de Venise, Domaine de Durban, Rhone Valley, France*

Full tasting notes are on page 318

"Some people call me Mr Hampshire, something I'm very proud of. I've built some great relationships and friendships with the producers that surround us."

Andrew MacKenzie, execututive chef,
Exclusive Chefs Academy

The Menu

Butternut espuma

Goat's cheese & watercress ravioli

Roasted lamb saddle & slow cooked shoulder

Apple crumble, custard & sorbet

Chocolate tart

People call him Mr Hampshire and Andrew always modestly smiles when they do. Through the years he has made local produce the centrepiece of his menus and given great credit to those he's helped and have helped him and when he isn't inviting the local producers into his kitchen, he is taking his bread to their local markets. Andy's made quite a few friends along the way.

He arrived at *Lainston House* from *The Four Seasons* in Park Lane in 1986 intending a one-year stop over as pastry chef. His plans to build a life and reputation in France were soon forgotten as he quickly fell in love with life in the heart of Hampshire and all things 'Great British'. Nearly three decades later these elegant grounds are still his culinary home.

He's been *Hampshire Life Magazine's, 'Chef of the Year'*, two years running and has always been in the top three nominees. He's was one of the founder members of the *Create and Cook Competition* aimed at inspiring young people to cook with local food, that has now gone on to be a great success in Hampshire, Sussex and the Isle of Wight.

Andrew's new project, the *Exclusive Chefs Academy*, is giving him the opportunity to literally write the book on great British and local ingredients. One we can all enjoy a page or two from!

Tanguy's tips

Goat's cheese & watercress ravioli: *Semillon, Hunter Valley, Australia, 2012*
Roasted saddle & shoulder of lamb: *Monastrell, Spain, 2011*
Chocolate tart: *Chocolate martini cocktail*

Full tasting notes are on page 318

Butternut espuma

Serves 6 to 8

Equipment: fine sieve, espuma canister & nitrous oxide capsule

125 g butter

1 small white onion, finely sliced

2 cloves garlic, finely sliced

500 g butternut squash, peeled, seeds removed & chopped

800 ml hot vegetable stock*

100 ml double cream

2 slices of French bread, cubed

Preheat oven to grill. Heat the butter in a large saucepan then sweat the onion and garlic without colour. Quickly toss the bread cubes in the hot butter, transfer to a tray and place under the grill until golden.

Next add the squash to the butter and cook for 3 minutes. Cover with stock, bring to the boil and simmer for 15 minutes until the squash is tender then add the cream. Blend the soup with a hand blender until smooth then pass through a fine sieve and keep warm.

When ready to serve pour into the espuma canister and leave to cool a little before adding the nitrous oxide capsule. To make without an espuma canister whisk the soup with a hand blender until light and frothy. This will create a light soup but not as foamy.

* See *The basics*, page 356

Goat's cheese & watercress ravioli
with apple pearls & butter sauce (photo on p146-147)

Serves 6 to 8

Equipment: pasta machine, 1 large and 1 medium scone cutters, small melon baller

Watercress pasta

500 g strong flour (tipo 00)

3 free range eggs

20 g watercress purée*

2 egg yolks for sticking together

Filling

250 g soft goat's cheese

juice & zest of 1 lemon

1 small shallot, finely chopped

salt & pepper

2 apples, peeled, cored & balled

a bunch of watercress, stalks removed & coarsely chopped

Garnish (see page 348)

butter sauce

To make the pasta, form a well with the flour and crack the eggs into it. Working from the inside mix together to form dough adding the watercress purée in drizzles then knead vigorously for 5 minutes, until smooth and elastic. Add drops of water if dry or dust with flour if wet. Rest for 30 minutes and roll out into pats about the size of your hand then pass through a pasta press from 7 to 1. Cut the sheets to 30 cm lengths and leave to dry until ready to use.

To make the filling, mix the goat's cheese with the rest of the ingredients and with your hands roll into ping pong ball-sized portions.

To build the ravioli lay out a sheet of pasta, place the goat's cheese balls evenly, about 4 to a sheet. Next brush in-between the gaps with egg yolk then cover with another sheet of pasta. Gently press down around the ravioli mounds. Cut the ravioli with a large scone cutter then gently press around the outsides. Trim with a smaller cutter to form a good shape and repeat until you have 8 raviolis making sure the edges are tightly sealed. Blanch in simmering water for 2 minutes then plunge into ice-cold water to stop the cooking. Pat dry and store until ready to serve.

To build the dish, wilt the watercress and make a small bed. Drop the raviolis into boiling salted water for 3 minutes. Remove with a slotted spoon and pat dry. Season to taste, place on the bed of wilted greens and spoon over the butter sauce. Garnish with apple pearls a few fresh leaves and serve immediately.

* See *The basics*, page 356

Roasted lamb saddle & slow cooked shoulder *with potato fondant, red onion marmalade, carrot purée*

Serves 6-8

Equipment: food processor

Braised lamb shoulder

2 kg shoulder of lamb (bone in)

salt & freshly cracked black pepper

30 ml rapeseed oil

mirpoix: 2 medium onions, 2 large carrots, peeled & quartered, 2 celery stalks, quartered, 3 garlic cloves, chopped

400 ml good red wine

150 ml hot lamb stock (enough liquid to cover)

4 sprigs of fresh rosemary

Saddle of lamb

1 whole lamb saddle (ask your butcher to bone)

2 tbsp vegetable oil

salt & freshly cracked black pepper

a small bunch of parsley, finely chopped

Parsley & rosemary crumb

100 g fresh white breadcrumbs

20 g rosemary, finely chopped

½ garlic clove

30 g fresh parsley, chopped

salt & pepper

Garnishes (see page 348)

fondant potatoes

carrot purée

red onion marmalade

For the braised lamb shoulder, preheat oven to 160°C. Season the lamb on both sides and heat the oil in a large non-stick frying pan. Cook the lamb for 4 minutes on both sides until brown then transfer to a deep casserole with a lid or large non-stick roasting tin. Add the mirpoix and cook for another 3 minutes until brown.

Transfer all ingredients to the casserole adding the rosemary, wine, stock (and water if you need more liquid to cover), and bring to the boil. Reduce the heat, cover with a lid or large sheet of foil and transfer to the oven for 3 to 4 hours. Take the shoulder out of the cooking liquor, drain and cool slightly. Skim the fat off the cooking liquor and reduce.

Flake the meat from the bone and place into a mixing bowl, add a little of the reduced cooking liquor, mix and season to taste. Place the mixture in a cling film-lined tray 1 cm thick then cover with parchment and press with something flat like a small chopping board and refrigerate overnight. Next day cut in to 8, 3 cm shapes and place in the fridge until ready to serve.

For the saddle of lamb, once your lamb has been boned, you will have two flaps either side of the eyes of the meat. Cut down the middle so you have two identical pieces Trim any excess fat. Spread the parsley crumb over the flaps. Roll the flap over the eye of meat and trim any excess and tie every 2 inches with string. Trim to make neat.

Pre-heat oven to 200°C and pre-heat a roasting tray with the vegetable oil for 10 minutes. Season the lamb and place in the tray and roast for 15 minutes turning the lamb every 5 minutes. Remove from the oven and rest for 10 minutes. When ready to serve remove the string and carve into 3 cm slices.

For the parsley and rosemary crumb, blitz the parsley in a food processor to a bright green purée (you want the chlorophyll to release), add the rest of the ingredients and blitz to form a light crumb. Add more bread crumbs if too wet.

Chocolate tart
with Amaretto ice cream & nougat praline

Yield 1 28 cm tart

Equipment: ceramic baking beans, fine sieve, ice cream maker, silpat mat

170 g pastry*
450 g dark chocolate (70% cocoa solids), finely chopped
530 ml whole milk
175 ml double cream
2 eggs, lightly beaten

Amaretto ice cream
700 ml double cream
300 ml whole milk
1 vanilla pod, split
6 large egg yolks
180 g sugar
120 ml Amaretto

Nougat praline
62 g unsalted butter
25 ml simple syrup (see page 354)
20 ml cream
75 g sugar
20 ml glucose
40 g cocoa nibs
8 g cocoa powder
40 g hazelnuts, toasted & crushed

For the pastry, preheat oven to 220°C. Remove chilled pastry from fridge and roll out onto a lightly floured surface to 4 mm thickness. Using the rolling pin carefully lift the pastry and lay it over a 28 cm flan tin, gently pushing it into the trim. Trim off excess. Line the pastry with parchment and fill with baking beans (or rice) and blind bake for 15 minutes until lightly golden. Remove the paper and beans return to the oven and bake for a further 5 minutes. Remove from oven and allow to cool.

For the chocolate filling, reduce the oven to 110°C. Place the chocolate into a heatproof bowl. Bring the milk and cream to the boil then pour over the chocolate, whisking briskly to form a smooth and glossy mixture. Stir the eggs together without introducing air then stir into the chocolate. Pour mixture into the tart case and bake for 20 to 25 minutes until just set.

For the Amaretto ice cream, over medium-low heat, in a thick-bottomed pan bring the cream and milk to the boil. In a separate bowl, whisk together the yolks and sugar. Gradually whisk in the hot cream mixture. Return to a clean pan and stir over medium-low heat for 5 minutes until the custard thickens and coats the back of spoon. Stir constantly and do not allow to boil. Strain into a clean bowl and chill until cold then whisk in the Amaretto. Churn in an ice cream maker according to manufacturer's instructions. Transfer to covered container and freeze. (This can be made up to 1 week in advance.)

For the nougat praline, preheat oven to 170°C. Combine the butter, simple syrup, cream, sugar and glucose in a pan and bring to the boil. Add the cocoa nibs, powder and hazelnuts. Turn mixture out onto a silpat mat and bake in the oven for 10 to 12 minutes. Cut into shapes while still warm and pliable and let the shapes set hard before using.

* See *The basics*, page 356

Pear crumble, custard & sorbet

Serves 6 with 600 ml custard

Equipment: fine sieve, espuma canister with 2 nitrous oxide capsules, ice cream maker

Pear compote

3 Conference pears, peeled, cored & sliced

100 ml apple juice

50 g caster sugar

1 vanilla pod

½ cinnamon stick

Custard

500 ml milk

vanilla seeds from the pod

6 egg yolks

100 g caster sugar

1 tsp cornflour

Crumble mix

100 g flour

50 g butter

50 g Demerara sugar

Lemon sorbet

200 g sugar

275 ml water

juice & zest of 8 lemons

For the pear compote, place the prepared pears in a saucepan on low heat with the apple juice and caster sugar and stir to combine until the sugar is melted. Using a small, sharp, pointed knife, split the vanilla pod open lengthways and scrape the seeds from the pod and set aside for the custard. Add the pod husk and the cinnamon stick to the pear mixture, cover and bring the mixture to a low boil. Cook gently for 25 minutes, stirring the mixture frequently with a wooden spoon to encourage the fruit to break down. Remove the saucepan from the heat and allow to cool slightly. Leave in the vanilla husk and cinnamon stick while resting for added flavour just do not serve these bits.

For the custard, combine the milk and vanilla seeds in a saucepan. Warm gently but do not let the liquid boil. In a bowl, beat together the egg yolks, sugar and cornflour until creamy then whisk in the warm milk. Strain the mixture into a clean pan and cook, stirring constantly, until the custard slightly thickens and coats the back of a spoon. Leave to cool then place in an airtight container and store in the fridge until required. When ready to serve add the custard sauce to the espuma canister and charge with two capsules.

For the crumble, preheat oven to 160°C. Rub the butter into the flour using your fingers, add the sugar and spread over a flat tray and bake for 10 to 15 minutes until golden. Cool then break up the crumble and set to one side in an airtight container.

For the sorbet, place the sugar and water in a pan, bring to the boil and simmer for 5 minutes. Remove from the heat and allow to cool for a while. Add the lemon juice and zest and leave to steep for an hour then strain and place in the ice cream maker and follow manufacturer's instructions. Store in the freezer in a lidded container.

To build the pre-dessert add the pear compote to a small glass, top with custard espuma, sprinkle with crumble and top with a boule of sorbet.

Chef's tip: 'Chop-chop!' You need to build and serve this dish quickly as it all starts to break down. It is shown as a pre-dessert but also makes a lovely main pudding.

Stockbridge
Jane Dick, Sue Whiting
& Nic James

If you go down to the woods today, you won't find Sue or Jane!

For Sue and Jane the sustainability of our food chain drives every decision they make and business is literally mushrooming!

Unlike plants, mushrooms have no protection in law, so are at risk from commercial exploitation especially over-picking of wild varieties. Cultivated specialty mushrooms are an exciting alternative with more varieties to choose from. With sixteen current types, chefs have a range of diverse and flavoursome mushrooms including: fragrant 'hen 'o the woods', meaty 'abalone', delicate 'velvet caps' and delicious 'namekos'.

Based in Stockbridge, *Fundamentally Fungus* grows some of the more exotic speciality mushrooms at their farm and works closely with other specialist growers to offer a wide range of well-known varieties such as portobella and shiitake. The mushrooms are grown on organically-certified woodchip and the waste goes to green mulch to be reused in agriculture. It's a truly sustainable process.

Sue & Jane's morish mushrooms grace the plates of the very best chefs in Hampshire and across the country.

Stockbridge organic mushroom fricassée with poached baby leeks, rosemary linguini & Lyburn cheese

Serves 4

Equipment: pasta machine & drying rack

400 ml vegetable stock

200 g pasta dough

100 g rosemary sprigs

4 baby leeks

25 g parsley, washed & finely chopped

25 g banana shallots, finely chopped

1 clove garlic, finely chopped

600 g assorted Stockbridge organic mushrooms

3 plum tomatoes

a splash of vegetable oil

100 g unsalted butter

shavings of Lyburn (or Parmesan) cheese to garnish

Pasta

330 g 'tipo 00' flour

3 eggs

1 yolk

100 g rosmary sprigs

Pasta can take on so many flavours. Rosemary is a natural choice. Peppery watercress or spinach, pepper, oregano. Give it a go.

To flavour the pasta, place the fresh rosemary sprigs in the microwave for 20 seconds at a time checking each time until they are completely dry, then with a pestle and mortar crush until a fine dust add this to the pasta mix at the beginning.

Blend the flour, eggs and extra yolk together in a food processor until dough is formed. Leave to rest in a refrigerator for 1 hour before use.

Roll on a pasta machine to desired thickness. Usually linguini will go from 7 to 3. Hang to dry until ready to use.

Once rolled blanch for 20 seconds in boiling, salted, oiled water and refresh in iced water. You can then cook them in boiling water as you need them. (I find that just adding to a hot sauce such as alfredo finishes the pasta to a perfect al dente.)

For the baby leeks, clean the leeks to ensure all grit is removed. Bring 100 ml vegetable stock to a simmer and poach the leeks for 10 minutes. Drain on kitchen roll, season to taste and re-heat when ready to serve.

For the fricassée, make a persillade by stirring together the parsley, shallots and garlic. Next prepare a pot of boiling water and a bowl of ice water. Plunge the tomatoes into the boiling water for 8 seconds then transfer to the ice water. Once cool skin the tomatoes, cut into 4 wedges and scoop out and discard the seeds. Pat dry and finely dice. Next place a little vegetable oil in a hot frying pan and sauté the wild mushrooms until soft. Add 300 ml vegetable stock and the persillade and bring to the boil. Add the butter while stirring continuously and when ready to serve stir in the tomatoes. To serve, twist the linguini with a fork and place in the centre of a warm bowl. Perch a baby leek on the side, spoon the fricassee around the pasta and finish with shavings of cheese.

Tanguy's tip

Organic mushroom fricassee & linguini: *Fiano, Campania, Italy, 2012 Full tasting notes are on page 318*

THE THOMAS LORD

West Meon
An Upham Brewery pub
Fran Joyce & Clare Winterbottom

Reviving an old friend – new classics meet old

Thomas Lord, 1755-1832, was a cricketer and entrepreneur most famous for building the London cricket legacy and ground that still bears his name. When he hung up his bat, he retired to the charming village of West Meon, near Petersfield and sometime after that the village renamed their local pub in his honour.

In 2012, Hampshire's Upham Brewery bought the well lived-in village pub and under the dedicated care of chef Fran Joyce and his partner Clare, new life was breathed into one of the Meon Valley's cherished establishments. During the restoration, residents showed such interest and concern for their much-loved local that Fran & Clare found themselves giving regular guided tours, encouraging the community to feel part of the project.

Fran and Clare's unique approach to the restoration included the substantial kitchen garden. They contacted the Hampshire Horticultural Society and found three local gardeners, Rosanna, Phil & Chris, who have lovingly re-built the garden which today is run as a profit sharing enterprise. It's a labour of love and a wonderful success.

Fran and Clare's enthusiasm and commitment for supporting local trade and preserving tradition abounds. Fran's menus celebrate local organic farms and fisheries. The village and local countryside wraps itself around the *Thomas Lord* like a kid leather glove. At any time of year this is a warm and welcoming place, inside and out.

> *"Everyone deserves to be surprised by what a local pub can offer."*

Fran Joyce, head chef

The Menu

Bar snacks

Venison & black pudding scotch egg

Crispy lamb belly

Upham Tipster Ale rarebit

Portland crab & brown crab custard

The menu

Black pudding, squash, quail egg

Upham Tipster Ale battered hake & Fran's triple-cooked chips

Treacle tart, honey oat biscuits

For over a decade Fran has been refining his love of all things local. His North Devon roots have given him a love for the countryside and respect for the farmers on his doorstep. He's in his element when spending time 'on the farm' and sharing his concepts for new recipes, based on classic British dishes, that celebrate the people and bounty in his immediate reach.

Fran's eyes were first opened to molecular gastronomy a few years ago when he was working at the celebrated *Royal Crescent Hotel* in Bath under another Fran, Fran Snell. But for this Fran, scientific cooking and modern techniques means attention to detail and flavour. His food is presented in a relaxed and rustic style in harmony with its environment.

Tanguy's tips

Bar snacks: *Upham Brewery's Classic Ale, Hampshire*
Portland crab: *Weissburgunder, Erst+Neue, Südtirol Alto Adige, Italy, 2012*
Black pudding: *Pinotage, Ruins, South Africa*
Fish & chips: *Upham Tipster Ale*
Treacle tart: *Tokaji, Aszú, Hungary*

Full tasting notes are on page 318

Bar snacks

Venison & black pudding Scotch egg
with mustard mayonnaise

Serves 4

Equipment: deep fryer

200 g venison mince

200 g sausage meat

200 g black pudding

a small bunch of parsley
  and tarragon, chopped

salt & pepper

4 quail eggs

1 package panko
  breadcrumbs

plain flour

1 medium egg

1½ litres rapeseed oil
  for frying

ice

Place quail eggs in a pan of boiling water for 2 minutes and 37 seconds then plunge into a bowl of ice water to stop the cooking process. When cooled gently peel and set to one side.

Mix together the venison, sausage meat, black pudding, seasoning and chopped herbs until evenly mixed. Measure into 125g balls, roll and then flatten in the palm of your hand large enough to wrap the egg in. Place a quail egg in the middle of the patty and gently wrap the meat around the egg. Don't squash the egg! Gently press together the edges and roll in your hands to make into an egg shape making sure it is smooth with no holes or cracks. Repeat with all eggs and refrigerate for at least 1 hour.

Place out 3 bowls filling one with flour, one with beaten egg and one with breadcrumbs. Roll the scotch eggs in that order and return to the fridge for another hour.

Preheat oven and set deep fryer both to 180°C and fry the Scotch eggs for 2 minutes. Place on a tray lined with parchment and bake in oven for 8 minutes. (This will produce a perfect scotch egg with a runny yolk.)

Crispy lamb belly
with mint mayonnaise

Serves 6 to 8 as a snack
Equipment: deep fryer

500 g lamb belly, rolled & tied	1 litre lamb stock
2 carrots, chopped	1 egg
1 large white onion, chopped	50 g plain flour
4 stalks celery, chopped	50 g panko breadcrumbs
2 leeks, chopped	2 egg yolks
1 star anise	200 ml rapeseed oil
1 tsp fennel seeds	6 mint stalks, finely chopped
a small bunch fresh thyme	a splash of white wine vinegar
& rosemary	2 tbsp Demerara sugar

For the crispy lamb belly, pre-heat oven to 160°C. Place the belly in a heavy deep pan with the chopped vegetables and herbs. Cover with lamb stock, seal with foil, cover tightly and place in the oven for at least 3 hours or until the meat is nicely tender. Remove from the stock and allow to rest until cool. Pre-heat deep fryer to 180°C. Cut the lamb into 75 g pieces, lightly flour then dip in beaten egg yolks and coat with breadcrumbs. Fry until nicely golden and crispy. Serve immediately.

For the mint mayonnaise, beat the egg yolks until light then emulsify the oil into them. Whisk in the mint and vinegar and season to taste with the sugar. Chill until ready to serve.

Upham Tipster Ale rarebit
on toasted ale bread with apple chutney

Serves 6 to 8 as a starter with 2 loaves of bread &
1 large kilner jar of chutney

50 g plain flour	2 tsp English mustard
50 g unsalted butter	2 tbsp Worcestershire sauce
250 ml Upham Tipster Ale	2 egg yolks
300 g mature Cheddar, grated	

For the rarebit, prepare a roux by melting the butter in a pan on low heat and slowly adding the flour. Next add the ale, mustard and Worcestershire sauce. Bring to the boil then lower the heat and stir in the Cheddar until completely melted. Remove from the heat and allow to cool. Once cool, whisk in the egg yolks. Spread a thick layer over a slice of toasted of ale bread and grill until golden. Serve immediately with apple chutney.

Portland crab & brown crab custard
with kohlrabi remoulade & treacle bread

Serves 4 with 1 8" round loaf of treacle bread
Equipment: food processor, chef's blowtorch, fine sieve,
muslin cloth

	Crab custard
500 g Portland white crab	250 g brown crab
25 g mayonnaise*	300 ml milk
juice of ½ lemon	300 ml single cream
2 kohlrabi (or ½ celeriac), finely julienned	3 egg yolks, beaten
a handful of fine frisée leaves	1 tbsp tomato purée
sea salt	juice of ½ lemon
	salt & white pepper

For the crab & custard, pick through the crab to remove any shells and dress with mayonnaise. Season to taste with salt, pepper and lemon juice and then chill. To make the custard, simmer the milk and cream in a pan then over low heat whisk in the egg yolks and tomato purée making sure not to over cook. Stir constantly until thickening, remove from the heat and whisk in the crab. Pass through a fine sieve, season to taste with lemon juice, salt & white pepper and chill.

For the kohlrabi remoulade, generously salt the julienne, rest for 30 minutes then place in a muslin cloth to squeeze out excess water. Dress lightly with mayonnaise and wholegrain mustard. To serve place just enough crab custard to cover the bottom of a bowl. Using a blowtorch, lightly crisp the surface. Place a quenelle of crab and kohlrabi on top, garnish with frisée and serve with slices of toasted treacle bread.

* See *The basics*, page 356

Black pudding, squash, quail egg
with truffle yolk dressing & bacon fried croutons

Serves 4

Equipment: hand mixer or food processor

400 g *Owton's* black pudding
1 butternut squash, peeled
60 g butter
3 egg yolks, whisked until light
30 ml white wine
100 ml truffle oil
2 slices of bread, torn into croutons
100 g lardons
8 quail eggs
a splash of rapeseed oil
salt & pepper
a handful of watercress

For the puréed squash, melt the butter until foaming over medium heat in a large pan. Dice round part of the squash and place in the butter then cover with cling film and cook on low heat until very soft. Remove from the heat, strain and blitz with a hand mixer or in a food processor until smooth.

For the diced squash, slice the neck into ¾ inch rounds and chargrill on both sides. Cool, cut into small cubes and season to taste.

For the truffle egg yolk dressing, in a clean dry bowl over a bain marie whisk the yolks and wine together to the ribbon stage* of a sabayon then slowly drip in and whisk the truffle oil to a smooth emulsification. Season to taste.

For the croutons, fry the lardons until crispy and remove them from the pan retaining the hot fat. Add the croutons and evenly coat them then fry until lightly golden. Season to taste and allow to dry on kitchen paper.

To prepare the dish, coat a cold frying pan with rapeseed oil and fry quails eggs on low heat. When the whites are cooked carefully remove and keep warm. Put same pan back on medium-high heat and fry chunks of black pudding until coloured on both sides. Place all prepared components on a plate, drizzle with dressing and garnish with watercress.

* See *Glossary*, page 356

Upham Tipster Ale battered hake & Fran's triple cooked chips

with crushed peas, seared lemon & parsley & caper mayonnaise

Serves 4

Equipment: fine needle nose pliers, deep fryer, an accurate scale, hand blender

4 175 g hake fillets, skin & pin bones removed

150 g frozen peas, defrosted

4 large Agria potatoes (or King Edward), peeled & hand cut to chips

2 lemons

454 g self-raising flour and a little extra

3 g bicarbonate of soda

568 ml Upham Tipster Ale

258 ml fizzy water

a knob of butter

1 tbsp malt vinegar

salt

1½ litres rapeseed oil for deep-frying

Parsley & caper mayonnaise

½ cup mayonnaise

2 tbsp capers, crushed & chopped

3 small gherkins, chopped

2 tbsp parsley, finely chopped

Using pliers, remove the pin bones from the fillets. Make the batter by mixing together the flour, bicarbonate of soda and a pinch of salt. Whisk in the ale and fizzy water until just brought together. Don't over mix.

Preheat oil in a deep fryer to 180°C. Dust a fillet on both sides with flour, dip in the batter and place in the hot oil. Fry for 2½ minutes, flip over and cook for a further 2½ minutes. Place on kitchen paper and allow to rest for 2 minutes before serving in a warm oven. Repeat for each of the fillets.

For the chips, soak in cold water for 1 hour. When ready to cook, place in a deep pan with fresh cold water, bring to the boil and cook until tender but not falling apart. Drain into a colander then gently toss them to bring up some of the starch. They should be nice and fluffy. Place them on a parchment-lined tray and chill until cold. Preheat a deep fryer to 130°C and blanch the chips in batches for 12 minutes until the centres are soft. Drain on kitchen paper then chill until cold again. When ready to serve, preheat deep fryer to 180°C and fry in batches for 2 to 3 minutes until golden & crispy. Drain and lightly salt.

For the mayonnaise, mix all ingredients together and chill until ready to serve.

For the peas, blitz with a hand blender until completely crushed. Melt the butter in a saucepan until turning brown then slowly add the vinegar until completely emulsified. Stir in the peas. Season to taste and serve hot.

For the lemons, slice into ½ inch rounds and remove any visible seeds. Line a frying pan with a little oil and heat until smoking hot. Carefully add the lemons and sear until caramelised on both sides.

The Thomas Lord

Treacle tart & honey oat biscuits
with bay leaf ice cream

Yield 1 9 inch tart
Special equipment: fine sieve

Sweet pastry
250 g plain flour
50 g icing sugar
125 g butter
1 egg
a splash of milk

Treacle filling
300 g breadcrumbs
150 g beurre noisette
3 eggs
56 g double cream
a pinch of salt
675 g golden treacle
juice of ½ lemon
zest of 2 lemons

Bay leaf ice cream
125 ml milk
40 ml double cream
1 egg yolk
2 bay leaves

Oat & honey biscuits
120 g rolled oats
runny honey

To make the crust, line a 9 inch tart tin with parchment and preheat oven to 140°C. Crumb the flour, sugar and butter together then slowly mix in the eggs and milk. Wrap the dough in cling film and chill until firm (about 1 hour). Roll out the pastry and press into the tart tin.

For the filling, pour the golden syrup into a pan and bring to a simmer on medium-low heat. Stir in the butter, cream and salt then add the lemon juice and zest. Next stir in the breadcrumbs. Remove from heat, allow to cool slightly and whisk in the egg. Pour the filling into the pastry and bake for about 45 minutes or until set but don't let the surface brown.

For the ice cream, in a heavy bottomed saucepan bring the milk, cream, sugar and bay leaves to the boil. Next whisk the egg yolk into a clean glass bowl. Slowly whisk in the cream mixture until fully tempered. Pass through a fine sieve into sealable containers and freeze.

For the oat biscuits, preheat oven to grill. Spread the oats on a baking sheet and place under broiler until lightly toasted. Re-set the oven to 160°C. Mix the oats with just enough honey to make them sticky. Spoon dollops onto a sheet of parchment then press using a top layer of parchment. Place back onto the baking sheet and into the oven until lightly golden.

Richard's great grandfather was farming and making local cheeses in the Meon Valley over 100 years ago and he fondly remembers the story of his grandfather on coming home from the pub declaring to his wife that the cheese on the ploughman's was extraordinary. His grandmother simply replied, "Of course, I've been selling it to them for years!"

In 2008, *Hyden Farm Originals* was the proud winner of the *The Great Taste Awards, Organic Producer of the Year,* earning two gold stars for their beef and guinea fowl and one each for its pork and smoked duck breast. It was declared the best organic food producer in Hampshire and arguably, it still is. Richard's exacting standards haven't wavered.

Clanfield

Richard & Angela Jones

Long before European legislation could dictate, Richard, like his father before him, has always been an organic and free-range farmer. He believes solidly in the traditions of rearing original breeds and keeping them at the fore of fine produce. Today, his daughter Bethan is working alongside him to keep up the fine family tradition and highest quality standards and generation six, all seven grandchildren can be found chasing the Indian runner ducks and collecting eggs. We can only look forward to at least another six generations of Jones's to keep up with!

Duck breast & faggot, crackling & jus with rosti, kale, honey parsnip purée, celeriac & horseradish cured turnip & parsnip crisps

Serves 4: yield 10 75 g faggots

Equipment: fine chinois, water bath and vac pac (alternative recipe is also provided). Overnight preparation is required for the faggots & crackling

2 duck breasts

2 duck legs

sea salt

16-20 sprigs thyme, leaves only

200-250 g duck fat

400 ml veal stock

150 g duck liver, finely chopped

35 g jumbo rolled oats

10 g each, chervil, parsley, chives & tarragon, finely chopped

1 egg

caul fat* for wrapping faggots

150 ml Madeira

1 head of garlic, cut in half

2 bay leaves

5 black peppercorns

1 star anise, cracked

2 tbsp dark brown sugar

a knob of butter

salt & pepper

available from most butchers

For the faggots, confit the duck legs by placing the legs on a tray and sprinkling generously with salt and half the thyme leaves. Cover with cling film and refrigerate overnight. Next day, place the legs in a heavy frying pan over medium-low heat and cover completely with duck fat. Gently simmer for 2 to 3 hours until the meat is very tender. Remove the legs from the fat and allow to drain. (Reserve the duck fat to finish cooking the crackling and faggots if not using a water bath.) Carefully remove the skin and set aside for the crackling. Using a fork, pull the meat away from the bones. Next place the meat and veal jus in a pan and simmer over medium-low heat for a further 1 to 1½ hours, until the meat is quite broken down. Place in a clean bowl and chill.

For the final stage mix the duck with the rest of the ingredients (except caul) then roll into 75 g balls and wrap with a fine layer of caul. If using a water bath, seal the faggots in cling film and vac pac. Place in the water bath at 67°C for 1½ hours then immediately place in a bath of ice water. If cooking on the stovetop preheat oven to 180°C then heat some duck fat in a heavy frying pan. Gently and evenly brown the faggots, transfer to a roasting tin, cover and bake for 10 to 15 minutes.

For the crackling, carefully stretch the skin from the duck legs on a tray and allow to air dry for 24 hours. Cut into ¼ inch strips and fry until crisp in hot duck fat. Allow to drain on kitchen paper and season to taste.

For the breasts, score the skin on the breast in a crisscross pattern and place in a vac pac bag. Cook in a water bath at 55°C for 3 hours then immediately place in a bath of ice water to stop the cooking. When ready to serve remove from the vac pac. To finish place the breasts skin-side down in a medium-hot frying pan and season. Allow the fat to render 3 minutes until the skin is golden and crispy. Flip and cook for another 3

Tanguy's tip

Duck breast & faggot: *Syrah a Papa, Rhone Valley, France*
Full tasting notes are on page 318

minutes. Season to taste and allow to rest for 5 minutes and slice across the grain.

If not using a water bath, prepare the breast in the same manner and increase the frying time to 3 minutes skin-side down, then flip for 1 minute. Repeat 3 minutes skin down, 1 minute meat down twice more then rest for 5 minutes. While the breasts are resting, heat 75 ml veal stock in a pan. Add the faggots and as they heat continue to spoon over the stock until hot.

For the jus, deglaze the duck breast pan with Madeira making sure to scrape up all the bits then add the leftover stock from cooking the faggots. Pour this into a pan, add the remainder of the thyme leaves, garlic head, bay leaves, peppercorns, star anise and brown sugar and let simmer for 20-30 minutes. Add splashes of water or white wine if the jus gets dry. Pass the mixture through a fine chinois and return to the heat in a clean pan. Add a knob of butter and reduce to a nice consistency. Season to taste.

Serve with rosti, roast celeriac, kale, parsnip & honey purée, pickled turnips, parsnip crisps & fresh grated horseradish.

* See *Garnishes* page 348

Newchurch, Isle of Wight
Colin Boswell & family

When one imagines a perfect plait of garlic one's first mental stop is rarely the Isle of Wight, or so it used to be. Colin Boswell and his family changed all that. It's hard to believe only a few decades ago vegetables such as courgette, aubergine and of course garlic, were relatively unknown and considered exotic in the UK.

Colin's parents started farming on the island in the 1950's. Norah, Colin's mother, was a keen gardener and had fallen in love with the idea of bringing the Mediterranean into her British post-war garden. To her delight garlic had already arrived.

During WWII the Isle of Wight was a base for the Free French Forces and Charles De Gaulle's determined resistance fighters couldn't be without one of the foundations of their daily rations so they packed some stock in their kit. A few years later a few bulbs found their way into Nora's exotic garden and by the 1970's she had adapted her varieties and they began to flourish.

Returning to the farm in the late 70's, Colin and his wife Jenny had even bigger plans for the mighty bulb. Through another 30 years of many trials and few errors they developed the sustainable and unique varieties of garlic that are now staples in UK kitchens and beyond.

The Garlic Farm is a going family concern. Norah is still busy in her garden, Colin and Jenny never sit still but enjoy letting their children infuse their creativity into everything garlic and the next generation of Boswell garlic experts are busy helping everyone.

"I love that garlic first came to the Isle of Wight and my family via French Resistance freedom fighters."

Charlie Bartlett, chef
Natasha Edwards, manager & author

The Menu

Tomato & lentil smoked garlic soup

Garlic Farm asparagus & eggs

Best ever pigeon Kiev

Cheeses & chutneys: IoW brie & blue

There isn't anything that Colin's daughter, Natasha Edwards doesn't know about garlic and her vast knowledge equals her undying enthusiasm. Indeed, she helped her father plant his first commercial crop as a toddler in 1977. After her university years at Oxford and working abroad, Natasha returned to the farm with her own young family to carry on the garlic tradition.

In her two books, *Garlic The Mighty Bulb* and *The Garlic Farm Cookbook*, Natasha's recipes are a compilation of her travels and work abroad, family tradition and developing the dishes for the *Garlic Farm & Restaurant*. The restaurant serves up a completely unique experience of the versatility of this unique food.

Tanguy's tips

Tomato & lentil soup: *Herbis, Franck Massard, Rueda, Spain*
Asparagus & eggs: *Roter Veltliner, Klassik, Leth, Wagram, Austria*
Pigeon Kiev: *Shiraz, Spotswood, Charlie Herring, Western Cape, South Africa*
Cheeses & chutneys: *Chardonnay, Saint Romaine, Burgundy, France & Port, Douro, Portugal*

Full tasting notes are on page 318

Tomato & lentil smoked garlic soup
with garlic & rosemary focaccia

Serves 8 as a starter

Equipment: hand blender, sieve

2 red onions, finely chopped

2 cloves smoked garlic, finely chopped

4 rashers smoked streaky bacon, chopped

2 tins chopped tomatoes

170 g red lentils, (pre-soaked weight)

a dash of Worcestershire sauce

1 tbsp tomato purée

1 tbsp chilli paste (or to taste)

800 ml vegetable stock

a splash of vegetable oil

salt & pepper

Garlic & rosemary focaccia

400 g strong flour, plus extra for dusting

7 g packet fast acting yeast

1 tsp salt

400 ml warm water

1-2 tsp sugar (or honey)

4 tbsp olive oil, plus an extra splash

4 cloves garlic, crushed

3 sprigs of fresh rosemary, leaves only, finely chopped

sea salt

For the soup, sweat the onions and garlic in a splash of oil in a large saucepan without colour then add the bacon and cook until slightly caramelised. Stir in the tomatoes, lentils and stock then add the remaining ingredients checking seasoning as you go. Bring to the boil for 10 minutes stirring occasionally then simmer for 1 hour until the lentils are tender. At this point you can serve as a hearty, chunky soup or blitz with a hand blender and pass through a sieve for a fine, light soup. Season to taste and serve hot with warm focaccia.

For the focaccia, mix together the flour, yeast and salt in a large bowl. Make a well in the centre. Mix together the water, sugar (or honey) and olive oil and pour in stages into the flour stirring with a wooden spoon or hands to bring the dough together. Continue to add liquid until the dough is slightly wet and easily workable. Turn out onto a floured work surface and knead for 10 minutes until smooth and elastic. Place in a clean bowl coated with olive oil and cover with lightly oiled cling film and leave in a warm place to rise until doubled in bulk. When the dough has risen, knock it back on a floured surface and shape the dough into 2 oval, flattish loaves. Transfer onto trays and leave to rise for 20 minutes.

Preheat oven to 200°C. Mix 2 tbsp olive oil with the garlic and rosemary. When the dough has risen using your fingers make dents over the surface and pour over the oil mixture so it pools in the dents. Sprinkle generously with sea salt and bake for 30 minutes until golden and hollow sounding when tapped from the bottom. Cool on a wire rack.

Garlic Farm *asparagus & eggs*

Serves 4 as a starter

Equipment: ramekins

8 large Isle of Wight asparagus spears, trimmed

4 eggs, cracked into ramekins

2 tbsp white wine vinegar

70 g butter, melted

1 red chilli, finely chopped & seeds removed

4 tbsp Greek-style set yoghurt

2 cloves Solent Wight garlic, finely chopped

salt & pepper

Bring 2 pans of water to the boil, 1 lightly salted for the asparagus and the other with vinegar for the eggs. Cook the asparagus for about 7 minutes, until tender but not soggy and transfer to kitchen paper to drain then keep warm until ready to serve. Next stir the chilli into the melted butter and mix the garlic into the yoghurt. In the second pan, carefully slide the eggs from the ramekins into just simmering water, swirl the perimeter of the water with a spoon and cook the eggs for 3 minutes. Remove with a slotted spoon and drain on kitchen paper. To serve, place 2 asparagus spears on each plate topped with an egg. Spoon on some yoghurt and drizzle the asparagus tips with butter. Season to taste and serve with warm crusty bread to mop up the butter.

Best ever pigeon Kiev *with garlic mash*

Serves 4

8 pigeon breasts, skin removed
12 garlic cloves, crushed
juice of 1 lemon
1 tbsp fresh tarragon, chopped
1 tbsp fresh coriander, chopped
a handful of fresh wild garlic, chopped
250 g butter, slightly softened
2 tbsp plain flour
1 free range egg, beaten
10-12 tbsp fresh breadcrumbs

Garlic mash
1 kg potatoes (Maris piper), peeled
    & chopped
1 bulb garlic, cloves peeled
2 bay leaves
500 ml milk
a knob of butter
salt & freshly ground black pepper

Preheat oven to 180ºC. Place the garlic, lemon juice, herbs and butter into a bowl and mix until well combined then roll it in cling film to create a sausage shape and refrigerate until firm.

Using a sharp knife make a pocket in the middle of each pigeon breast, large enough to hold a pat of garlic butter. Divide the butter into 8 and stuff into the centre of each breast. Pane the breasts in flour, beaten egg and breadcrumbs to coat completely, shaking off any excess. Heat a little oil in an ovenproof frying pan and fry on all sides until lightly browned. Transfer to the oven and bake for 5 minutes until golden-brown and cooked through. (The breasts are delicate and cook quickly so be careful not to over-cook.)

For the garlic mash, place the potatoes, garlic, bay leaves, milk and enough water to completely cover in a large saucepan. Bring to the boil then simmer until completely cooked through. Drain the potatoes retaining ¹/₃ of the liquid. Mash the potatoes with a knob of butter adding liquid until creamy. Season to taste and serve warm.

Gazpacho & bruschetta

1 kg ripe tomatoes, chopped
2 spring onions, chopped
3 garlic cloves
1 large cucumber, chopped
75 ml olive oil
juice of 1 lemon
2 tbsp sherry vinegar
a handful of basil leaves, finely chopped
a few stems of flat parsley, finely chopped

The Garlic Farm bruschetta
1 loaf garlic & rosemary ciabatta
3 large garlic cloves, peeled
400 g ripe plum tomatoes
1 red onion, finely diced
a handful of basil leaves
250 g black olives, pitted & crushed
1 red chilli, finely chopped
marinated white anchovies
olive oil
ice
freshly cracked black pepper

Place the tomatoes, spring onions, garlic and most of the cucumber in a blender and whizz until smooth. Pass through a sieve then pour the mixture back into the clean blender. With the blender running on low slowly add in the oil, lemon juice and vinegar and finally stir in the herbs. Season to taste and chill until ready to serve.

For the crostini, heat oven to 160°C. Slice the ciabatta and brush each side with olive oil. Toast on a tray until lightly golden then rub with garlic cloves.

For the tomato topping, score the tomato tops with a knife and blanche in boiling water for about 5 minutes or enough time for the skin to easily peel off with the fruit remaining firm. Plunge in ice water then peel the skins, quarter, remove the seeds and finely dice. Mix together with onion, a few torn basil leaves and a splash of olive oil.

For the tapenade, simply crush the olives into a paste using a drizzle of olive oil and season to taste.

Spread the toppings on the crostini and top with a twist of black pepper.

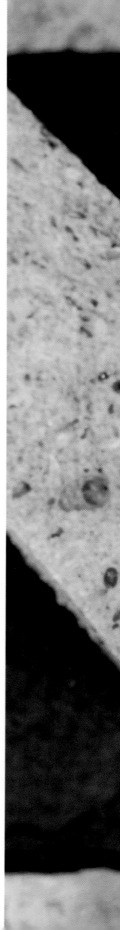

Mezze

A sharing plate for 4 people

Equipment: deep fryer

Pickled garlic with lemon & limes

3 tbsp mustard seeds

1 tbsp fenugreek seeds

2 tbsp groundnut oil for frying (or rapeseed)

1 tsp turmeric

1 tbsp red chilli powder

3 unwaxed lemons, cut into small chunks

3 unwaxed limes, cut into chunks (rinds on, seeds removed)

2 garlic bulbs, cloves peeled

3 tbsp sea salt

Tzatziki

200 ml set-style Greek yoghurt

½ large cucumber, peeled, de-seeded & finely diced

2 garlic cloves, peeled & crushed

1 tbsp parsley, finely chopped

1 tbsp mint, finely chopped (plus extra for garnish)

1 tbsp olive oil

1 tbsp lemon juice

salt & pepper

Broad bean & pea hummus

300 g broad beans, shelled & boiled (fresh or frozen)

100 g peas (fresh or frozen)

4 large garlic cloves

a handful of mint leaves & a few for garnish

2 tbsp olive oil

100 g crème fraiche

juice of 1 lemon

salt & pepper

Devilled whitebait & aioli

600 ml milk

450 g whitebait

30 g plain flour

1 tsp cayenne pepper

sea salt

zest of 1 lemon

1 tsp smoked paprika

1½ litres sunflower or rapeseed oil
   for frying

Aioli

3 large garlic cloves

2 egg yolks

1 tbsp Dijon mustard

300 ml olive oil

1 tbsp lemon juice

salt & pepper

For the pickled garlic, using a pestle and mortar lightly crush the mustard and fenugreek seeds. Heat the oil in a pan and gently fry all the seeds with the spices for 2 minutes then add the fruit, garlic and salt. Place in an airtight container so that the mixture is well packed to limit extra air. Leave to pickle in the refrigerator for at least 10 days, turning occasionally.

For the tzatziki, simply stir all the ingredients together adjusting the seasoning with salt, pepper & lemon juice. Chill until ready to serve and garnish with a couple mint leaves.

For the hummus, mix together the beans, peas and garlic with a stick blender to make a paste. Stir in the crème fraiche and season to taste with the lemon juice, salt & pepper. Top with a couple mint leaves.

For the devilled whitebait, pour the milk over the whitebait let soak for 10 minutes. Drain and discard the milk. Preheat a deep fryer to 180°C. Place the flour, cayenne and salt in a large sealable plastic bag, shake then add the fish and shake again until well combined. Remove the fish and place onto a plate, or baking tray. Fry in batches for 2 to 3 minutes until lightly golden in colour. Drain onto kitchen paper then toss with lemon zest, a pinch of salt and paprika, until well combined.

For the aioli, crush the garlic with a bit of salt with a pestle and mortar to a paste then whisk the garlic, egg yolks and mustard together until well combined. Emulsify by pouring a fine stream of oil into the egg mixture until thickened. Balance the seasoning with salt and lemon juice. If you prefer a sauce to mayonnaise, add a bit of water.

Tanguy's tip

Mezze: *Assyrtiko, Thallasitis, Gaia wine, Santorini, Greece*
Full tasting notes are on page 318

Barton-on-Sea
Mike Caddy, proprietor

Barton-on-Sea is perched on the spectacular cliff-edge at the mouth of the Solent Way. It has been a civilised community as far back as the Bronze Age and likely earlier. The 35 foot cliffs are geological wonders and tell vivid stories of Britain's evolution. Around the turn of the last century the village and surrounding land was owned by one of William the Conqueror's chums, Roger de Montgomerie, 1st Earl of Shrewsbury, and through the centuries became renowned as a smuggler's haven, so much so that in the late 19th century rows of Coast Guard cottages were established to house armed guards to police and protect the cliffs, seafront and waterways. They still stand today but the smugglers have been replaced by golfers, walkers and paragliding enthusiasts.

After fifteen years in the UK hospitality industry followed by a spell in the luxurious Carmel Valley in California, owner Mike Caddy returned to his native shores. He had a vision to bring together a unique approach that combined the extraordinary drama of the South Coast of England, exquisite classic cuisine and attention to detail, served in laid back Californian style. The result is *Pebble Beach*.

"I never tire of the endless possibilities our local produce presents and I never tire of the view from my office. J'adore ma cuisine!"

Pierre Chevillard, head chef

The Menu

Crab & lobster cakes

Grilled sea bass

Raspberry tiramisu

Pierre has been a head chef for several decades and he's still as in love with food today as he was growing up in one of France's gastronomic centres, *Le Couteau*, near Lyon. Over the years he's gained quite a fan club and held a Michelin star for more than 24 years.

He cut his teeth in a one Michelin-starred restaurant before moving to the famous three starred *Troisgros*, in Roanne. He then came to England in 1979 and joined *Chewton Glen* as sous chef where he quickly took over as head chef and remained for 24 years, winning and retaining his Michelin star for the duration.

Pierre blends effortlessly the traditions of French and English cuisine. He's a stickler for detail and many of his young and now famous protégés learned patience, perseverance and technique under his careful watch.

Modestly, Pierre prefers his kitchen to notoriety and for him smiling diners are his highest achievement. Pierre and *Pebble Beach* are a match made in heaven. Relaxation and patience are in harmony here. As Pierre's diners relax and gaze out over the West Solent and Isle of Wight, Pierre patiently concocts delightful dishes and even he never tires of the view.

Tangny's tips

Crab & lobster cakes: *Chardonnay, Eric Forest, Burgundy*

Grilled sea bass: *Nossa, Calcario, Bairrada*

Raspberry tiramisu: *Licor de Tannat, Canelones Region, Uruguay*

Full tasting notes are on page 318

Crab & lobster cakes

with potato crust, fondue of fennel and bouillabaisse jus

Serves 4

200 g fresh crab, flaked
200 g lobster tail, diced
1 stick celery, diced
1 red pepper, diced
1 green pepper, diced
100 g white bread, crusts removed, diced
2 eggs
1 tbsp mayonnaise
salt & pepper
2 potatoes, finely julienned
oil for frying
1 mango, diced

Fennel fondue
2 fennel bulbs
butter
250 ml white wine
150 ml double cream

Bouillabaisse jus
mirpoix: 1 onion, chopped; 1 carrot,
 chopped; 1 ½ leeks, chopped; 1 fennel
 bulb, sliced; 2 garlic cloves
1 tsp butter
100 ml white wine
1 tsp tomato purée
3 cloves
2 bay leaves
a few saffron threads
100 ml Pernod
11/4 litres fish stock
2 tbsp lobster butter*
salt & pepper

For the crab and lobster cakes, combine the crab flakes, lobster, celery, red and green peppers, cubed bread, eggs and mayonnaise and season to taste. Form into four round cakes and cover with julienne strips of potato. Fry in hot oil on both sides and keep warm.

For the fondue of fennel, slice the fennel bulbs finely and sauté in a little butter until soft. Add white wine and reduce completely, then add cream and reduce until thickened.

Arrange cakes on plates and surround with portions of fennel fondue and diced mango pieces.

For the jus, lightly sauté the mirpoix in butter then add the seasoning, tomato purée and spices. Pour in the Pernod and white wine and reduce to half then add fish stock and cook for thirty minutes to reduce again. Strain and finish with the lobster butter. Sprinkle the jus over the crab cakes.

* See *Garnishes*, page 348

Grilled sea bass *with braised leeks & thyme*

Serves 4

**Equipment: hand blender
or food processor**

4 225 g sea bass fillets
juice of 1 lemon
2 leeks, diced into 5 cm batons
1 tbsp butter
5 tbsp white wine
250 ml double cream
salt & pepper

Fish & thyme jus
450 g fish bones, rinsed
125 ml olive oil
1 onion, diced
125 ml dry white wine
a sprig of thyme
250 ml veal stock

Garnish
sautéed oyster mushrooms
small new potatoes
strips of leek, blanched, patted dry
    & crisped in the oven on parchment
    at lowest setting

Prepare all the components of this dish in advance of grilling the fish.

For the fish & thyme jus, sauté the fish bones in olive oil until lightly browned. Add the onion and stir over low heat until onion is transparent. Pour in the white wine and reduce to half. Add thyme and veal stock and reduce to half. Simmer until thickened. Strain and keep warm.

Sauté the leek batons in butter until translucent then add white wine and reduce until liquid has evaporated. Pour in the double cream and simmer until the leeks are cooked and the cream is reduced. Season to taste.

Season the fish fillets with salt, pepper and lemon juice and grill on both sides. Do not overcook.

To serve, arrange the leeks in the centre of the plates and place the fish on top. Pour the jus around the dish and garnish with oyster mushrooms, new potatoes and crisped leek strips.

Raspberry tiramisu

Serves 6

Equipment: fine chinois

340 g mascarpone
4 egg yolks
110 g granulated sugar
110 ml Kahlua
110 ml double cream, whipped
125 ml espresso
250 ml milk
250 g fresh raspberries
60 boudoir biscuits
30 g cocoa powder

Kahlua coffee sauce
600 ml single cream
30 g instant coffee
6 egg yolks
120 g caster sugar
120 ml Kahlua

Raspberry sauce
500 g fresh or frozen raspberries
juice of ½ lemon
100 g caster sugar

chocolate sticks for decoration

Soften the mascarpone cheese by stirring it with a fork. Whisk the egg yolks with the sugar over a bain marie until thick and fluffy. Remove from heat and whisk to cool. Add the softened mascarpone cheese, half of the Kahlua and fold in the whipped cream.

Mix together the remaining Kahlua, espresso and milk then draw the boudoir biscuits through this and line a 20 ml oval dish, bottom and sides, or sprinkle with the liquid after the dish has been lined. Spread a third of the mascarpone cheese over the biscuits and place a layer of moistened boudoir biscuits on top and press down lightly. Spread another layer of mascarpone on top and cover with raspberries masking them with mascarpone. Top with moistened boudoir biscuits and finish with the remaining mascarpone. Refrigerate for two hours until set. Sprinkle with cocoa powder and cut into wedges. Decorate with chocolate sticks and serve with Kahlua coffee sauce and raspberry sauce.

For the Kahlua coffee sauce, bring the cream and instant coffee to the boil. Whisk together the egg yolks and caster sugar. Pour the boiling cream onto the egg yolks whisking all the time. Return mixture to a rinsed-out saucepan and cook gently for a few minutes stirring constantly until the mixture coats the back of a spoon. (Cautious cooks would use a bain marie but providing you do not allow the mixture to boil there is no need.) Remove from heat and add the Kahlua liqueur.

For the raspberry sauce, purée the raspberries in a blender, add the lemon juice and sugar and stir until the sugar is dissolved. Pass through a fine sieve and refrigerate until ready to use.

Sopley Farm
near Christchurch
Dan Tanner, owner &
Rob Cox, farm manager

As fresh as it gets

Hanging onto the very edge of the southwest corner of the New Forest, *Sopley Farm* has been growing over twenty varieties of soft fruit and vegetables for over thirty years. It's a fabulous place where the energetic can pick their own seasonal produce including: strawberries, raspberries, blackberries, tayberries, gooseberries, blackcurrants, redcurrants, plums, runner beans, broad beans and pumpkins and for the less energetic, a simple stroll into the farm shop delivers a cornucopia of asparagus, rhubarb, courgette, marrow, potatoes, garlic, sweetcorn and varieties of squash. Everyone on the farm gets a real buzz from watching families charging about the place, learning first hand where the food they normally buy in cellophane bags comes from but if you can't make the drive down, their fruit and veg can also be found at most markets across the South.

Rob Cox has been managing the *Sopley Farm* for the past three years. A native of Cornwall, he brings with him boundless energy and creativity. Walking through the fields, the vitality of the place is palpable. You can almost hear the plants singing as they bask in their rich New Forest soil and slightly salt-tinged air.

The varieties of plants that Rob selects are chosen for their flavour not shelf life. The focus is on growing fruit and veg that's tastier than anywhere else by limiting the volume of each crop so they can spend more time caring for it. For Rob, 'fresh' isn't a word on a package in a supermarket, its picking something and popping it in your mouth. It's not unusual for customers, chefs and retailers alike, to have to wait a few minutes while their produce comes in from the field. They know its worth it and this is a standout reason why fruit & veg suppliers throughout the world favour *Sopley Farm* produce.

Poached duck egg in pastry & Sopley Farm asparagus

with dry sherry & morel sauce

Serves 4

4 duck eggs

4 puff pastry cases 8 cm square
   & 3 mm thick

1 egg yolk, lightly beaten

a splash of milk

24 *Sopley Farm* asparagus, cooked
   for 5 minutes

200 g fresh morel mushrooms

30 g shallots, finely chopped

60 g butter

100 ml dry sherry

100 ml chicken stock

200 ml double cream

4 tbsp white wine vinegar

10 sprigs of chive

For the puff pastry, preheat oven to 170°C. Place the pastry cases on a baking tray, egg wash with egg yolk and a dash of milk and bake for 12 to 15 minutes. Keep warm.

For the sauce, heat a pan with 40 g butter, add the shallot and morels and sweat for 3 minutes then add the dry sherry and reduce until completely evaporated. Add the chicken stock and reduce by half then add the cream. Season to taste and cook gently until the sauce coats the back of a spoon and set aside.

For the asparagus preheat oven to grill. Melt the rest of the butter and cut each asparagus tip to 1 inch long, place on a baking tray and brush with the melted butter and gently warm under the grill. Thinly slice the remaining asparagus and add to the sauce.

For the poached duck eggs, bring a medium-sized pan of water to the boil, add 4 tbsp of vinegar, break each duck egg into a cup then carefully pour each into the simmering water and poach for 5 minutes. Remove with a slotted spoon and keep hot.

To serve, open the pastry case and create a cavity, put 2 spoons of sauce inside, then place the asparagus tips around the edge of the case, wedge the egg in the middle and sprinkle with chives. Pour the remaining sauce around and serve.

Tanguy's tip

Poached duck egg: *White Rioja, Spain*
Full tasting notes are on page 318

The Oak Inn

Bank, near Lyndhurst
A Fuller's pub, Martin Sliva, manager

A quintessentially English watering hole

Tucked into the southeast corner of the New Forest is the medieval hamlet of Bank and *The Oak Inn* has been at its centre since the 17thC. The 1800's saw it as a thriving cider house supporting local orchards and workmen and feeding travellers on the Dorset to London road.

It's Dickensian charm attracted literary figures including the Victorian 'queen of sensation', Mary Elizabeth Braddon, who scandalised English society with her novel, *Lady Audley's Secret* and her son, author and playwright WB Maxwell spent his childhood in the family country home. It was also where, in 1904, Virginia Woolf and her siblings celebrated Christmas and brought in the New Year.

Most intriguing though the wood-burning fireplace was moved to the inn from the residence of the Liddle family. Alice Liddle was CS Lewis's muse. She was *Alice in Wonderland*.*

The hamlet and inn's charm have changed little. Martin Sliva and his team pride themselves on timeless hospitality. They still tend to horses for local riders and four-legged friends are as welcome as their two-legged companions.

For more than a decade, Martin has also built on the time-honoured tradition of supporting local producers. *The Oak Inn*'s food is a celebration of traditional pub fare made from seasonal, local ingredients. It really is a delightful glimpse of the New Forest's rural past.

*Alice's gravesite can be found in the nearby Lyndhurst cemetery under the name Mrs Reginald Hargreaves. (The original surround and mantle were severely damaged so local artisans crafted a replica.)

> *'It's hard to improve on what the land, sea and sun give us in the New Forest and it's our responsibility to make sure it continues to remain healthy and plentiful.'*

John Lightfoot, chef

The Menu

Solent grilled mackerel

Owls Barn cider braised belly of pork & crackling

Elderflower panna cotta

John has been cooking up New Forest classics since 1986 and he never tires of finding fresh seasonal produce and working with local farmers and artisans. His recipes regularly feature native foraged ingredients. For John, most days include a trip to his favourite seaside patch to collect fresh sea beet, samphire and other edible treasures.

Back in the kitchen John likes to keep things simple. If a local artisan has a superb product, he'll use it. His approach is fitting for a traditional pub. He combines his skill and experience and love of the outdoors using ingredients from nature's great larder.

Tanguy's tips

Grilled mackerel: *Sauvigon Blanc, Marlborough, New Zealand*
Braised belly of pork: *Maccabeo, Pays D'Oc, France*
Panna cotta: *Moscatel Naturalmente dulce, La Mancha, Spain*

Full tasting notes are on page 318

Solent grilled mackerel
with gooseberry sauce & wilted sea beet

Serves 4

2 large mackerels, filleted*

juice of half a lemon

1 tsp extra virgin olive oil

½ tsp dried wild fennel seeds

2 handfuls of sea beet per person
   (use spinach if not available)

25 g butter

250 g gooseberries, top and tailed

75 ml double cream

1 tsp caster sugar

salt & pepper

For the mackerel, preheat oven to grill and brush the fillets with olive oil and lemon juice, sprinkle with fennel seeds and lightly season. Place on a tray skin-side up and grill for 4 to 5 minutes. Serve hot.

For the sea beet, wash and remove any thick stalks and pat dry. In a pan over low heat melt a knob of butter then add sea beet. Warm until just wilted and season to taste. To assemble the dish, place sea beet in the centre of the plate, top with the mackerel and spoon a light amount of sauce around the plate.

For the gooseberry sauce, heat the butter in a saucepan over low heat then add the gooseberries. Gently simmer for 10 minutes until soft and starting to break up then lightly mash. Add the sugar and cream, season to taste. Cook for another 5 minutes then cover and keep warm.

*see *The Basics p356* or ask your fishmonger to fillet for you.

Owls Barn cider braised belly of pork & crackling *with celeriac purée, spiced apple compote & potatoes dauphinoise*

Serves 4

Equipment: butcher's string, hand blender

2.2 kg pork belly
1 tsp salt
1 garlic bulb, cut in half
1 onion, peeled & quartered
8 juniper berries
8 whole black peppercorns
1 star anise
3 bay leaves
sprigs of fresh thyme & rosemary
550 ml dry cider
vegetable stock (if required)

Celeriac purée

300 g celeriac, peeled & diced
600 ml whole milk
40 g unsalted butter
salt & pepper

Apple compote

1 kg cooking apples (Bramley), peeled, cored & diced
4-5 tbsp caster sugar
25 ml brandy

Potatoes dauphinoise

1 kg potatoes, peeled (Maris piper or Desiree)
2 cloves garlic, crushed
500 ml double cream
salt & pepper
herbs de Provençe

For the crackling, pre-heat oven to 200°C and slice the pork skin into long thin strips. Place on a tray, sprinkle with salt and bake for about 15 minutes until crispy. (These can be done well in advance and stored in an airtight container.)

For the pork belly, pre-heat oven to 160°C, remove the fat and ribs, roll and tie.* Place the rest of the ingredients in a deep roasting tin or oven proof dish deep enough for the pork to sit in ¾ covered with cider. Top up with some vegetable stock if required. Cover with lid or tin foil and cook for about 3 hours until tender. Leave to cool.

Place the celeriac, milk and butter in a heavy bottomed pan and cook until tender. Strain reserving the liquor and liquidise the celeriac with a hand blender adding some of the strained milk to get a smooth and creamy consistency. Season to taste and keep warm until ready to serve.

Place the apple pieces in a large, heavy bottomed pan on medium-low heat. Sprinkle with sugar and add brandy. If required add a bit of water to prevent the apples catching on the bottom. Cook on gentle heat stirring constantly. When apples start to break up remove from heat or if you prefer a smoother compote cook until completely soft.

Pre-heat oven to 160°C and slice the potatoes about 3mm thick, put them in an ovenproof dish. Heat the cream, garlic and a good pinch of mixed herbs, salt and pepper. Pour the cream mixture over potatoes so that the cream is just under the top layer of potatoes. Bake for about 1½ hours or until the potatoes are completely tender. You can press the potatoes and leave to go cold then cut them into portions then re-heat them or serve straight from the oven.

* Your butcher will do this for you. Save the ribs they're great for a bbq.

Elderflower panna cotta

with lavender shortbread & blood orange sorbet

Serves 4

*John serves Jude's blood orange
sorbet with this dish*

Panna cotta

100 ml whole milk

400 ml double cream

40 g caster sugar

1 vanilla pod, split & seeds removed

3 gelatine leaves

juice of 2 lemons

4-5 heads of elderflower, lightly washed
and bugs removed (or elderflower
cordial to taste but use less sugar)

Lavender shortbread

350 g unsalted butter

150 g caster sugar

4 tbsp icing sugar, sifted

2 tbsp lavender, finely chopped
(less or more to taste)

zest of 1 lemon

325 g plain flour

65 g corn flour

a pinch of salt

For the panna cotta, soak the gelatine in cold water until soft. Place milk, cream, sugar, lemon juice and vanilla in a saucepan and bring to the boil, add the elderflowers and simmer for 5 minutes. Next add the softened gelatine and stir lightly until dissolved. Remove from the heat and allow the elderflowers to infuse for about 20 to 30 minutes. Pass through a fine sieve or muslin cloth and pour into glasses and refrigerate until set. (If using cordial there is no need for infusing or sieve.)

For the shortbread, pre-heat oven to 170°C and line a baking sheet with parchment. Place all the ingredients together in a mixer and blend until all ingredients bind together to form smooth dough, (you shouldn't need to add any liquid). Roll out to about 2.5 cm thick and cut into preferred shapes. Place on the lined baking tray and refrigerate for about 1 hour. Next, bake for 18 to 20 minutes until just starting to go brown at the edges. Remove from the oven and sprinkle with sugar while still hot, allow to cool. These can be kept in an airtight container for several days.

Fuller's Brewery & Foraging on Lepe Beach

Gales Seafarers Ale, *rock samphire, sea purslane & sea beet*

The Oak Inn's chef, John Lightfoot delights in the Hampshire coastline where he forages for the rock samphire, sea purslane and sea beet that regularly feature in his dishes. He and his dogs take regular romps on Lepe Beach carefully picking plants in the rocks and like all good foragers, making sure that plants aren't over picked and it's only natural that the inn's specials board regularly features dishes that combine fruits of the sea, like sustainably caught Lyminton crab with foraged sea vegetables and *Fuller's* own *Gales Seafarer Ale*.

Gales Brewery was acquired by *Fuller's* in 2005 and as one of Hampshire's oldest and established breweries, Fuller's has kept up the *Gales* traditions of producing some of the county's finest ales.

Lymington crab croquette & Gales Ale battered sea vegetables

with foraged salsa verde

Serves 4

Equipment: deep fryer

Crab croquette

2 large potatoes

100 g white crab white meat plus
    50 g brown meat

1 tbsp chopped parsley

zest of 1 lemon

50 g plain flour

2 free range eggs beaten

50 g breadcrumbs

1½ litres vegetable oil for frying

cayenne pepper

Gales Ale battered sea vegetables

150 g each: rock samphire, sea purslane
    & sea beet

juice of 1 lemon

60 g plain flour

100 ml Gales Real Ale

¼ tsp cayenne pepper

sea salt

Foraged salsa verde

a handful of:

    three-cornered leeks

    wild sorrel

    rock samphire

4 anchovies, finely chopped

6 tbsp olive oil

zest of 1 lemon

a pinch of cracked black pepper

1 tbsp Dijon mustard

2 tbsp red wine vinegar

For the croquette, preheat oven to 180°C and bake the potatoes until tender and completely cooked through. Scoop out the flesh and mash until smooth, set to one side until cool. When cool add the white and brown crabmeat, parsley, lemon, cayenne pepper to potatoes and then roll mixture into fat sausage shapes about 5cm in length. Roll the crab mix into the flour, then the egg mix and then coat with breadcrumbs. Chill but do not cover with cling film, as it will make the breadcrumbs soggy. Preheat deep fryer to 170°C for 2 to 3 minutes until crisp golden brown and warm through.

For the sea vegetables, blanch the rock samphire, sea purslane and sea beet in boiling water for 30 seconds then refresh under cold water and pat dry. Whisk the ale, lemon juice and cayenne pepper into the flour to make a smooth paste-like batter. Preheat deep fryer to 170°C and roll the sea vegetables in flour then into the batter and deep-fry. Cook until golden brown and crispy, sprinkle with a little sea salt and serve.

For the salsa verde, chop the vegetables, mix together with the rest of the ingredients to make a course salsa and season to taste. You can use other greens foraged such as alexanders, ground ivy, hogweed, borage, nettles (blanch first) wild chervil, sea beet, ramsons, whatever is in the cupboard.

Tanguy's tip

Lymington crab croquette: *Vinho verde, Adega de Monacao, Portugal*

Full tasting notes are on page 318

Come in ..... sit down ....relax ......
... enjoy the local produce .....
.....great food ...... & fine wine !!

DANˢ KITCHEN

St Helen's, Isle of Wight
Dan & Carla Maskell,
chef & proprietors

St Helen's is a charming village perched above the northeastern coast, overlooking the fishing harbour of Bembridge. It has an air of prosperity about it and standing on the vast village green one can almost hear the whispers of the famous folk that have enjoyed its relaxed atmosphere. In 1795 the adventurous daughter of an erstwhile fisherman, Sophie Dawes, was born. She was a bit of a wild child in her time and famously became the mistress to Louis Henry II, Prince of Condé until he married her to make her the Baroness de Feuchère. It's also said that Horatio Nelson's last view of Britain was St Helen's as he sailed to fight the Battle of Trafalgar. In more recent times, The Beatles are said to have been resident while attending the *Isle of Wight Festival*. One can imagine John Lennon sitting at the pub across the green penning the infamous words, 'She's got a ticket to ride and she don't care.'

Across the green from that pub is *Dan's Kitchen,* where Dan and Carla Maskell delight locals and tourists alike with Dan's accomplished cuisine and Carla's smiling hospitality. Like Sophie Dawes, they are both native to St Helen's so understand the importance of keeping local trade thriving.

Nothing pleases chef Dan more than concocting imaginative plates featuring his friends ingredients and equally, nothing pleases Carla more than serving them with a warm and welcoming smile.

'I'm an island boy through and through. It's a privilege to know the families that provide the best of the Isle of Wight's produce, that are the foundation of everything I cook.'

Dan Maskell, chef

The Menu

Confit of duck burger

BLT

Chicken & spiced sweet potatoes

IoW strawberries, shortbread & cream cheese

Chef Dan started his career at the beautiful, *Royal Hotel* in Ventnor, where he spent fifteen years. He moved on to gain further experience on the mainland at Michelin-starred *JSW*, in Petersfield, but the island called him home. In 2011 he took the plunge and set up shop on the Green in St Helen's, much to the delight of the locals and visitors alike.

Dan is a modern chef that thinks on his feet. He looks at the fish, tomatoes, honey, whatever local producers bring his way and has the imagination to step out of his repertoire box to do new things. He applies his unique sense of humour as well but the result is skilled. Dan plays with modern ideas, turning them into scrumptious plates. Perhaps Dan has soaked in some of the adventurous spirit of St Helen's first lady, the irrepressible Sophie Dawes.

Tanguy's tips

Burger: *Carmenére Single Vineyard, Errazuriz, Valle de Aconcagua, Chile*
BLT: *Terra Alta, Rosé, Catalunya Spain*
Chicken & spiced sweet potatoes: *Muscat, Hugel, Alsace, France*
IoW strawberries & cream cheese: *Blanquette Méthode Ancestrale, Doux, Antech, Limoux, France*

Full tasting notes are on page 318

Confit of duck burger *with pickled vegetables*

Serves 4 as a starter

Equipment: 50 & 60 mm pastry cutters, food processor, fine sieve

220 g duck leg, confit (2 legs)
500 g duck fat (or more if needed)
60 g shallots, finely diced
40 g capers, chopped
30 g tomato ketchup
a splash of sherry vinegar
4 flat mushrooms (60 mm diameter)
4 slices *Island Bakers* brioche
2 thin slices Gruyere cheese
a sprinkling of poppy seeds
sea salt

Pickled vegetables

*Dan suggests you use any vegetables
of your preference*
1 carrot, thinly sliced
1 slender celery stick, peeled & sliced
a few cauliflower florets, cut into
   tiny florets
250 ml Chardonnay vinegar
2 g sea salt
375 ml water
125 g sugar
1 bay leaf
2 black peppercorns

Orange purée
1 small seedless orange
100 g sugar
25 ml sherry vinegar
175 ml orange juice
50 ml water

For the confit of duck leg preheat oven to 150°C. Place the legs in a cast iron casserole with enough duck fat to completely cover the legs. Cook for 3 hours until the meat falls away from the bone. Pull and coarsely shred the lean meat. Lightly salt the shallots and cook without colour then add the capers and ketchup. Let the mixture cool then mix with the duck meat, add few drops of sherry vinegar, check seasoning and press into 50 mm pastry moulds.

For the pickled vegetables, bring the water, bay leaves and peppercorns to a simmer then add the sugar, salt and Chardonnay vinegar, stir until the sugar has dissolved. When cool add your choice of vegetables and leave for a minimum of 6 hours.

For the orange purée, score the orange from top to bottom 6 times, place in a pan, cover with cold water and bring to the boil, simmer for 3 minutes drain and refresh in ice water. Repeat this 5 more times and on the last time simmer the orange for 20 minutes, by then the orange should be completely soft. Place the orange in food processor and blend to a smooth purée. Place the sugar in a pan with 50 ml water and melt to a dark golden caramel. Add the orange juice (be careful as the caramel may pop and spit), followed by the vinegar then whisk in the orange purée, keep on the heat and whisk until it becomes a smooth caramel. Pass through a fine sieve and cool.

Lightly fry the mushrooms then drain excess moisture on kitchen paper then using a 60 mm pastry cutter, cut slices of brioche and cheese.

To serve, stack the 'burger' with the brioche on the bottom followed by the compressed duck, cheese, top with the mushroom cap and sprinkle on a few poppy seeds. Serve with pickled vegetables and a drizzle of the orange purée.

BLT *with black pepper cream cheese*

Serves 4

**Equipment: cast iron casserole,
2 trays with weights (such as bricks),
hand mixer**

1 whole pig's cheek (ask your butcher
    to prep)
1½ litres court bouillon (see page 355)
sea salt

Black pepper cream cheese
200 g cream cheese
100 g cream
2 gelatine leaves, soaked in cold water
cracked black pepper to taste
lemon juice

a selection of fresh tomatoes (kept
    at room temperature)
a few oak roasted tomatoes*
mixed salad leaves
vinaigrette (see page 356)

For the crispy pig's cheek, soak the cheek in cold water for 12 hours. Preheat oven to 100°C. Place the cheek in a cast iron casserole and cover with bouillon, cover with a lid and cook for 12 hours. Remove the casserole from the oven and allow the meat to cool in the liquor. Then drain and flatten the cheek between 2 trays adding some weight to press it. (A couple bricks work nicely.) Place in the fridge and when cold, slice thinly and sprinkle with sea salt. Preheat oven to 180°C. Bake until golden and crispy draining off any excess fat during cooking.

For the cream cheese, using a hand mixer, beat until soft, add the black pepper to taste and a few drops of lemon juice, warm the cream, squeeze excess water from the gelatine and dissolve in the warm cream then fold into the cream cheese. Place in fridge to set.

Lightly season the tomatoes just before serving.

* These are a specialty of the Isle of Wight's, *The Tomato Stall.*

Chicken & spiced sweet potatoes

with onion bhaji, carrots & mango

Serves 4

Equipment: deep fryer, hand blender, squeeze bottle

4 chicken breasts, skin on
flour for dusting
curry spice (see below)
½ lime
1 large sweet potato, peeled & chipped
a splash of lemon juice
1 carrot, finely diced
a few small cauliflower florets
baby spinach leaves
a few sprigs of micro cress

Onion bhaji
90 g onions, finely sliced
2 g salt
100 g pasta flour
5 g baking powder
160 g water
3 g turmeric
3 g cumin
6 g chilli powder
1 lime
vinaigrette (olive oil & sherry vinegar)
1 ½ litres vegetable oil for deep frying

Mango purée
1 ripe mango, peeled & stone removed
a splash of sherry vinegar
sugar

Curry spice

1 tsp ground coriander	¼ tsp ground cloves
¼ tsp ground cardamom	¼ tsp fenugreek
½ tsp ground cumin	½ tsp turmeric
½ tsp ground ginger	¼ tsp cayenne
½ tsp ground mustard	

For the chicken preheat oven to 180°C. Rub the breast skins with flour and curry spice, pan fry skin-side down and when nicely coloured finish in oven with half a lime.

For the onion bhaji, preheat deep fryer to 180°C. Mix the flour and spices together then add the onions, followed by the baking powder and then water. Form the bhaji into loose bunches and cook in a deep fryer until golden. Season and add a good squeeze of lime juice.

For the sweet potato chips, preheat oven to 180°C. Blanch the chips until just cooked, lay out on a tray and season with curry spice and a bit of lemon juice and then roast until crispy.

For the mango purée using a hand blender, mix with the few drops of sherry vinegar and a little water until smooth. Taste and depending on the mango maybe season or add a bit more vinegar or sugar. Pour into a squeeze bottle.

Steam or blanch the carrots and cauliflower.

To serve, slice the chicken breasts and arrange on plates with the chips, and vegetables then dress with a few dots of purée, spinach leaves, coriander micro cress and a sprinkle of vinaigrette.

IoW strawberries, shortbread & cream cheese *with lemon curd & Champagne jelly*

Serves 4

Equipment: hand blender, fine sieve, ice cream maker, blender

Shortbread

125 g plain flour

75 g unsalted butter, softened

30 g sugar

Lemon curd

juice and zest of 2 lemons

70 g egg yolk (approximately 3 medium eggs)

150 g caster sugar

½ tsp cornflour

125 g unsalted butter, diced and kept cold

Champagne jelly

300 ml Champagne

50 g sugar

3 gelatine leaves, soaked in cold water

Cream cheese

125 g mascarpone cheese

125 g cream cheese

55 g sugar

1 vanilla pod, seeds only

2 gelatine leaves, soaked in cold water

150 ml whipping cream

Strawberry sorbet

500 g very ripe IoW strawberries, hulled

110 g caster sugar

35 g powdered glucose

a handful of fresh IoW strawberries, not refrigerated

For the shortbread, using a hand blender, beat the butter and sugar until light and fluffy, and then slowly sift in the flour until it forms a dough. Wrap in cling film and refrigerate for 1 hour. Preheat oven to 150°C Roll out to about the thickness of a £1 coin, place on a baking sheet and bake until lightly coloured, cool for a minute or two and then slide off on to a cooling rack. When cool break into bite-sized pieces.

For the lemon curd, bring the lemon juice and zest to the boil then remove from the heat. In a separate bowl, whisk the yolks, sugar and cornflour together. Whisk the juice into the yolks and return back to a saucepan. Cook over a medium heat stirring constantly until the mixture has thickened (be very careful not to boil as it will scramble). Remove from the heat and let the mixture cool a little, then start whisking in the butter small bits at a time, making sure it melts before adding the next bit, when all the butter is added, pass through a fine sieve and set in the fridge.

For the jelly, warm 75 ml of the Champagne and sugar to dissolve the sugar, squeeze out excess water from the gelatine and add to the warm liquid, stir to ensure that the gelatine and sugar has completely dissolved, add to the remaining Champagne, pour into a shallow tray and refrigerate to set.

For the cream cheese, beat together the two cheeses, sugar and vanilla seeds. Warm 50 ml of the whipping cream, squeeze out excess water from the gelatine and dissolve in the warm cream. Whisk the remaining whipping cream to soft peaks then whisk in the warm gelatinised cream and then fold in the whipped cream, spoon into a piping bag and refrigerate until ready to use.

For the sorbet, blend all the ingredients in a blender for 5 minutes until the sugar has dissolved, pass through a fine sieve and churn in an ice cream maker as per manufacturer's instructions.

To serve, daintily arrange all the components on plates on a swipe of lemon curd and top with a few fresh strawberries.

Captain Stan's
BEMBRIDGE
FISH STORE

Bembridge, Isle of Wight
Mike & Ruth Curtis

Mike and Ruth did what so many only dream of. They served notice on their day jobs and decided to take a few risks and have some fun. Mike's education and experience was in business and Ruth was a health and safety manager. Along the way they built a thriving B&B in Cornwall.

Mike got his first job when he was twelve. It was a foggy night in the Hamble and a fisherman needed someone to lend a hand. Young Mike was hooked, literally. By the age of fourteen, he was working on a 'set net' boat called, *The Shooting Star*. This type of commercial fishing takes time and skill. It's recognised by all governing bodies as sustainable. It doesn't damage the environment and the fishermen have to know their waters and seasons because they can only catch a bit of what's swimming by and that suited Mike just fine.

Mike was just forty, he and Ruth had sold the B&B and new adventure, knocked, again, literally. The owner of the boat that Mike worked on as a youth was standing on their doorstep offering to sell him *The Shooting Star* and the rest wasn't history it was just the beginning.

All of the pieces of their past experience have come together. Today, *The Shooting Star* selectively fishes from the Isle of Wight's northeastern Bembridge harbour and the fish go directly to their busy shop in town where daily, Ruth and shop manager Vesko keep customers and chefs anticipating what the morning's catch will be.

These days the business of commercial fishing is a complex and often controversial undertaking. There are risks involved and it's expensive, especially to do it well. And that's just where Mike and Ruth's adventures have landed them. Did they really drop out?

Plaice fillets & lemon risotto

with IoW mushrooms and broad beans

Serves 4

Equipment: thermometer, fine sieve

4 150 g plaice fillets

1 litre court bouillon (see page 355)

a pinch of celery salt

a selection of Isle of Wight wild
  mushrooms

100 g young broad beans, blanched
  & husked

200 g risotto rice

1 small onion, finely diced

1½ litres fish stock, hot

25 g butter

40 g Parmesan, grated

a squeeze of lemon

a handful of bean tops

salt & pepper

Pea purée

200 g peas

65 g milk

40 g whipping cream

ice

a leaves of micro-cress for garnish

For the plaice, poach the fillets in court bouillon heated to 70°C until just cooked (about 4 minutes for a thick fillet). When ready to serve season with celery salt.

For the risotto, in a heavy based pan over a low heat, melt 5 g of butter and cook the onion without colour. Increase the heat to medium and stir in the rice to coat evenly with the butter. Add the stock a ladle at a time, stir constantly and allow the rice to absorb the liquid. Continue until the rice is cooked 'al dente' then add the remaining 20 g of butter and the Parmesan. Season to taste with a bit of lemon juice.

For the pea purée, bring the milk and cream to the boil, add the peas and simmer for 2 minutes. Transfer to a blender and blitz until smooth, adjust the seasoning, pass through a fine sieve into a bowl set over ice and set aside cool.

Sauté the mushrooms in a splash of oil and a knob of butter, lightly season and warm the broad beans.

To serve, pass a swipe or two of purée on plates then spoon on a bed of risotto, top with the plaice and garnish with vegetables and a few sea beet leaves.

Tanguy's tip

Plaice: *Viognier, The Wingwalker, Alpha Domus, Hawkes Bay, New Zealand*
Full tasting notes are on page 318

CHEWTON GLEN

HAMPSHIRE

New Milton, New Forest
Luke Matthews, executive head chef

Chewton Glen is synonymous with luxury. From being remembered fondly as an author's family retreat to voted the *Best Country Hotel in the World,* it's a remarkable place with many stories to tell.

The original house was built around 1732 and owners of varying nobility, politics and enterprise have shaped it to what it is today; a lovely collage of old, new, country, chic, seaside and forest.

In 1821, an esteemed Royal Navy officer, Lieutenant Frederick Marryat was commissioned to watch over Christchurch Bay and police its notorious smuggling activities. Frederick was no ordinary officer, he was also an established author who kept company with the likes of Charles Dickens and influenced the works of Joseph Conrad, Mark Twain and Ernest Hemmingway. In 1837, his brother, Lieutenant George Marryat bought *Chewton Glen* and so it was that Frederick was able to soak up the atmosphere of the house, surrounding forests and paths to the seaside that feature in his classic children's novel, *Children of the New Forest.* One can only wonder if his imagined vast country house, *Arnwood*, was indeed *Chewton Glen.*

In the mid-twentieth century it was transformed into an English country house hotel and since 2007 the sumptuous spa, golf course, tree house suites, vast kitchen gardens and fine dining have come into their own.

On most days executive head chef, Luke Matthews and his team can be found planning their seasonal dishes with head gardener, Darren Venables, or smuggling ingredients back to the kitchen to delight their guests.

> *"I'm inspired by the flavours our regional produce offers. Everyday we experiment with endless combinations in our kitchen and garden to reach the sublime."*

Luke Matthews, executive chef

The Menu

Heritage beetroot & Fjordlings smoked duck

New Forest venison poivrade

Beaulieu strawberry vacherin

Luke first came to Chewton Glen aged 20. Just one week of work experience had him hooked but he learned his love of food in his mother's kitchen in nearby Christchurch. He never stopped working in local restaurants and still loves big kitchen banter and camaraderie.

Luke's journey led him to the South of France where he honed his skill in French classics as sous chef at *Hotel Les Bories* in the village of Gordes-en-Provence. He couldn't get enough of the Mediterranean's endless variety and uncomplicated style but his native south coast was calling so in 1993 he came full circle, back to *Chewton Glen*.

In 2003 Luke took the reins as executive head chef. Since then, his vision and energy have included developing an extensive kitchen garden and non-stop support of local and national events to promote local producers. When he's not in the kitchen Luke delights in exploring new ideas with his wife Claire and children, Chloe and Jamie.

Tanguy's tips

Heritage beetroot & smoked duck: *Pinot Noir, Pfalz, Germany*
New Forest venison poivrade: *Saint Emilion, Bordeaux, France*
Beaulieu strawberry vacherin: *fresh strawberry daiquiri*

Full tasting notes are on page 318

Heritage beetroot & Fjordlings smoked duck
with truffle & Rosary goat's cheese cromesquis

Serves 4 as a starter
Equipment: food processor, deep fryer

1 smoked duck breast, finely sliced

Roasted beetroot
2 yellow beetroot
2 red beetroot
2 candy stripe beetroot
2 white beetroot
a splash of rapeseed oil
1 tbsp balsamic vinegar
1 garlic clove, puréed
1 bay leaf
1 sprig of thyme

Beetroot purée
200 g cooked purple beetroot, peeled
    & chopped
100 ml orange juice
20 g Demerara sugar

Rosary goat's cheese cromesquis
200 g Rosary goat's cheese
a drizzle of truffle oil to taste
1 (10 g) fresh New Forest truffle, grated
plain flour for dusting
1 egg, beaten
1 pkg Panko breadcrumbs
1½ litres rapeseed oil for deep-frying

vinaigrette*
micro watercress
sea salt & pepper

For the roasted beetroot, preheat oven to 170°C. Wash and trim the tops and tails of the beetroots, coat them with a mixture of the rapeseed oil, balsamic vinegar, garlic, bay leaf and thyme. Wrap tightly in tin foil and roast for 2 to 2 ½ hours until soft. Allow to cool then peel off the skins.

For the purée, blend the beetroot in a food processor until completely smooth. Over low heat, reduce the orange juice and sugar until completely dissolved and only a tiny amount remains. Add to the puréed beetroots and season to taste.

For the cromesquis, preheat a deep fryer to 180°C. Mix together the goat's cheese, truffle and a little truffle oil and roll into 10 g balls. Dip into the flour, egg wash and coat with panko crumbs and fry until lightly golden. Lift out with a slotted spoon and allow to drain on kitchen paper.

To assemble, spread some of the purée onto a plate, dress the beetroots in some vinaigrette* and season, arrange on the plate with the deep fried goat's cheese, thinly slice the duck and lay over the beetroot and finish with some micro watercress.

* See *The basics*, page 356

New Forest venison poivrade
with polenta chips, roasted root vegetables & blueberry sauce

Serves 4

Equipment: fine sieve, deep fryer

4 180 g medallions of venison saddle,
    save bones & trimmings
a handful of black peppercorns, crushed
curly kale, wilted & dressed with
    vinaigrette*
salt & pepper

Polenta sticks
500 ml milk
50 g Parmesan cheese, grated
50 g red onion, diced
125 g polenta & a little extra
1½ litres vegetable oil for frying

Venison Sauce
1 kg venison trimmings & chopped bones
mirpoix: 200 g each diced onion, carrots,
    celery & leek
200 ml red wine vinegar
500 ml red wine
2 litres veal stock
5 juniper berries
1 sprig of thyme
a knob of butter

Garnish
4 baby carrots with the top, peeled &
    cut in half lengthwise
2 purple beetroot, peeled & sectioned
2 golden beetroot, peeled & sectioned
½ celeriac, cut into batons
8 baby leeks, blanched
a splash of olive oil
1 garlic clove, crushed
1 sprig of rosemary

For the polenta sticks, sweat the red onion in a pan, add the milk and bring to the boil then add the polenta and cook for about 6 minutes until the mixture leaves the side of the pan and starts to form a ball (this is critical for the frying). Add the Parmesan and turn out onto a lightly oiled tray to set. Once set cut into sticks and then roll in a little dry polenta. These can be made and frozen ahead of time. When ready to serve preheat a deep fryer to 180°C and fry the polenta until lightly golden, drain on kitchen paper and season to taste.

For the venison sauce, preheat oven to 180°C. Roast the trimmings and bones until browned then drain. Colour the mirpoix in the pan with the juniper and thyme, deglaze the pan with the red wine vinegar and reduce until almost gone then add the red wine and reduce by ²/₃. Add the stock, bones and trimmings, bring to the boil and simmer for 3 hours skimming all the time, pass through a fine sieve and reduce to a sauce consistency and stir in a knob of butter. Season to taste.

For the garnish, preheat oven to 180°C and roast all of the vegetables with olive oil, garlic and rosemary till golden. Keep warm.

For the venison, preheat oven to 200°C. Roll the meat in the pepper, heat a frying pan with a little oil and seal off on all sides then roast in the oven for about 5 minutes, turn halfway through then rest.

To assemble arrange the polenta on plates with the vegetables, warm the sauce and stir in a knob of butter. Carve the meat and arrange on top of the vegetables and polenta and serve with the sauce.

* See *The basics*, page 356

Beaulieu strawberry Vacherin

Serves 4

Equipment: hand mixer, piping bag, and deep metal rings

Vanilla cream
100 ml double cream
½ vanilla pod, seeds removed

Marinated strawberries
500 g strawberries
20 ml Grand Marnier
juice & zest of 1 lime
icing sugar

Vacherin
100 g egg whites, fresh
200 g sugar
½ vanilla pod, seeds removed
40 ml water
5 ml white wine vinegar
10 g cornflour

For the vanilla cream, add the vanilla seeds to the cream and whisk until stiff. Chill until ready to use.

To marinate the strawberries trim and cut into halves or quarters depending on size then add together with the Grand Marnier, lime juice and zest and a bit of icing sugar to taste.

For the Vacherin, pre-heat oven to 100°C and line 2 baking trays with parchment. Using a hand mixer, whisk the egg whites to almost soft peaks, then slowly add the sugar in 3 stages adding the cornflour with the 3rd lot of sugar on a medium speed to form soft peaks. At the same time bring the water to the boil, add the vanilla seeds and vinegar then pour onto the meringue. Continue to mix on full for a further 3 to 5 minutes. The mix should reach stiff peaks at this stage. Spoon the meringue into a piping bag.

Before piping, splash the parchment lightly with water and a soak metal ring in hot water then place on the parchment and pipe ¾ of the way up the ring, carefully slide the ring off, re-heat in the hot water and repeat. Bake for 1 hour, then turn the oven off and leave in the oven for another 20 minutes. Remove and cool on wire racks. If preparing the meringues in advance make sure they are packed away between parchment and wrapped tightly in a container with cling film.

To assemble, place a teaspoon of the cream in the centre of each plate to glue the meringues down. Spoon the cream onto the meringue and arrange the strawberries drizzling a little of the juice around.

LAVERSTOKE PARK FARM

Overton
Jody & Claire Scheckter

Jody Scheckter started *Laverstoke Park Farm*, in North Hampshire in 1996, with the aim of producing the best-tasting, healthiest food, without compromise, for himself and his family. He has never wavered from this philosophy and it is applied every day, across every aspect of the land, people, animals and produce that make it such a special and important agricultural centre.

The 2,500 acre organic and biodynamic farm is certified as organic by the Soil Association and has the only licensed 'soil foodweb laboratory' in Europe. It offers comprehensive analysis of the biological health of soils for research centres, farmers and horticulturalists as well as consultancy services to growers throughout the UK and Europe.

The farm creates a healthy and natural environment using time-honoured tradition based on slow-growing plants and animals combined with the most up-to-date technology and equipment. Biodynamic preparations enrich their compost that is then applied to the soil, nourishing the grasses that feed the animals and create nutrient-dense food. At *Laverstoke Park Farm*, they believe that this is why its produce tastes like homegrown food used to taste. It is research working in harmony with nature.

Amoungst *Laverstoke Park Farm's* superb selection of produce is their famous buffalo mozzarella. Jody wanted to create his own bit of Italian heaven. He originally went to see the buffalo out of curiosity as they fit the farm's philosophy that slower-growing, rare breeds produce healthier animals that also taste better; buffalo are the least developed bovine. The more he learned, the more he liked; from their higher-protein milk and lower cholesterol meat, to their naturally curious and tactile nature. He knew he wanted to have Asian water buffalo at the farm. He started with a herd of 250 and now husbands over 2,060 of the lovely beasts.

He's also pretty serious about the cheese! After extensive research he brought the equipment and experts from Italy to Hampshire. *Laverstoke Park Farm* buffalo mozzarella is second to none.

Thank-you Mr Scheckter, for your vision and commitment. For looking to the past to improve the future and creating superb products like your buffalo mozzarella to grace our finest tables.

Inka tomato salad

with Laverstoke Park Farm mozarella & tapenade

Serves 4

Equipment: food processor

a variety of coloured Isle of Wight
    tomatoes around (2 to 3 per person)
tapenade
Laverstoke buffalo mozzarella bocconcini
micro basil cress
sea salt & pepper

Tapenade
150 g black olives
25 g capers
½ garlic clove, puréed
2 tbsp olive oil

Basil mayonnaise
1 whole egg
1 egg yolk
2 tsp Dijon mustard
1 tsp grain mustard
½ garlic clove, puréed
a small bunch of basil
400 ml peanut oil (or sunflower)
50 ml white wine vinegar

Vinaigrette
100 ml sherry vinegar
300 ml olive oil
1 shallot, finely diced
Rye toast to serve

For the tapenade, put everything into a food processer and blend to a paste and season to taste.

For the basil mayonnaise, put eggs, mustard, garlic, basil and vinegar into a food processor and blend, drizzle in the oil to emulsify and season to taste.

For the dressing, whisk together the sherry, oil and shallot.

To assemble, cut the tomatoes into halves and quarters depending on their size and season lightly with a little of the vinaigrette. Arrange on a swipe of the basil mayonnaise dotting around the mozzarella (mozzarella should be served at room temperature) and tapenade and finish with the basil cress.

Serve with ultra thin slices of rye toast.

Tanguy's tip

Inka tomato salad: *Vermentino, Tuscany, Italy*
Full tasting notes are on page 318

THE ROCKINGHAM ARMS

PUB . RESTAURANT

Canada, West Wellow
Upham Brewery Group
Mark & Penny Thornhill & family

Hugging the Northeast corner of Canada Common in the New Forest lie the villages of East and West Wellow and just inside the park gates is the adjoining hamlet of Canada where, taking centre stage, is *The Rockingham Arms*. Built in 1840 as the first dwelling of this Victorian Hamlet, this traditional village pub has recently been given a bright and often humorous lift by the Upham Brewery Group.

Wellow, like its neighbouring Test Valley parishes, is built on layers of quiet history and a few interesting celebrity daughters. On his death in 899AD, King Alfred bequeathed 'the toune of Welewe' in his will to his eldest daughter Ethelgifu and she, like many dutiful princesses of the time turned her hand to prosperous milling and fulling in the wool trade. In more recent times, the local Wellow School was established by a gift of the Nightingale family and their famous daughter, Florence, is buried in the nearby 13thC parish church of St Margaret of Antioch.

In modern times the filial theme lives on. For Mark and Penny Thornhill, experienced international publicans, and their daughters Amelia and Poppy, it's a family affair. They love their industry, the pub, the locals and the area and it shows. Their daughter Amelia is Michelin-trained and she expertly shares all aspects of the day-to-day management. Poppy is always on hand to share her point of view.

Chef Brian Ahearn's experience and style match perfectly. His menus are a delightful balance of traditional pub food and modern sophistication. Along with the Thornhills, he has a reputation for working with local farmers and producers and all they have to do is walk out their front door to find the best of just about everything.

A leisurely lunch, dinner or just a thirst-quenching pint or two is time well spent with the folks at the 'pig that rocks'.

'For me great food is all about flavour and to achieve this you need the best ingredients and that's exactly what we have right here at home.'

Brian Ahearn, head chef

The Menu

Warm smoked salmon

Steak, kidney & Coleman's pie

Jacob's ladder

Pimm's & Langley's Gin jelly

South London lad, Brian earned his stripes under the world's finest. At just 13 he was invited to a work experience day at *The Savoy*, it changed his life and future. Determined to become a great chef, at 15 he returned to complete two weeks work experience before, a year later, starting his three and a half year apprenticeship working his way through every aspect of the disciplined kitchen set up by Georges Auguste Escoffier.

Over the next few years Brian worked in top establishments including Bruno Loubet's, *L'Odean* in London, the exclusive *The White Barn Inn* in Kennebunk, Maine, *Wentworth, Pennyhill Park's St James Restaurant*, as head chef, then on to Madrid, India and Australia. Wild oats sown, Brian returned to London as executive sous chef at Albert Roux's, *Brasserie Roux* in St James's followed by opening the doors of one of Belgravia's poshest pubs, *The Thomas Cubitt* as head chef.

Soon Brian's feet were itching again. The residents of northern Hampshire have been the lucky benefactors of his boundless energy. He has re-developed and launched successful pubs and inns including: *The Woolpack Inn*, Candover Valley, *The Willow*, Winchester and *The Derby*, Odiham. He's no stranger to taking on the challenge of delighting the locals and enticing hungry visitors.

Tanguy's tips

Warm smoked salmon: *California Chardonnay*
Steak, kidney & Coleman's pie: *The Punter Bitter, Upham Brewery, Hampshire*
Jacob's ladder: *Chateau Montus, Madiran, Southwest France*
Pimm's & Langley's Gin jelly: *'Sorrelade' - a lemonade made with sorrel, lemon & honey*

Full tasting notes are on page 318

Warm smoked salmon
with quail's eggs & potato & watercress scone

Serves 6 as a starter

Equipment: bbq, home warm smoker* & alder or applewood chips, thermometer, food processor, 2 squeeze bottles

* To prepare the smoker you will need a roasting tin with a lid, a wire rack that fits inside it, wood chip or sawdust and a bbq. Smoking can also be done on a stovetop but it's better to keep the smoke outside.

1.5 kg salmon, skinned, filleted & pin boned
a handful of fennel seeds
a handful of sea salt
12 quail's eggs
salt & pepper

Watercress, horseradish & shallot purée
140 g watercress
1 banana shallot, finely chopped
1 tbsp fresh horseradish, grated
ice

Beetroot & apple juice purée
4 pre-cooked beetroot, chopped (store bought are fine)
a few splashes of apple juice

Olive snow
40 ml olive oil
15-20 g maltodextrin (see page 355)

To smoke the salmon, rub the flesh with salt and fennel seeds, wrap in cling film and allow to cure in the refrigerator for 6 hours (4 hours per kilo). When ready to smoke, rinse well under cold water and pat dry. To prepare the smoker, line the bottom of a roasting tin with wood chips or sawdust and place the wire rack above so it isn't touching the wood. Heat a bbq to 80°C and place the tin in. When the wood begins to smoke, lay in the fish, cover tightly and smoke for 45 minutes making sure to control the temperature. The salmon can be served hot or cold.

For the scones, preheat the oven to 180°C. Sift the flour, salt, mustard powder and baking powder into a bowl. Rub in the butter with your fingertips until the mixture resembles fine breadcrumbs. In another bowl, stir the milk into the mashed potato then add the watercress and blend well. Add to the dry ingredients and stir with a fork adding a splash of milk, if needed, to form soft dough. Lightly knead the dough on a floured surface until smooth then roll out to 2 cm thickness. Place on a greased baking sheet. Mark into batons that will match the size of the salmon batons with a sharp knife. Brush with beaten egg and bake for 15 minutes until well-risen and golden brown.

For the watercress purée, bring a saucepan of salted water up to the boil, add the watercress, cover and return to the boil. Plunge immediately into ice water then drain watercress well. Blend the drained watercress, shallot and horseradish in a food processor with four ice cubes adding splashes of water to form a smooth purée. Season to taste and pour into a squeeze bottle.

For the beetroot and apple juice purée, place the beetroot in a food processor adding splashes of apple juice to form a smooth purée. Season to taste and pour into a squeeze bottle.

For the olive snow, mix the two ingredients together to form a light fluffy powder.

To serve, trim the scones and salmon into batons, gently fry the quail's eggs, dress the plate with dots of the purées, sprinkle on some olive snow and garnish with sprigs of watercress.

Steak, kidney & Coleman's pie

Serves 4

Equipment: individual pie moulds, baking beans

1 kg steak, trimmed & diced (2mm)

250 g ox or lamb's kidney, trimmed & diced

350 g short pastry

2 shallots, chopped

3 carrots, chopped

a knob of butter

a sprig of thyme

a sprig of rosemary

2 tablespoons flour

100 ml red wine

1 tbsp Coleman's mustard

10 g yellow mustard seeds

10 g brown mustard seeds

a splash of vegetable oil

salt & pepper

1 egg, beaten

For the filling, heat a large frying pan with a little oil. Season the steak with salt and pepper and add to the pan. Fry until well coloured and completely sealed. Season the kidneys and braise quickly to seal and colour in a hot pan then transfer to the beef.

Melt a knob of butter in another pan and cook the shallots, carrots, rosemary and thyme for 2 to 3 minutes, deglaze the pan with a splash of wine then add to the meat. Add the mustard and mustard seeds and rest of the wine and cook until the sauce thickens and the steak is very tender adding more wine or water if it evaporates too quickly. Season to taste.

Preheat the oven to 220°C. Roll the pastry to ¼ inch thick and press into a pie dish crimping the edge, cover with parchment and baking beans and blind bake. Add the filling, brush the rim with beaten egg and apply the crust top. Making sure the pastry top is bigger than the dish. Push down around the sides, trim and crimp for a neat finish. Brush completely with egg wash and bake for 30 to 40 minutes until golden.

Jacob's ladder

with caramelised onion mash & savoy cabbage

Serves 6

Equipment: potato ricer

3 kg short rib of beef

mirpoix: 2 carrots, chopped; 2 onions,
   chopped; 2 celery sticks, chopped

750 ml red wine

salt & pepper

Caramelised onion mash

4-6 potatoes (Maris piper),
   peeled & chopped

1 onion, peeled & sliced

a splash of vegetable oil

a splash of milk

several knobs of butter

Savoy cabbage, shredded

a knob of butter

For the beef, preheat oven to 220°C. Place the beef, mirpoix, wine and a bit of seasoning in a roasting tin. Cover and roast on high heat for 30 minutes then reduce the temperature to 180°C. Continue to roast for several hours until the meat falls from the bone. Rest for 10 to 15 minutes before serving.

For the potatoes, caramelise the onion in a pan in a splash of oil until deep golden and set aside. Boil the potatoes until soft. Pass through a ricer then whisk in a splash of milk and 3 to 4 knobs of butter. Stir in the onions, season to taste and serve hot.

Pimm's & Langley's Gin jelly
with strawberry salad & Champagne sorbet

Serves 4

Equipment: ice cream maker

600 ml Pimm's
50 ml Langley's Gin
100 g sugar
6 gelatine leaves, softened in cold water
zest of 1 lime
a punnet of strawberries, trimmed & finely sliced

Champagne sorbet
225 g sugar
juice of 1 small lemon
300 ml Champagne or sparkling wine

For the jelly, warm the Pimm's, gin and sugar in a saucepan until the sugar is completely dissolved. Add the softened gelatine and stir until it is dissolved then continue to cook for another 2 minutes. Pour into a shallow tray and refrigerate until set.

For the Champagne sorbet, place the sugar in a medium-sized pan with 500 ml cold water. Bring to the boil, stirring until the sugar dissolves. Simmer for 10 minutes then remove from the heat and cool. Add the lemon juice and Champagne or sparkling wine and stir well. Pour into an ice-cream maker and follow manufacturer's instructions.

To serve, cut the jelly into fine cubes and sprinkle with lime zest and top with quenelles of sorbet.

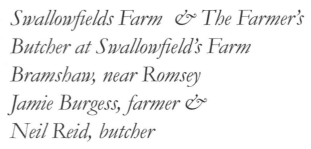

Swallowfields Farm & The Farmer's Butcher at Swallowfield's Farm Bramshaw, near Romsey Jamie Burgess, farmer & Neil Reid, butcher

300 years after they were hunted to extinction the wild boar are back in the New Forest, thanks to Jamie Burgess. He spent a year adapting his land to create a secure enclosed natural environment that saw to the animal's distinct characteristics without domesticating them.

An adult boar can weigh in at more than twenty stone, stand over a metre tall, reach speeds of up to thirty miles per hour and jump six feet so far be-it for any farmer to get between them and their insatiable desire to forage the forest floor.

Jamie also makes sure their diet is as close as nature intended as possible. The boar are slow growing and keeping them in an unforced, natural environment results in higher protein and lower fat meats with a fuller, usually nuttier flavour.

It's not the easiest choice of animal husbandry but he's always had a fascination for these lovely creatures. Admittedly, it takes patience, imagination and a dangerous wild animal license to start but Jamie isn't farming for the mass market. He is committed to encouraging people to buy from their local producers and he gives them something unique and something you can't buy in the high street.

Butcher Neil Reid along with his wife Rachel, run the butchery and shop right on the farm providing the public and top chefs with excellent beef, pork and of course, unique New Forest wild boar.

Swallowfield's Farm *wild boar chop & smoked duck egg, caper & shallot remoulade* with sautéed potatoes & *crispy shallots*

Serves 4

Equipment: deep fryer, bbq, home warm smoker & alder or applewood chips, thermometer

4 wild boar chops
a knob of butter
2 duck eggs
a handful of capers, chopped
3 banana shallots
flour & milk for pane
4 potatoes, peeled
salt & pepper
1 ½ litres vegetable oil for deep frying

For the wild boar chops, preheat oven to 200°C. Cut away the rind and reserve to make crackling garnish, lightly season and sear on both sides on a hot griddle. Place the pan in the hot oven for two minutes until the meat is pink but cooked through. Return to the stove top and baste in foaming butter. Season to taste and rest for five minutes before serving.

For the smoked duck remoulade, prepare a stovetop smoker as per the smoked salmon recipe (page 36). Hard-boil the duck eggs and peel. When the wood begins to smoke, place the eggs in a flameproof container into the smoker, cover and let cure for five minutes. Remove the eggs and set aside to cool then chop roughly. Peel and chop two shallots and mix these together with the duck egg and capers. Season to taste.

For the sautéed potatoes, parboil the potatoes so they are just soft through. Drain and cut into wedges. Melt a knob of butter and a splash of vegetable oil in a frying pan and sauté the potato wedges until they have a nice golden crust. Season to taste.

For the crispy shallots, preheat deep fryer to 180°C. Peel two banana shallots and slice into rings. Pane the rings in flour, then milk, then back in the flour and place in the oil with a slotted spoon. Fry until golden and crispy, then remove with the slotted spoon and place on kitchen paper to drain.

While the deep fryer is still hot scrape away excess fat from the boar rinds and cut into strips then deep fry until golden and crispy and drain on kitchen paper.

Serve the chop with the rest of the components hot on a board.

Tanguy's tip

Wild boar chop: *Cabernet Franc, Finger Lakes, New York*
Full tasting notes are on page 318

Emsworth, near Portsmouth
Ramon & Karen Farthing, chefs & patrons

36 On The Quay overlooks the picturesque Emsworth Channel. Through the ages it has maintained an air of prosperity and spirit of diversity. Since 1239 Emsworth has been a market town as well as a port once famous for its wine importing, lumber exporting, shipbuilding, rope making, flower growing, local flour was once ground by tidal mills and there was also a thriving oyster trade. By the 19th century the railway helped turn it into a fashionable seaside resort where the wealthy could discretely bathe in seawater. It boasted more than 30 pubs and beer houses and the weekly market and annual fete were second to none. Emsworth is a bit more tranquil these days. The tidal nature of the harbour is no longer suitable for modern shipping and encroaching development tainted the water and saw out the oyster beds but its still as pretty a spot as ever and right on the tip of the docks is one of Hampshire's culinary jewels, *36 On The Quay*.

Ramon and Karen Farthing opened the restaurant in 1996. Ramon had previously worked as personal chef to Lord and Lady Spencer at Althorpe. He earned his first Michelin star at *Calcot Manor* in Tetbury and was awarded a successive star during his four years at *Harveys Cellars* in Bristol and only one year after opening *36 On The Quay* was awarded his third successive Michelin star in 1997 and has maintained it ever since. While Ramon's been minding the kitchen, his wife Karen has been at the front seeing to every detail. On top of that, she is also an experienced chef de partie and was formerly senior pastry chef at *The Royal Crescent* in Bath.

Today, the Farthings are looking forward to spending a little more time enjoying the fruits of their labours and sharing the responsibilities with Ramon's protégé, chef Gary Pearce and Martyna, his lovely wife.

'I'm home. I love what I do and where I do it. 36 on the Quay is my past, present and future. I'm a happy man!"

Gary Pearce, head chef

The Menu

Emsworth Harbour canapés

Pea panna cotta & lovage soup

Local asparagus & slow cooked egg yolk

Fresh roast plaice & confit chicken

Meadowsweet rice pudding

Gary once had a reputation for being a bit of a wild child. One of those youngsters who has a lot of creativity and energy and nowhere to channel it, in his words, "One day I just woke up and thought I have got to sort my life out and I knew I wanted to be a chef." Gary did his training at South Downs College and never looked back.

In 1999, with haute cuisine calling, he walked into Ramon Farthing's Michelin-starred kitchen and simply asked for a job and his industriousness paid off. After apprenticing at *36 on the Quay,* he joined two Michelin-starred chef David Everitt-Matthias at *Le Champignon Sauvage* in 2006 where he worked up the ranks then went to work on the Continent.

Gary came home to Hampshire from the celebrated *De Wulf,* in Belgium, with refined skill and a head full of ideas. Once again he walked into Ramon Farthing's Michelin-starred kitchen and simply asked for a job. He was welcomed back with open arms and the two of them have been working side-by-side ever since.

Tanguy's tips

Canapés: *Langley's 008 Gin Cocktail, Hampshire*
Pea panna cotta: *Spatburgunder Rosé, Ahr, Germany*
Local asparagus: *Muscat, Alsace, France*
Plaice & confit chicken: *Sequillo white, Malmesbury, South Africa*
Meadowsweet rice pudding: *Sparkling Shiraz, Barossa Valley, South Australia*

Full tasting notes are on page 318

Emsworth Harbour canapés

Crispy chicken skins with honey mayonnaise & hedgerow herbs

Serves 4
Equipment: food processor

skin of 4 whole chicken breasts
salt & pepper

Honey mayonnaise
160 g egg yolk
70 g honey
5 g salt
0.5 g xanthan gum (optional) (see page 355)
5 g sherry vinegar
75 g rapeseed oil

Hedgerow herbs (a combination of dandelion, yarrow, chervil flowers, fennel & pea shoots)

For the crispy skins, preheat oven to 180°C. Stretch out the skins with the inside facing up and scrape off any excess fat then place them on a tray lined with greaseproof paper. Sprinkle with a bit of salt and pepper cover with another sheet of greaseproof then set another tray firmly on top and cook until crisp. Drain on kitchen paper.

For the mayonnaise, blend all ingredients except the oil in a food processor at medium speed. Continue mixing and slowly drizzle in the oil until emulsified. To serve, dress with hedgerow herbs.

Seed biscuits with cheese cream & pickled radish

Serves 4 as a snack
Equipment: food processor, thermometer, hand blender, squeeze bottle or piping bag

100 g butter, cut into small cubes
100 g Parmesan, grated
100 g Cheddar, grated
12 g flour
6 g salt
3 egg yolks
20 g sesame seeds
10 g onion seeds
10 g linseed
10 g flaxseed
10 g poppy seed
10 g sunflower seeds

Cream cheese
500 ml milk
200 g strong Cheddar, finely grated
8 g kappa carrageenan (see page 355)
8 g salt

Pickled radish
50 g radishes, very finely sliced
100 ml white wine vinegar
50 g sugar
50 ml water
a pinch of thyme

For the biscuits, preheat oven to 180°C and line a baking tray with greaseproof paper. Mix all the ingredients together to the texture of a sable pastry. Roll into a thin sheet on a lightly floured surface, cut into desired shapes and bake until lightly golden. (Make in advance and store in an airtight container.)

For the cream cheese, heat the milk to 80°C. Add the cheese and kappa carrageenan and stir until melted and smooth then add the salt checking the seasoning as you go. Pour into a clean bowl and set aside to cool and set. When set, blitz with a hand blender and spoon into a squeeze bottle or piping bag and refrigerate until ready to use.

For the pickled radish, boil the vinegar sugar, water and thyme then allow to cool then pour over the radishes and allow to stand for 30 minutes. The remainder can be stored in a sterilised jar and kept chilled for a couple days.

Flaxseed crisps & salted brill roe

Serves 6 to 8 as a snack
Equipment: micro-plane (an ultra-fine grater)

Flaxseed crisps
300 g flaxseed
500 g water
a pinch of salt
a knob of butter

Salted brill roe
2 500-700 brill roe sacks
500 g coarse sea salt

For the crisps, preheat oven to 100°C and line a baking tray with greaseproof paper. Place all ingredients into a pan and cook slowly until the mix binds together but still a bit sloppy. Spread thinly onto the tray and dry in the oven until crisp. When cool, break into bite-sized pieces.

For the salted brill roe, preheat oven to 70°C. Gently wash the sacks under cold running water, place on a tray and cover with salt. Let stand for 30 minutes then rinse thoroughly. Dry on a rack in the oven until very dry. Dust a few biscuits per person with a fine layer of grated roe. (The rest will keep for several months when sealed and stored airtight in the refrigerator and is an excellent natural salty seasoning.)

Pea panna cotta & lovage soup
with salt baked beetroot, pea shoots & pansies

Serves 4 as a starter

Equipment: hand blender, fine sieve, dariole moulds, food processor

Pea panna cotta

300 g peas, blanched (frozen are fine)

100 ml milk

400 ml double cream

2 g powdered agar agar (see page 355)

salt & pepper

Lovage soup

500 g lovage

2 medium potatoes (Maris piper), peeled & chopped

2 onions, chopped

a knob of butter

500 ml milk

200 ml chicken stock

salt & pepper

Salt-baked beetroot

3 large beetroots

Salt crust

750 g plain flour

750 g coarse sea salt

100 g caraway seeds

40 ml rapeseed oil

362 ml water

flour for dusting

micro pea shoots & pansies for decoration

For the pea panna cotta, make a pea purée by blitzing the blanched peas with a hand blender and pass through a fine sieve then season to taste. Next bring the milk and cream just to the boil, add the agar agar until completely dissolved then add the pea purée. Check seasoning, pour into dariole moulds and refrigerate to set. When ready to use, run the moulds under warm water, give them a little spin and gently jiggle to coax the panna cottas out.

For the lovage soup, sweat the onions in butter without colour. Add the potatoes, milk and stock and simmer until the potatoes are very soft. Blitz with a hand blender until smooth adding the lovage a bit at a time. Pass through a fine sieve, season to taste and chill until ready to serve. Can be served warm or chilled.

For the salt-baked beetroot, preheat oven to 180°C. Make the salt crust dough by combining all ingredients in a food processor to make a dough. Roll out the dough on a lightly floured surface to about 1 cm thick then wrap and seal the beetroot and bake for 1 hour. When ready to serve cut away the crust, trim and slice.

Local asparagus & slow cooked egg yolk _with brown butter purée, fresh ricotta, whey,_

forget-me-nots & marigolds

Serves 4 as a starter

Equipment: thermometer, blender, fine sieve, muslin cloth, plastic squeeze bottles or piping bag

16 asparagus spears
ice
4 chicken eggs

Brown butter purée
250 g unsalted butter
300 ml water
30 g caster sugar
10 g cornflour
6 g xanthan gum (see page 355)

Whey
You can get this from specialist cheese shops
1 litre whey
1 g xanthan gum

edible forget-me-nots & marigolds
  for decoration

For the asparagus, trim the ends and peel the spears to the heads. Blanch in salted boiling water for one minute then plunge into ice water. Drain on kitchen paper. Warm just before serving.

For the eggs, place in a pan of 64°C water for 1 hour. Use a thermometer to maintain a constant water temperature. Serve immediately. (Alternatively the yolk can be traditionally poached)

For the brown butter purée, melt the butter in a medium saucepan until golden brown then slowly add 25 g water being careful not to split the mixture. Add the sugar and bring to the boil then whisk in the cornflour and remaining water until smooth. Pour into a blender adding the xanthan gum and blitz. Pass through a fine sieve, pour into a plastic squeeze bottle or piping bag and chill.

For the whey, bring the whey to the boil then reduce slowly to 300 ml. Pass through a muslin cloth then add the xanthan gum. Refrigerate until ready to use.

To serve, pass a swipe of the whey across the plate and add a few dots of the purée and ricotta then place the egg yolk in the centre and 4 warm asparagus on top. Decorate with a few flowers and serve.

Fresh roast plaice & confit chicken wings *with caramelised cauliflower & Alexander buds.*

Serves 4

Equipment: food processor, fine sieve, fine mandolin

4 200 g plaice filleted & skinned
(ask your fishmonger to do this)
12 chicken wings
a handful of coarse sea salt
2 sprigs of thyme, leaves only
1 garlic clove, crushed
100 g duck fat, melted
1 small cauliflower
100 g butter and a bit extra
a splash of milk
200 g Alexander buds
a couple knobs of butter
a splash of vegetable oil
a splash of white wine
salt & pepper

For the plaice, preheat oven to 160°C. Lay the fillets back-to-back and head-to-tail and wrap in cling film and refrigerate until ready to use. Prepare the fish when all other components of the dish are ready.

For the chicken wings, trim and cut the wings, removing the tip so you have drums and flats (save the trimmings to make a sauce). Cover with sea salt and let stand for 20 minutes then roast until golden brown. Season the duck fat with thyme and garlic then cover the wings and cook for another 30 minutes until the bones pull out easily. Drain on kitchen paper.

To make the sauce, sear the chicken trimmings with a bit of oil in a hot pan until they are very brown. Discard the trimmings and deglaze the pan with a bit of white wine, add the tarragon and butter and reduce to a light sauce consistency. Season to taste and pass through a fine sieve.

For the caramelised cauliflower, preheat oven to 180°C. Trim the leaves but keep the stalk and cut into 1 cm slices. Melt 100 g butter in a roasting tin, toss in the cauliflower making sure all the slices are coated and roast until golden. Transfer to a food processor, add a splash of milk and blitz. Season to taste, pass through a fine sieve and chill.

For the Alexander buds, gently sauté in a knob of butter for 1 minute tossing constantly until warm through.

To serve, in a lightly oiled pan fry the fillets for 1 minute each side. Add a knob of butter and baste for 1 minute. Warm the caramelised cauliflower then pass a swipe on each plate. Arrange the fish and chicken wings and sprinkle with cauliflower shavings and Alexander buds.

Meadowsweet rice pudding
with fresh strawberries & strawberry chips

Serves 4

Equipment: fine sieve, silpat mat, large ring moulds or scone cutters

30 g meadowsweet flowers
350 ml milk
75 g pudding rice
50 g sugar
25 g double cream, semi-whipped
1½ gelatine leaves, softened in cold water

Strawberry chips
500 g strawberries, trimmed
a generous dollop of runny honey

500 g strawberries, trimmed and sliced
a few bright flowers for decoration

Meadowsweet is a wonderfully diverse plant. Probably most famous as being one of the common ingredients in aspirin for its concentrated salicylic acid, it is also a digestive aid. It grows in abundance in damp areas such as pond edges, soft meadows, hedges and riversides.

For the rice pudding, bring the flowers and milk to the boil then gently simmer for 20 to 30 minutes then remove from heat. When cool, pass through a fine sieve. Next, in a saucepan add the rice, sugar and infused milk. Cook on medium heat until the rice is soft, add the gelatine then place in refrigerator. When cold, fold in the semi-whipped cream.

For the strawberry crisps, preheat oven to 100°C. Blitz the strawberries and honey together then pass through a fine sieve. Spread a thin layer onto a silpat mat and dehydrate in the cool oven for 12 hours until crispy. When cool break into bite-sized shards.

To serve, spoon the rice into moulds and top with fresh strawberries and strawberry crisp shards and decorate with a few delicate flowers.

Sorrel & apple ice

Serves 4 as a pre-dessert

Equipment: food processor, fine sieve

500 g sorrel, washed in cold water
1 litre apple juice
150 g sugar
juice of 3 lemons
40 g glucose

Place the sorrel, apple juice, sugar and ⅔ of the lemon juice in a food processor and blitz until smooth. Check the flavour and add further lemon to taste. Pass through a fine sieve into a non-metallic airtight container. Place in the freezer and fold the mixture every 15 to 20 minutes as it freezes.

Portsmouth
Andrew Johnson & Family

In 1975, Andrew Johnson's dad, Bernard, established a market on the Camber Dock to provide local fishermen a place where they could land and sell their daily catches. As a lad, Andrew cut his teeth in the fishing trade there.

Within a few years *Johnson's*, along with 3 other fishermen, bought its first beam trawler and over the next 20 years expanded to 7 trawlers, employing over 60 people. Andrew started as a deckhand and worked his way through every possible responsibility deep sea commercial fishing demanded and soon earned his skipper's ticket. Over 21 years he skippered 6 trawlers and worked in every UK and Dutch fishing ground.

In the late 1990's the fishing industry hit difficult times, with soaring fuel prices, new EEC legislation and fish quotas, Andrew and his father decided to sell their trawlers and call it a day. It was Andrew's sister Cheryl and Johnson's marketing manager, David Dench that convinced him to take another look at things so the new *'Johnson's Enterprises'* was born, or in a sense, the old *Johnson's* was back. In 2000, Andrew returned to his father's original trade of providing local fishermen a place to sell their catches.

Today, with skill only decades of experience offers, they buy local day-boat fish and shellfish from south coast fishermen and also source fish from most other UK fishing ports. All are processed and distributed daily to fine fishmongers, retail markets and restaurants.

Roast brill, sauerkraut, hazelnut gnocchi & local foraged mushrooms

with fermented rye soup

Serves 4

Equipment: deep fryer, ricer, digital scale

1 kg brill, filleted & skinned (have your fishmonger do this)

500 g sauerkraut

a selection of exotic mushrooms

1 garlic clove, crushed

a knob of butter

a splash of white wine

salt & pepper

Hazelnut gnocchi

1 kg potatoes (King Edward), baked

100 g potato flour

100 g roasted hazelnuts, chopped

3 egg yolks

100 g Parmesan

10 g salt

50 ml hazelnut oil

Fermented rye soup

300 g rye flour

500 ml water, boiled and cooled to blood temperature

4 garlic cloves, lightly crushed

2 onions, diced

10 g juniper berries

100 g smoked sausage, chopped

500 ml chicken stock

salt

nasturtium leaves & three-cornered garlic flowers

The rye fermentation is chef Gary's wife, Martyna's Nan's traditional recipe and takes 3 days to make. Its Polish name is Zur and can be bought online or at specialty Polish shops. Gary also makes his sauerkraut but recommends that good quality store bought is also fine.

For the brill, lay the fillets back-to-back and head-to-toe and wrap in cling film and refrigerate until ready to use. Prepare the fish when all other components of the dish are ready.

For the gnocchi, scoop out the potato flesh and pass through a ricer. Add the rest of the ingredients and mix until well combined. Roll into 3 g balls. Blanch in boiling salted water until they rise to the top then drain on kitchen paper. When ready to serve pre-heat deep fryer to 180°C and fry until golden. Season to taste and serve hot.

For the soup, mix together the rye flour, water and garlic in a sterilised jar and rest in a warm place for 3 days stirring everyday. It should smell a bit sour. When ready, sweat the onions and juniper in a pan then add the sausage. Pour in the rye mixture and simmer for a few minutes. Add the stock in small portions allowing the soup to reduce until you have a nice consistency. Season to taste.

To serve, in a lightly oiled pan fry the fish fillets on both sides for 1 minute each, add a knob of butter and baste for 1 minute. Dress the plate with the fish, gnocchi and little rondelles of warm sauerkraut and decorate with the nasturtium leaves and garlic flowers. Serve the warm soup on the side.

Tanguy's tip

Roast brill: *Fiano white, Adelaide Hills, South Australia*

Full tasting notes are on page 318

THE PIG

Brockenhurst, New Forest
James Golding, chef director

The New Forest is Europe's largest surviving ancient pasture woodland. William the Conqueror claimed this vast area as his hunting ground in 1079 and to this day, alongside deer and wild boar the cattle, ponies, donkeys and pigs of the commoners graze freely and at its heart stands *The Pig*.

The Pig is so much more than a charming Victorian country house. It's a showcase for the remarkable kitchen garden at the core of chef James Golding's philosophy about food. The restaurant exists to celebrate the garden and anything head gardener, Alex Coutts and his team can't grow and forager, Garry Eveleigh can't find, James sources within a 25 mile radius. Their trademark '25 Mile Menu' is truly a celebration of everything local.

Continuing his commitment to local provenance James has built partnerships with gardeners, farmers and producers from the area. Local organic farm, Sunnyfields advises on garden development and along with local butcher Alan at T Bartlett & Sons, James has created, *A Pinch of Salt*, a unique range of cured meats using his own smoke house.

This place is designed to enjoy the creation of food from garden, forest, field and stream. What a delight it is to stroll through herb, vegetable and fruit gardens, past the hens and quail and who wouldn't miss a chance to make new friends with *The Pig*'s friendly pets – the pigs of course!

> *"I think our local farmers and producers are the finest so I put them at the fore of everything we serve at The Pig."*

James Golding, chef director

The menu

Piggy bits:
    Brock eggs & Coleman's dressing
    Smoked bacon & apple arancini
    A Pinch of Salt **Karma ham & olives**

Dorset cockles

Crispy pork belly & fennel salad

The Pig's **extraordinary Bath chap
    on a board**

Forager's fizz

Dorset buttermilk blancmange

If one were to look up the words provenance and food one might see a picture of James Golding.

For James, heading *The Pig* is literally coming home. Just like his signature '25 Mile Menu' he grew up just a few miles away. At just 16, James entered the *Académie de Culinaire de France*, founded by Albert Roux and Richard Shepherd and while still studying won his first post at the legendary *Savoy Hotel* in London and in three short years had worked his way through every station in its classically French kitchens.

In 1998 James joined *Le Caprice* as chef de partie and three years later joined its sister restaurant *J Sheekey* as sous chef. It was during this period that his love of local and British really took hold but James still had some exploring to do so he went to run the kitchen at *Soho House* in New York and adding a touch of sparkle to his already glamorous career was one of its chefs serving at their exclusive Oscars party in Hollywood.

In 2006, as a new dad, James returned home to the south coast of England bringing with him a style that's completely unique; a quirky mix of London elegance and New York chic with lashings of California cool on top of meticulous and disciplined classic French.

Tanguy's tips

Piggy bits: *7 Fuentes, Valle de la Orotave, Tenerife, Spain*
Dorset cockles: *Gruner Veltliner, Krempstal, Austria*
Crispy pork belly: *Chablis 1er Cru, Burgundy, France*
Bath chap: *traditional English bitter, Hampshire, England*
Dorset buttermilk blancmange: *Late Harvest Zinfandel, Mendocino, California*

Full tasting notes are on page 318

Piggy bits

Brock Eggs

Serves 6 to 8 as a sharing
dish or starter

Equipment: deep fryer,
food processor

2 ham hocks

½ pig's head

mirpoix: 1 onion, leek, carrot & celery
    stick, chopped

1 tsp black peppercorns

1 bay leaf

2 sprigs of thyme, leaves only,
    chopped

sea salt

12 quail eggs, cooked for exactly
    2½ minutes

a small bunch of parsley, chopped

a pinch of celery salt

pepper

pane mix: flour, egg & breadcrumbs

Coleman's vinaigrette

1 tbsp pasteurised egg yolk

2 tbsp white wine vinegar

1 tbsp English mustard

salt & pepper

rapeseed oil

**Smoked bacon &
apple arancini**

Serves 4

Equipment: deep fryer, hand
blender, fine sieve

100 g Arborio risotto rice

8 rashers dry-cured smoked streaky
    bacon, diced

1 onion, diced

1 large apple (variety your choice),
    peeled & diced

2 litres vegetable or chicken stock

100 g flat leaf parsley, chopped

50 g mature English cheese

50 ml rapeseed oil

salt & pepper

2 eggs

300 g fine white bread crumb

200 g flour

Spiced tomato sauce

5 Isle of Wight tomatoes, de-seeded
    & chopped

5 garlic cloves, finely chopped

75 ml white wine vinegar

75 g brown sugar

½ tsp ground ginger

½ tsp sea salt

½ tsp smoked paprika

½ tsp cayenne pepper

½ tsp dry mustard seed

½ tsp clove

½ tsp ground allspice

2 star anise

A Pinch of Salt **Karma ham & olives**

Here's a dollop of inspiration from
James on how to make a simple snack
elegant. His delicious karma ham
is described on page 317 and he's
dressed it with green olives, pickled
golden beetroot and a few flowers.

Brock eggs

Preheat oven to 180°C and place the mirpoix, herbs and spices into a large roasting pan with the ham hocks and pig's head, cover with cold water and cook for 2 ½ hours until the meat falls off the bone. When cool enough, pick off all the meat and shred by hand into a large bowl then add chopped parsley and season to taste.

For the quail eggs, place the eggs in boiling water for exactly 2½ minutes then plunge into ice water to stop the cooking process. When cooked very gently peel.

Next spread the meat into thin circles on a clean work surface and wrap the quail eggs in the meat. Chill for 30 minutes. Pane in breadcrumbs and deep fry. (You can also colour in a non-stick pan and flash through the oven for a healthy option.) When crispy, season with celery salt and serve with Coleman's mustard vinaigrette.

For the Coleman's vinaigrette, place the egg yolk, vinegar & mustard in a food processor and while mixing slowly add the oil until emulsified and thickened. Season to taste and dress under the Brock eggs.

Smoked bacon & apple arancini

For the arancini, sauté the bacon in oil then add the onion and cook until soft then add the apple and cook until it has a little colour. Add the rice and sweat down for 5 minutes to release a little starch. Bring the stock to the boil and add a ladle at a time to the rice stirring all the time. Continue until rice is cooked al dente then remove from the heat, stirring continuously for about 5 minutes to take the residual heat out and stop the mixture over cooking. Once cool add the chopped parsley and season to taste.

Preheat a deep fryer to 190°C. Roll the rice into 35 g balls. Make a dent through to the middle with your finger and stuff with 10 g of cheese and re-roll into balls. Set out the flour, beaten eggs and breadcrumbs on plates, pane each rice ball and deep fry for 3 minutes until perfectly golden.

For the tomato sauce, blend the vinegar, cloves and garlic together in a heavy saucepan and cook without colour then add the rest of the ingredients and cook slowly for 35 minutes until thick and pulpy. Blitz with a hand blender until smooth and pass through a fine sieve. Season to taste.

Dorset Cockles *with foraged sea vegetables*

Serves 4 as a light dish

Equipment: deep fryer

250 g Dorset cockles

2 tbsp shallots, chopped

1 garlic clove, chopped

100 ml white wine

50 g butter

100 ml double cream

a pinch of parsley, chopped

salt & pepper

6 pieces of deep fried lava weed

a handful of samphire, sea beet & purslane, washed & blanched

1½ litres rapeseed oil for deep-frying

crusty bread to serve

In a heavy bottomed pan heat the butter, garlic and shallot and cook without colour. Add the cockles and white wine and cover with a lid. When the cockles have steamed open add the double cream, season to taste and bring back to the boil for 1 minute then keep warm until ready to serve. Just before serving add the parsley and sea vegetables and leave for 30 seconds to cook in the sauce.

For the seaweed, preheat a deep fryer to 180°C. Make sure the seaweed is washed and dried to avoid spitting. Carefully place it into the fryer and fry until crispy (it will only take a few seconds), remove with a slotted spoon and drain on kitchen paper. Serve with ample crusty bread and a glass of chilled white wine.

Crispy pork belly & fennel salad

Serves 6 as a starter

Equipment: deep fryer

½ pork belly
sea salt
1 garlic clove, crushed
1 bay leaf
2 sprigs of thyme
10 peppercorns
1½ litres rapeseed oil for deep frying

Dressing
a pinch of smoked chilli flakes
2 tbsp runny honey
1 tbsp soy sauce

Pickled Fennel
1 large bulb fennel, shaved
½ litre white wine vinegar
1 litre white wine
2 bay leaves
10 peppercorns
150 g sugar or to taste

mizuna or rocket and edible flowers
   to garnish
sesame seeds, lightly toasted

To marinate the pork, sprinkle generously with sea salt and the rest of the herbs & spices, seal tightly in cling film and refrigerate overnight.

Prepare the dressing at least 2 hours in advance by whisking the ingredients together and let stand to infuse.

For the pork belly, preheat oven to 200°C. Place the pork on a baking tray, season and cook for 1 hour until cooked through. Cool and slice 1 cm thick by 5 cm long. Preheat deep fryer to 180°C then deep fry the pork pieces until crispy (or pan roast for a healthy option). Drain the pieces on kitchen paper. When ready to serve, place in a large bowl and drizzle with dressing until completely coated.

For the pickled fennel, bring all ingredients except the fennel to the boil in a pan then while hot pour over the fennel. Balance the flavour with sugar to taste and let stand until cool.

To serve, place the crispy pork belly on top of a generous amount of pickled fennel. Dress with some mizuna or rocket, place on top and drizzle some more dressing around and over. Garnish with sesame seeds and edible garden flowers.

The Pig's extraordinary Bath chap on a board

This is an historic West Country dish traditionally served as a cold, pressed meat dish. James Golding's dramatic version is taking its own place in history.

Serves 1 lower jaw per person

1 lower pig jaw, including bone & teeth
1 garlic clove, chopped
2 sprigs of thyme
10 peppercorns
2 bay leaves
sea salt
rapeseed oil, enough to coat

Roasted beetroot
2 beetroot, peeled & diced
a splash of rapeseed oil
2 sprigs of thyme
1 bay leaf
a splash of red wine
salt & pepper

Apple sauce
2 to 3 Bramley apples or the same weight of crab apples, peeled & cored
a pinch of sugar

To prepare the Bath chaps, use a sharp knife to score all the skin off the chap, rub with oil and seasoning, wrap in cling film and refrigerate overnight. Next day rub all over with sea salt then leave for 30 minutes. Preheat oven to 220°C, rub off all excess salt and place on a roasting tray. Cook for 30 minutes then drop the temperature to 180°C for 60 minutes, then cook until crispy on the outside and well cooked through. Serve with roasted beetroot & apple sauce.

For the roasted beetroot, preheat oven to 180°C, lightly coat the diced beetroot with oil and vinegar, season with thyme and bay leaf and roast until just cooked through. Season to taste.

For the apple sauce, cook the apples with a little moisture until very soft, season with a pinch of sugar and stir until smooth.

Forager's Fizz: bog myrtle granita

Serves 8-10 as a pre-dessert

Equipment: ice cream maker, fine chinois

1½ tbsp air-dried bog myrtle buds
2 litres fresh apple juice
300 g sugar
edible flower for decoration

Bog myrtle grows throughout the UK and much of Central & Northern Europe and North America. It's particularly known as an aromatic and insect repellent. In medieval times it was a staple ingredient in beer and fragrant seasoning.

In *The Pig*'s kitchen James challenges his team to create an amuse bouche, pre-dessert or cocktail using what's left of each day's foraged bounty.

For this fizz they pick the buds before the shrub goes into full leaf. The smallest buds are picked and allowed to dry in a warm place before use.

Gently heat the buds in a pan until the aroma is released. Add the fresh apple juice and sugar and reduce to 1.4 litres. Cool, then pass through a fine chinois. Check the flavour for sweetness adding a touch more sugar to taste but don't over sweeten. Follow ice cream maker's instructions for a granita. Serve with a pretty edible flower.

Buttermilk blancmange
with damson gin purée & jelly

Serves 6

Equipment: fine chinois, dariole moulds, hand blender

Blancmange
125 ml milk
150 ml double cream
75 g sugar
1½ gelatine leaves
250 g buttermilk (or yoghurt)

Damson gin purée
300 g plums, stones removed
500 ml damson gin
125 g pears
a pinch of sugar if needed

Jelly
125 ml pear poaching liquor
75 ml damson gin
add 1½ gelatine leaves

Crumble
100 g soft light brown sugar
100 g butter
100 g plain flour
40 g porridge oats

edible flowers for decoration

For the blancmange, bring the milk and sugar to a simmer and soak gelatine in cold water. Add the soft gelatine to the warm milk and whisk until dissolved. Stir in the cream, followed by the buttermilk and pass through a fine chinois then pour into dariole moulds for at least six hours until set.

For the damson gin purée, cook the plums in a little water until they have softened, then cook down gently in 300 ml damson gin until stewed. Poach the pears in a 500 ml water and 250 g sugar syrup (reserve the syrup to make the jelly). Using a hand blender, blitz the plums and pears together and adjust the flavour as required, (add a little gin if its not very boozy), to make a fine purée.

For the jelly, soak the gelatine leaves in cold water until softened and warm the pear poaching liquor with the fresh damson gin. Add the gelatine and stir until dissolved. Check the taste, it should be slightly boozy and fruity. Pass through a fine chinois into a cling film-lined 1 litre tub.

For the crumble, preheat oven to 165°C. Rub all the ingredients together, spread on a tray and bake for 10 to 15 minutes until golden then break up while still warm.

To serve, smooth a layer of the purée on plates. Remove the blancmange from the moulds by running them under a hot tap and spin to release from all sides for a couple of seconds. Give the mould a shake to release the vacuum and if necessary use your fingertips to tease the blancmange out of the mould. Place in the centre of the plate, dot with cubes of jelly and sprinkle with crumble & a few edible flowers.

T. BARTLETT & SONS

A Pinch of Salt Curing Company

"As James's family butcher I saw him grow from a young man to an accomplished chef so when he came back from New York and asked me to work with him to create a range of British charcuterie for The Pig, *I didn't hesitate. We set about creating a range of cured meats that now consists of 18 month, air-dried hams, coppa, lomo, red wine salamis, chorizos and bresaola. James started to rear pigs at* The Pig *so it was also a great opportunity to showcase their own pork."*

Alan Bartlett carries on the legacy that his grandfather and father established in 1938. Whilst other butchers have come and gone, *T Bartlett & Sons* remains a bustling business with an unwavering commitment to supporting its local farms. Recently Alan and James Golding collaborated to create *A Pinch of Salt*, a brand of cured meats and charcuterie made of hand-selected meats cared for by Alan using James's recipes and the smoke house that he built at *The Pig*.

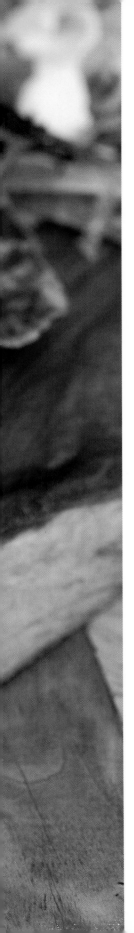

A Pinch of Salt
cured meats platter

Serves 4

Hampshire Lomo
Coppa
Karma Ham
Chorizo
Red Wine Salami
Bresaola

Hampshire Lomo

Lomo is Spanish for tenderloin. Lomo embuchado is dry-cured with the flavors of smoked paprika, oregano and James leaves a little fat on to give a sweeter flavor where the traditional Spanish style would not.

Coppa

Coppa is made from the muscle running from the neck to the shoulder of a pig. It originates from the Tuscan word, capocollo meaning 'head and neck'. It is usually served very thinly sliced like its cousin prosciutto but it isn't brined as ham is. *A Pinch of Salt*'s coppa is air-dried for 3 months and uniquely flavoured with fennel and cinnamon.

Karma Ham

Dry-cured ham comes from the gammon or leg. Styles are as varied as there are pork-producing regions around the world. All *A Pinch of Salt* hams are aged to a minimum of 16 months using a traditional method of air-drying. Karma Ham is seasoned with pepper, thyme and oregano.

Chorizo

Chorizo pre-dates the Roman Empire and originated in the Iberian Peninsula. It takes its rich colour and flavour from chillies and paprika and is frequently used as seasoning to dishes as well as on its own. James cures his traditionally using spicy paprika and blends the smokey flavour with fennel to make his recipe strong and unique.

Red Wine Salami

Salami is made in varieties the world over and is possibly the granddaddy of all cured eats. This air-dried and frequently fermented sausage can be made from any variety of meat. Its exceptionally long shelf life has made it a Southern European staple. *A Pinch of Salt*'s gold medal winning salami is air-dried and flavoured with red wine, savory and black pepper.

Bresaola

Bresaola comes from Northern Italy. The word is taken from the Lombardy dialect, 'bresada', meaning braised. James makes his from rump of Pennington beef, seam butchered and marinated in red wine with bay and rosemary and hung to air dry for four to six months.

Tanguy's tip

A Pinch of Salt cured meats platter: *Palo Cortado, Tio Pepe, Jerez, Spain*
Full tasting notes are on page 318

Tanguy Martin
Sommelier

For Tanguy Martin, wine encompasses every aspect of life: education, history, culture, food, travel, discoveries, friendship & family. He can even manage to talk about football and wine in the same conversation!

Born in Lyon, France, Tanguy studied oenology in the *Lycee viticole de Beaune* in Burgundy then went on to the prestigious *Centre de Formation Professionnelle* in Montpellier to take a diploma in winemaking and winegrowing.

Having grown up on the cusp of Southern Burgundy and the Northern Rhone regions and armed with a degree in oenology and full qualification from two of the finest professional wine related institutions, Tanguy had his eyes set on forging a career in the wine regions of New Zealand and Australia but his stars were aligned differently.

One day he was perusing the internet looking for interesting antipodean destinations when he came across information about Gerard Basset and *TerraVina*. Not many aspiring youngsters would shoot an email to one of the world's most experienced and celebrated wine experts, but Tanguy did and the rest is history.

Hampshire was a lot closer to home than down under and the opportunity to work under and learn from *TerraVina*'s then master sommelier Laura Rhys and under the tutelage of Gerard was something special. So in 2011 Tanguy popped across the channel and took Hampshire and The New Forest to heart.

In May 2013, Tanguy took the reins as *TerraVina*'s head sommelier with responsibility for its extensive and rather exclusive cellar with the daunting responsibility for continuing to build what Gerard Basset OBE and Laura Rhys started.

For Gerard, the success of his protégés is a great reward. Tanguy was awarded the *Chaîne des Rôtisseurs* coveted *Young Sommelier of the Year for 2014* and a bronze medal at the *Moët & Chandon Sommelier of the Year 2014*. There is only one thing that Tanguy can't quite agree with his Loire Valley native mentor. Whilst he thinks Gerard is the wine equivalent to the best La Ligue coach that ever lived, in his view Olympique Lyonnais is a far superior vintage to St Etienne.

Tanguy's taste

Lime Wood

Coda uova affumicato & pickled fennel with radish, crackling & rye
Looks appetising doesn't it? We need to start gently then, and for this, I recommend something light, refreshing and possibly not very well known but so surprising; Greek Ouzo. This aperitif is made of spirit, anise and fennel, star anise and other herbs and spices. It's so smooth and quaffable, the creamy texture matches the pickled fennel nicely so if you have the chance, taste: **Ouzo of Plomari, Isidoros Arvanitis, Greece.** *(I was just sipping one while writing these notes.)*

Squid ink garganelli with crab & parsley
Let's open a beer, fresh and cold, not a classic Italian beer, but one coming from the east of Milano. Try a style of lager with a smooth palate, lightly sparkling and with almost the pretention of ale, my recommendation is: **Puro Malto, Oro di Milano, 5.1%abv.**

Double agnolotti with chicken, polenta, peas & broad beans
When serving a light meat dish with this double agnolotti, you could have either a white wine or a red, but let's stay Italian with a lightish red wine from Piedmont made of the Dolcetto grape. Dolcetto gives a light and fresh berry note, try: **Dolcetto d'alba Monte Aribaldo, Marchesi di Gresy 2012.** *(It's delicious when young and it can age for a few years.)*

Halibut with sweet peas & heritage tomatoes
We need a wine that stands out here, a wine with depth. Not just any rosé but a famous one, from a classic and well known appellation: a Bandol from the South of France, made of mainly Mourvedre, the Bandol wines are very enjoyable with sea food: **Chateau de Pibarnon, Bandol, Provence, France 2012.**

Milk & honey: goat's milk panna cotta with honey jelly
Honey, honey, I'm sure nobody will mind if we open a fabulous bottle to finish well, a nice Sauternes perhaps.

It's sweet, with a long and lively acidity, the vintages do vary but the wines are in great demand. Let's try: **Chateau Suduiraut, Sauternes, Bordeaux, France, 1999**

Strawberry cream puff with white chocolate mousse
Let's finish with a Canadian wine, a sweet and reputed one from the Easern Parts of the country, in Ontario, Peller Estates is well known for it's icewine. It's an exceptional style of wine. The grapes have to be picked under -8 degres Celcius. It's cold but so cool! It delivers some ripe tropical fruits, peach, apricot, a hint of orange blossom, absolutely fantastic. My recommendation: **Vidal, (grape variety), Icewine, Peller Estate, Niagara Peninsula, Ontario, Canada, 2010.**

The art of the smokehouse board
Mix & match, smoke & smart, it's a lovely appetiser, white or red, it doesn't matter. You just need either pure, mineral white or a light, smoky red. Pure or smokey like some of the Jura wines in the pre-Alps, Arbois appellation for white and red are great. Chardonnay for the white with a touch of dry nuts and salty minerality. The reds are lively, fruity and smoky try Poulsard. This indigenous grape will please Pinot Noir, Gamay or Cabernet Franc drinkers. For a top producer go for: **Stephane Tissot.**
White: **Arbois, Chardonnay, Empreinte, Jura, France, 2011.**
Red: **Arbois Poulsard, Les Bruyeres, Jura, France 2011.**
(These wines will wake up your palate and get it ready for the dishes that follow!)

The Plough

Trout tartare
The fresh water fish and scotch eggs…make me think about the Loire Vallée. A Sauvignon Blanc will be ideal here. Let's go for a classic appellation with a terroir influence: **Sancerre, Les Monts Damnés, Gérard Boulay, Loire Vallée, France, 2010.**

Surf & turf braised pork belly with cockles, sausages & white bean cassoulet
It's complex to match a wine with a dish of this complexity but you should look for a wine with good structure and balance. I suggest a wine from Piedmont; Barolo is a good example: **Barolo, Serralunga d'Alba, Fontanafredda, Piedmont, Italy, 2005.**

Chocolate mousse with sea salt & hazelnut ice cream
Lovely! Some of my favorite flavors! I recommend a wine with the same type of character: sweet & nutty with chocolate notes. Go for a sweet Sherry, a tawny port, or Madeira. My suggestion is: **Sweet Madeira, D'Oliveiras, 10 Years Old.**

Charlie's kid's menu
Sliders on brioche buns
Mama Mia pizza
Chocolate & honeycomb clusters
Baked hedgehogs Alaska
Create a mocktail for the kids. How about nice refreshing drinks such as: **New Forest mist,** made from ginger beer, lime juice & almond syrup and: **Monkey Boy's Cosmonaut,** made from peach purée, cranberry juice, lime juice, grenadine syrup & Fentimans rose lemonade.

The Chesil Rectory

Wood pigeon with caramelised walnuts, chicory, pickle, Stockbridge mushrooms & Secretts beetroot dressing
To complement the gamey, earthy and forest flavours of the dish, serve a lively and fruity red wine with similar flavours. Beaujolais will complement the dish bringing a fresh touch of red and wild berries. Such as: **Morgon, M.Lapierre, Beaujolais, France, 2012.**

Hampshire Dexter beef fillet, rump & bone marrow bon bon with Secrett's parsnip purée, potatoes dauphinoise, shallot crisps & red wine jus
This calls out for some ripe red and velvety berries and maybe a touch of eucalyptus. How about: **Plexus, John Duval, Barossa, South Australia, 2006. (***Why not? Chef Damian will appreciate this if he is an Aussie fan!***)**

Poached rhubarb & crème vanilla
What do the unique flavors of the rhubarb need? Some exotic notes? Some citrusy flavors and touch of honey? Ah yes, here we are*:* **Chenin Blanc, Late harvest, Rudera winery, Stellenbosch, South Africa, 2010.**

Crown of Blackmoor Game pheasant with parsnips & sweet & spicy red cabbage
I could taste this dish just reading it and I imagined it being washed down with a velvety wine with delicate flavours, a wine both elegant and racy. An extraordinary blend of Syrah and Viognier (white grape); coming

from the Northern Rhone, a Cote Rotie, try a small and talented wine maker: **Côte Rotie, E.Guigal, Rhone Valley, France 2009.**

The Little Gloster

Scandinavian breakfast: *poached egg & bacon with asparagus*
I bet, you don't want an alcoholic drink at 9am in the morning, but if it was a big party the night before, or even if it wasn't, you can add a bit of tomato and spice to this breakfast and it's almost a full English. Opt for a **Bloody Mary** with **Reyka Iceland Vodka.** Just find the right balance between the alcohol, tomato juice, a touch of Worcestershire sauce, pinch of pepper, celery salt and some freshly squeezed lemon juice and there you are.

Gravadlax & caviar
Mmm, this sounds cool, cold, and intense. Forget wine and be traditional, try a chilled glass of: **Linie Aquavit** from Norway. The spirit is perfectly flavoured with caraway and dill, or if you are a James Bond fan, go for a **Dry Martini** using **Dry Lillet Vermouth, Reyka Iceland Vodka,** ice and olives.

Roast Gurnard
For this dish, I recommend a white wine with high minerality, good structure, some spice and a long finish, something like a Chenin Blanc will work very well. Let's try a natural wine: **Saumur, l'Insolite, Thierry Germain, Loire Valley, France, 2010.**

Tarte tatin with calvados caramel
Make your own cocktail: **'God bless The Queen Apple'**, from 1 part **Hill Farm Juice Clear Apple Juice,** 1 part **Calvados 8YO Roger Groult Calvados, Normandy** and 1 part of the traditional **Kings Ginger Liqueur.**

The Little Gloster celebration burger on Island Bakers brioche buns with Gallybagger cheese & pickled cucumbers
Hee hee! My first food experience in UK four years ago was a great burger and a nice pint of beer. Burger & beer, for me is like a French guy and his baguette, never the first without the second! Let's try a beer handcrafted in Lymington, **The Vibrant Forest Brewery.** Kevin handcrafts all his beers to have distinctive character. I will opt for: **The Nova Foresta** with the burger. It's amber bitter with a refreshing, light palate, and a generous

amount of spicy and fruity English hop to balance the soft maltiness.

The Wellington Arms

Twice baked cheese soufflé with goat's cheese & grilled vegetables

Goat's cheese is always fun to pair with white wine and here you have hundreds of choices, but **Sauvignon Blanc** is always the perfect match; from France or New Zealand, it has to be fresh, grassy, and zesty. Let's be daring and go for a South African instead: **Sauvignon Blanc, Waterkloof, Stellenbosch, South Africa, 2013.** A great find with a very impressive terroir influence!

Terrine of tiger prawns & leeks with Marie Rose sauce

A nice start to any meal. Let's choose a nice wine to enjoy with this terrine, something zesty, fruity and bone dry. The Albarino grape is great; it's classic in Spain but popular further away as well. Let's go down under: **Albarino, The Bell Ringer, Coopers Creek, Gisborne, New Zealand 2013.**

Crying leg of lamb

What is it crying for? I would be happy to eat it! It's not a sad story; it's a fine dish! To match this a Mourverdre is perfect, traditionally from South of France it also does well in the McLaren Vale, South Australia, with robust flavors and velvety texture. Try: **Mourvedre, Yangarra Estate, McLaren Vale, South Australia, 2010.** *(Even though Simon and Aussie Chef Jason like their French wines, I think they'll agree with me on this one.)*

Jelly of Wellington Arms elderflower cordial with raspberry ripple ice cream

A delicate flower with a hint of berries and nothing is better than a sweet wine with fragrance and slight fizz to go with this quintessential summer treat. It has to be: **Moscato d'Asti, Canelli, Cerutti, Cassinasco, Piedmont, Italy, 2013.**

Ricotta & Parmesan stuffed pumpkin flowers with homegrown leaves & lemon & honey dressing

It would be nice to find a wine with flowery aroma and a hint of citrus, mellow on the palate with a hint of stone and green fruit. Sound impossible? Well you have more than one choice but I think you will enjoy a traditional French grape with an English twist. It's delicious when combined with food and I'm sure you will want to visit the vineyard after being spoilt with this wine: **Madeleine Angevine, Danebury Vineyards, Stockbridge, Hampshire, UK 2010.**

TerraVina

Swiss chard & pine nut galette with confit salmon, sorrel sauce & Avruga caviar

Make a change and go for a rosé: **Whispering Angel, Caves d'Esclans, Sacha Lichine, Cotes de Provençe, 2013.** This rosé has got more roundness and body but is still well balanced and will perfectly match the bitter taste of the Swiss chard, although other Cotes de Provence could work very well.

Roast loin, braised leg & faggot of New Forest venison with red cabbage & parsnip

The terroir is there, the venison is tasty, juicy and delicate. A deep and powerful red must be appreciated: **Vinha Pan, Luis Pato, Beira, Portugal, 2005.** This wine is a spectacular concentration of flavors; earthy, fruity and spicy yet still elegant. *(This dish deserves this wine.)*

Blackcurrant soufflé & apple ice cream

Banyuls is always a safe option when it comes to black fruits, so try: **Banyuls Rimage, Le Clos des Paulilles, Cazes, Roussillon, France, 2006.** It's a complex blend of black and red fruits, complemented by a touch of sweet nutmeg and cinnamon that should work well with the apple ice cream.

Pork, wild leek & pear

Here the terroir of the New Forest is evident, I suggest Pinot from a small appellation in Burgundy: **Chambolle-Musigny, Domaine Hudelot-Baillet, Burgundy, France, 2005.** One of the most feminine Pinot Noirs with some delicate notes of cherries, maraschino, a touch of dried roses, silky tannins and a long and fine finish.

Lobster, carrot & buttermilk

An off-dry wine will complement this dish as the minerality will bring up the flavors of the lobster and add a touch of citrus to the buttermilk, I recommend **Riesling, Château Belá, Egon Müller, Štúrovo, Slovakia, 2010.**

Acorn, chocolate & sugars
This dish will surprise you. It's very sweet and intense.
I recommend a wine to complement the sweetness:
**Rutherglen Muscat, Stanton & Killeen, Victoria,
Australia, NV.** A liquid version of Christmas pudding,
it is complex, rich, intense and absolutely sumptuous!

The Globe & The Chestnut Horse

Avington smoked trout mousse
Fresh and summery, let's bring some grapefruit, lime,
lemon and orange blossom; the whole citrus family:
**Gros Manseng, Domaine des Cassagnoles, Côtes de
Gascogne, South West, France, 2013** will be superb!

Rabbit & game terrine
Have you ever tried a rabbit from Chile? Me either but
I have tried a Pinot Noir from Chile and it would be
perfect with the rabbit: **Pinot Noir, Cahuil Vineyard,
Leyda, Leyda Valley, Chile, 2012.**

Simon's pie
This is sumptuous home-cooked comfort food. It's great!
The lamb delivers rich flavour. I think a full-bodied,
lamb-friendly Merlot from Chile: **Petit Verdot, Casa
Lapostolle, Rappel Valley, Chile, 2010.**

Tarte citron with raspberry coulis
Sweet & zesty. Shake it, shake it, it's cocktail time! Make
a **Lemontini** using **Hendricks Gin, Limoncello** and
lemon juice. *(You may need a rest on a comfy sofa after.)*

**Traveller's ploughman's with flowerpot bread,
piccalilli & chutneys**
A blonde for the lady traveller, please! Or was that a lady
for the blonde traveller? It's a pint of blonde or should
I say a delicious fruity crafted blond ale: **Bood Doggle,
Ringwood Brewery, Hampshire, 4.2% ABV.**

Verveine

**Smoked treacle wholemeal bread, & home
smoked sea bass**
Let's fizz again! Just to open your senses, make yourself
comfortable enjoy a nice English sparkling from
Hampshire, Auxerrois & Rulander. Yes I am still speaking
about wine! These two grapes make a great harmony;
bring some notes of fresh brioches driven by a delicate
citrus acidity and vibrant finish…a great way to start the
tasting menu. The wine: **Cossack, Danebury Vineyards,
Hampshire, UK. 2006**

Brixham turbot & smoked pig's cheek
Fish and meat are always interesting to pair, I love it! The
turbot is dense and the cheeks bring richness to the dish.
I think a modern wine with a lovely mix of Roussanne
and Marsanne from the Languedoc. It's a nice balance
between richness and persistence: **Les Muriers, Mas
Bruguiere, Côteaux du Languedoc, Languedoc,
France 2011.**

Scallops & pickled rhubarb
'Peak Pool de Pea Net'. I just love the sound of it.
Picpoul de Pinet is fun, light, crisp, and a great seafood
friend! It goes perfectly with this dish. Its wine from
the South of France produced specifically for oysters,
scallops and other seafood: **Picpoul de Pinet, Domaine
de Font Mars, Languedoc, France, 2013.**

Seared tuna
Tuna is fish that doesn't always require white wine; in
fact some light, fruity reds go very well. Pair this dish
with a light Pinot Noir; even better a natural one. Try this
juicy, fruity, earthy wine: **Pinot Noir, Cotes D'Auxerre,
Domaine Goisot, Burgundy, France 2012.**

Chamomile smoked wild sea trout
Dry or off-dry I wonder. Germany produces the most
amazing Riesling on the planet. If I may, I would suggest
an off-dry Riesling from the Mosel: **Riesling Kabinett,
Wehlener Sonnenuhr, Joh Jos. Prüm, Mosel,
Germany, 2007.** A fabulous vintage and very complex
wine mixing sweetness and lively minerality with exotic
notes to reveal the flavours of the chamomile and the
delicacy of the sea trout.

Langoustines & Granny Smiths
Maria Gomes, sounds like a tennis player but it's just a
fantastic grape variety from the Beira region of Portugal.
This grape has lovely texture with gentle spices and
delicate notes of grapefruit. It's lively, refreshing and my
choice for this dish: **Maria Gomes, Luis Pato, Beira,
Portugal, 2013.**

Pear tree

The apple, and pear never falls far from the tree and so this Pear tree dessert after a long meal suggests a brandy but not any brandy: A Calvados. This spirit is a distilled cider made from apples and pears. My recommendation: **AOC Calvados Domfrontais Reserve, (minimum 30% pear) Victor Gontier, Normandie, France, 2008.** Lovely, ripe and spiced notes of pear and compote finishing with a hint of vanilla.

Lainston House

Herring with purple carrot, mooli, shallots, bacon & apple

Fresh and crisp, I can see a wine, which is very well known and sometimes forgotten; a wine aged for a short period of time on the lees to give it balance and complexity without hiding its freshness to reveal the oilyness of the fish. Perhaps a: **Muscadet Sèvre et Maine, Sur Lie, Clos des Allées, P. Luneau-Papin, Loire, France, 2012.**

Lamb, sweetbreads & broad bean falafel with mint emulsion & tomato

Wine is great when you taste something new, something different that you won't forget. Something different. In Turkey they make cracking wines, especially when they blend their native grapes with international ones. My latest discovery is: **Vourla Urla, Ukuf Mevkii, Turkey, 2010 (Cabernet, Merlot, Bogazkere, and Syrah).** A full-bodied wine, with very good balance and a long finish; outstanding and unexpected!

Lemon, basil chocolate & kiffir with honey jelly & yoghurt sorbet

Hmm, a zesty and soft dessert with nice limey flavours and a touch of summer from the chocolate mint. Let's travel far away, to Tasmania, and grab a bottle of sweet Riesling. They can't be compared to the top German sweet wines but in the New World, Tasmania is great for late harvested Riesling. It has a large palate of lime and lemon zest, lemon curd, balanced with some very delicate sweet spices such as cinnamon. The wine is full-bodied, intense and definitely, moreish: **Botrytis Riesling, Tamar Ridge, Tamar River, Tasmania, 2010.**

Strawberries & cream with whey sherbet & burnt cream

Some of my best memories of my home in the South of France are picking strawberries in the garden for dessert and sipping sweet wines with them. What a great education. I always have a bottle of Muscat in the fridge during the summer: **Muscat de Beaumes de Venise, Domaine de Durban, Rhone Valley, France, 2010.**

Exclusive Hotels Chefs Academy

Rosary goat's cheese & watercress ravioli

Sauvignon Blanc is a classic pairing with goat's cheese. If you want to be adventurous, try something like a Semillon from the New World. It has an oily palate that brings a touch of lemon, lime and a bit of passion fruit: **Semillon, Brokenwood, Hunter Valley, New South Wales, Australia, 2012.**

Roasted saddle & slow cooked shoulder of lamb with potato fondant, red onion marmalade & Jerusalem artichoke purée

For this dish you can add some powerful flavors such as ripe, dark cherries, the tannins of the wines must be ripe and sweet. Let's try a full body red like a: **Monastrell, Juan Gil, Jumilla, Spain, 2011.**

Chocolate tart & caramel ice cream

Bartender, may I have a: **Chocolate Martini** please? Imagine **Russian Vodka** mixed with **Mozart Chocolate Liqueur** and a touch of Aztec bitter chocolate. (*Try to sip it but it won't last!*)

Organic mushroom fricassee & rosemary linguini with poached baby leeks & Lyburn cheese

A suave and exuberant style of wine with a herbal note will be good here. With linguini, an Italian Fiano: **Fiano di Avellino, Feudi di San Gregorio Pietracalda, Campania, Italy, 2012.**

The Thomas Lord

Bar snacks

Venison & black pudding scotch egg
crispy lamb belly with mint mayonnaise
rarebit on toasted homemade ale bread
While you are snacking, why not try a local bitter: **Classic Ale, Upham Brewery, Hampshire.** It has an initial sweetness and this smoothly spiced bitter will be ideal and prove more than acceptable company.

Black pudding, squash, quail egg, truffle with egg yolk dressing & fried bread croutons
Taste something traditional, a light Pinotage with hints of red berries and a touch of smokiness and a lively and juicy palate to match this versatile dish: **Pinotage, Ruins, Robertson, South Africa, 2011.**

Portland crab & brown crab custard with treacle bread & kohlrabi remoulade
Light and crisp wine from Italy: **Weissburgunder (Pinot Blanc), Erste+Neue, Südtirol Alto Adige, Italy, 2012.** With some soft white peach and nectarine and a delicate hint of pear drop, this wine will bring a gentle breeze to this dish.

Upham Tipster Ale battered hake with hand-cut chips, crushed peas and caper & parsley mayonnaise
Another bitter will go well, in fact try the same used in the dish: **Tipster Ale, Upham Brewery, Hampshire, 3.6% AB.** It's light and crisp with notes of citrus and a bitter finish. This beer will bring some smooth flavor to the fish.

Treacle tart with honey oat biscuit & bay leaf ice cream
Tokaji Aszú, 5 Puttonyos, Crown Estate, Hungary, 2002. Marmalade, honey, vanilla and nuts are the main characters and will pair comfortably with the treacle through the natural concentration of flavors and the acidity of the wine. The richness of the dessert will be released!

Breast & faggot of duck with rosti potato, honey parsnip purée, celeriac & horseradish cured turnip
You may need a wine with some savory notes here. It will go well with the character of the duck and match with the spicy notes of the horseradish. Try a Syrah: **Syrah a Papa, Stephane Montez, Rhone Valley, France 2012.**

The Garlic Farm

Tomato & lentil smoked garlic soup with garlic & rosemary focaccia Bread
Fresh and lively with a hint of herbs, delicate spices and light almond blossom. Let's go for it, go for a Viura from Rueda in Spain. My choice is: **Herbis, Franck Massard, Rueda, Spain, 2013.**

The Garlic Farm asparagus & eggs
Asparagus is always the star of early summer, a very pleasant bitterness and normally it calls for a fresh style of wine too. If you have different choices, you can try a white from Austria; they are normally clean and fresh with a hint of ginger and pepper. Try: **Roter Veltliner, Klassik, Leth, Wagram, Austria, 2012.**

Best ever pigeon Kiev with garlic mash
This is a nice game dish. Syrah or Shiraz? I think both are a good match. The wine has to be juicy, with ripe fruit intensity and savoury finishing on a spicy note. So not just any Syrah then. Let's be adventurous and support a local guy: **Shiraz, Spotswood, Charlie Herring, Western Cape, South African, 2008.** This wine has the temper of the Rhone Valley with the sun of South Africa but the winemaker is from Lymington!

Cheeses & chutneys
IoW brie & blue cheese for the soft and tawny port: A buttery, creamy, and almondy Chardonnay for the IoW Brie, just to play with the creaminess of the cheese; a great Burgundy: **Saint Romain, Domaine Deux Montille, Burgundy, France, 2009,** warm vintage for more body. For the blue, classic Port, or even better, a nice Tawny, aged in barrique for 10 years: it will develop some delicious flavours of nuts, raisin, caramel: **Otima 10, Warre's, Douro, Portugal 10YO.** (Love it!)

Gazpacho & bruschetta
Mezze
pickled garlic with lemon & limes
tzatziki
broad bean & pea hummus
devilled whitebait & aioli
Imagine yourself, starting an evening al fresco by the blue sea, dreaming about holidays, sunshine, a warm climate, and this plate of Mezze. It sounds almost as if you are on a Greek island. So let's go with the Assyrtiko grape. A specialty from Santorin. It's dry, full-bodied, distinctive minerality, with a delicate note of honeysuckle: **Assyrtiko, Thallasitis, Gaia wine, Santorini, Greece, 2012.** (Perfect to sip and more!)

Pebble Beach

Grilled sea bass with braised leeks & thyme.
A great combination of flavors here, you may need a unique wine, rich and mineral at the same time. Portugal offers some unique styles of white wine: **Nossa, Calcario, Filipa Pato and William Wouters, Bairrada, 2012.** (I'm a fan!)

Crab & lobster cakes with potato crust, fondue of fennel & bouillabaisse jus
Chef Pierre Chevillard is from Lyon, as Burgundy is not very far from his place of origin, we suggest a classic Chardonnay, smooth & steely, with a salty finish: **Pouilly-Fuissé, L'ame Forest, Eric Forest, Burgundy 2011.**

Raspberry tiramisu
A great wine made as vintage port, but with an unusual grape variety called Tannat: **Licor de Tannat, Familia Deicas, Canelones Region, Uruguay.** It's a must try and good alternative to other sweet red wines.

Poached duck egg in pastry & Sopley Farm asparagus with dry sherry & morel sauce
Sherry makes me think of Spain and the eggs bring some viscosity to the dish. I would go for a young, traditional white Rioja. It's a mix of apple, fresh lemon, green vegetables with a creamy texture and hint of pastry and nutty flavors. Two grapes can be used, Viura and Malvasia. Try: **Muga (white), Barrels Fermented, Rioja, Spain, 2013.**

The Oak Inn

Solent grilled mackerel with gooseberry sauce & John's foraged wilted sea beet
This dish calls out for a fresh, aromatic white wine. The oiliness of the fish and the gooseberry sits easily with an exotic Sauvignon Blanc: **Sauvignon Blanc, Little Beauty, Marlborough, New Zealand, 2013.** Delicious aromas and a zinging acidity!

Owls Barn Cider braised belly of pork with celeriac purée, spiced apple compote, & potatoes dauphinoise
Go for something new and exuberant that's suave, mineral and complex. Something different: **Maccabeo, Figure Libre, Gayda, Pays D'Oc, France, 2010.**

Elderflower panna cotta with blood orange sorbet & lavender shortbread
A sweet wine will go well so find something with floral notes; orange blossom and elderflower are perfect and found in Moscatel. My recommendation: **Moscatel Naturalmente dulce, Finca Antigua, La Mancha, Spain, 2011.** Viva Espana!

Lymington crab croquette with Gales Ale battered sea vegetables & foraged salsa verde
Salsa Verde, fiesta and sunshine takes me to Northern Portugal where the wines are light and crisp, with citrus character and a delicious hint of saltiness that sings on the palate. Try: **Vinho Verde, Adega de Monacao, Portugal, 2013.**

Dan's Kitchen

Confit of duck burger with pickled vegetables
Explosive green pepper, blueberries, cassis and blackberries. I think a nice fruity and spicy red wine. A Chilean grape that disappeared from Bordeaux but is doing well in Chile comes to mind, Carmenere. It has an easy style: **Carménère Single Vineyard, Errazuriz, Valle de Aconcagua, Chile, 2010.**

BLT with black pepper cream cheese
Summer terrace, a light breeze and rosé! What else? I don't think you can go wrong with a Spanish wine from Catalunya: **Mas Amor, Terra Alta, Catalunya, Spain, 2012.**

Chicken & spiced sweet potatoes with onion bhaji, carrots & mango
It has to be aromatic and fresh to gently soften the spices. I would try a dry Muscat from Alsace: **Muscat, Hugel, Alsace, France, 2012.**

IoW strawberries, shortbread & cream cheese with lemon curd & Champagne jelly
Let's fizz again with an off-dry style of sparkling, famous in Southwest France. It's said that the sparkling method was invented in Limoux but I don't want to upset my friends in Champagne, so I will leave the debate to you: **Blanquette Méthode Ancestrale, Doux, 'Frisson' Antech, Limoux, NV.**

Plaice fillets & lemon risotto with IoW mushrooms and broad beans
Risotto and rich white wine, perfect. Bring some texture, some cream, butter, spices, as well as delicate almond blossom notes and a long after taste…Go for a rich Viognier, a great aromatic grape, produced around the world but stop in New Zealand: **Viognier, The Wingwalker, Alpha Domus, Hawkes Bay, New Zealand, 2012.**

Chewton Glen

Heritage beetroot with Fjordlings smoked duck, Dorset truffle & Rosary goat's cheese cromesquis
This is a lovely dish, a mixture of traditional flavors with contemporary style. What about a Pinot Noir with a fine and subtle palate from an unexpected region: **Pinot Noir Réserve, Oliver Zeter, Pfalz, Germany, 2010.**

New Forest venison poivrade with polenta chips, roasted root vegetables & red wine sauce.
Left or right, rich and powerful or intense and complex, a Bordeaux, it will be! **Chateau Lassegue, Saint Emilion Grand Cru, Bordeaux, France, 2005.**

Beaulieu strawberry Vacherin
Imagine, the banks of the river in Beaulieu, a sunny day and a cocktail. Cuba is not very far after all: **Fresh Strawberry Daiquiri.** *(and a sun-lounger!)*

Inka tomato salad with Laverstoke Park Farm buffalo mozzarella & tapenade
You can taste summer in this dish, if you are not on the border of the Beaulieau River, go to Tuscany where the white wines are clean, zesty and slight spicy with a touch of Mediterranean herbs: **Vermentino, Tenuta Guado al Tasso, Antoniri, Bolgheri, Tuscany, Italy 2012.**

The Rockingham Arms

Warm smoked salmon with quail eggs & watercress scone
Delicious flavours, a rich salmon and the watercress to bring some freshness. What about a really complementary Chardonnay from a warm climate that's buttery, rich and mellow. Let's go to California: **Grand Reserve Chardonnay, Kendall Jackson, California, 2011.**

Steak, kidney & Coleman's pie
A Bitter would be a good match, give a taste to a local one: **Punter, Upham Brewery, Stakes Farm, Upham, Hampshire, 4.0% ABV.** The rich earthiness and the nuttiness of the beer will match well with this dish.

Jacob's ladder with caramelised onion mash & savoy cabbage
Opulent, rich, tannic, robust and complex, I would like to bring you to the Southwest of France. Tannat is the grape: **Chateau Montus, Madiran, South West France, 2005.** *(That is a big boy in a big bottle!)*

Pimm's & Langley's gin jelly with strawberry salad & Champagne sorbet
Should we add any more alcohol to this? The flavours are attractive and intense so I suggest something refreshing: **a Sorrelade**, sorrel mixed with lemon juice and honey, like a lemonade but made of sorrel. In small quantities sorrel is a really pleasant flavour and a good digestive, soft with some intense flavours to bring a new sensation.

Wild boar chop, smoked duck egg & shallot remoulade
Wild and gamey, sounds more like a good hunting party. What about an adventurous destination like New York. Away from the tall buildings, a bit further inland, and more precisely not very far from the Niagara Falls, some fantastic wines are made from international grapes. A good example is Cabernet Franc. Light, fresh, oriented to the red and black fruit and driven by green pepper spice, it would be delicious with this dish. My choice is: **Cabernet Franc, Hermann J.Wiemer, Finger Lakes, New York, 2008**

36 on the Quay

Emsworth Harbour canapés

Crispy chicken skins with honey mayonnaise & fresh picked hedgerow herbs seed biscuits with cheese cream & pickled radish flax seed tuile & salted brill roe
Have a modern cocktail to start to wake up your senses and enjoy these little snacks: **Langley's 008.** A James Bond-style drink; shake 50 ml of **Langley's Gin, 12.5ml of St Germain Elderflower, 37.5ml of apple juice (Hill Farm of course), ½ lemon juice, and 4 basil leaves.**

Pea pannacotta & lovage soup with salt baked beetroot, pea shoots & pansy flowers
Refreshing, earthy and contrasting texture. It would be quite interesting to find a wine with crunch and fruit. I imagine a rosé with this dish, German is nice, Try: **Spatburgunder Rosé Meyer Näkel, Ahr, Germany 2013**.

Local asparagus & slow cooked egg yolk with brown butter purée, ricotta & whey
To match the balance between the freshness of the asparagus and the smoothness of the egg you should go for a floral and crisp wine. Try a Muscat d'Alsace, it's light and suave with delicate flavours and will work perfectly: **Muscat, Goldert, Domaine Zind-Humbrecht, 2011.**

Roast plaice & confit chicken wings with caramelised cauliflower & Alexander buds
Brilliant! The real challenge for a sommelier; fish and meat together. White or red? I'm going for a white that's rich and buttery, a wine original and complex blend including: Chenin Blanc, Palomino, Semillon Blanc, Grenache Blanc, Semillon Gris, Viognier, Clairette. Only one country is able to grow all these grapes at the same time, South Africa. The wine: **Sequillo white, Sequillo Cellars, Malmesbury, South Africa, 2011.**

Meadowsweet rice pudding with fresh strawberries & strawberry chips
Nothing is best to finish the dessert with than a nice glass of bubbles, White or rosé? Prosecco or Champagne? What about a sparkling Shiraz ? WHAT? Yes, it's brilliant, with the dark fruit character it will just bring a fantastic roundness to this dessert: **Sparkling Shiraz, Peter Lehmman, Barossa Valley, South Australia, 2010**

Roast brill, sauerkraut & hazelnut gnocchi with foraged mushrooms & fermented rye soup.
That sounds like a rich, full and complex white wine dish. I've something exciting, a Fiano, not from Italy but Australia. Try the delicious and surprising: **Princess Fiano, Fox Gordon, Adelaide Hills, South Australia, 2011**.

The Pig
Piggy bits

Brock eggs & Coleman's dressing
Garden savory sausage rolls
Arancini
Cured ham & flowers
Red for the pig, salty and peppery, brambly and juicy, lively and windy, on the Tenerife Island the pigs will find good land: **7 Fuentes, Jose Pastor Selections, Valle de la Orotava, Tenerife 2012.**

Dorset Cockles with foraged sea vegetables
Add a mineral wine, with some flintiness, a touch of white pepper, ginger; some young Gruner Veltliner from Austria are superb! My recommendation: **Gruner Veltliner, Von der Terrassen, Sepp Moser, Krempstal, Austria, 2012.**

Duck egg with wild oyster mushrooms, nasturtiums & A Pinch of Salt pancetta
The Kimmeridgean soil of the Chablis region is what comes to my mind when I look in this dish The saltiness and strength of the Chardonnay grape is perfect: **Chablis 1er Cru Beauroy, Laurent Tribut, Burgundy, France 2010.**

Bath Chap
Tout est bon dans le cochon! All is edible from the pig. There probably isn't a more traditional English dish than this one. Live it up with a traditional bitter. Let's reveal the old days and try an old fashioned: **"XXXX" Porter 4.7% abv Ringwood Brewery.**

Buttermilk blancmange with damson gin jelly, pure cream & berries
Try a sweet red wine. The soft tannins should be absorbed by the blancmange: **Perli, Late Harvest Zinfandel, Edmeades Estate, Mendocino County, California, 2006.**

A Pinch of Salt cured meats platter
It's local meat, but there is a strong Spanish influence, so go for sherry. Palo Cortado is one of the most mysterious of sherry styles. It's nutty and almondy with a pinch of salt and ideal to start lunch or, if the terrace is open, to enjoy a bit of sun: **Eleanor, Palo Cortado, Tio Pepe, Jerez, Spain NV.**

Tanguy Martin

Hampshire's larder

Hampshire and the Isle of Wight's landscape encompasses just about everything: downland, farmland, heathland, woodland, coastline, fertile valleys and chalk streams. The region's diversity makes it completely unique. As a result, the variety and scale of its produce is vast including: fruit, vegetables, grain, dairy, meat, game, poultry, fish and seafood, beer, juice, wines, jams and chutneys, honey, cheese, baked goods, the list goes on. Hampshire's diversity, though one of its strengths, also presents challenges for the people dedicated to it. What it offers in variety it can lose in a lack of cohesion.

Food group *Hampshire Fare* was born out of this need for cohesion. Over 20 years ago, Hampshire County Council's Economic Development Office was approached by a group of local farmers and producers seeking support and a collective structure to develop, expand and market their produce. These were people who had made a conscious choice to work within their communities, maintain and, in some instances, revive local quality. Farmers wanted to meet like-minded farmers, jam makers wanted to meet fruit growers and most wanted to meet the chefs, publicans and shopkeepers responsible for putting it all in front of customers.

Hampshire Fare was set up in 1991 to give small farmers and producers a voice and promote the benefits of buying local food and drink. It set out to create opportunities for people from all aspects of the food industry to connect and it was considered pretty radical thinking at the time.

One success story is the month-long and countywide *Hampshire Food Festival*. Another was the initiative '*Preserving the Hampshire Hog*', a programme supported by The Prince's Countryside Fund and designed to help struggling pig farmers diversify into making their own charcuterie with training and support from one of the country's leading charcuterie experts. Sarah and John Mills at *Parsonage Farm*, near Andover, benefited from the scheme. Not only do they now specialise in making charcuterie, they even offer workshops on how to do it. For the Mills and other farmers like them, being given the opportunity to create multiple revenue streams meant the difference between keeping and losing the farm. It meant a lot.

Sarah also values *Hampshire Fare* giving her farm, and other small concerns like her's, an equal voice alongside other, larger producers such as *Laverstoke Park Farm* and *Leckford Estate*, (otherwise known as the *Waitrose Farm*). Today *Hampshire Fare* brings together more than 300 Hampshire and Isle of Wight businesses from across the entire food industry. It's one of the country's oldest food groups of its kind and it's logo is proudly displayed on the walls and shop fronts of the businesses it supports. For shoppers and diners it sends a message that the people presenting the produce, behind the counter or in the kitchen have a real commitment to supporting the community that supports them.

The Meon Spirit Company
Swanmore
Will Dobson

Will Dobson is now the man behind this family-owned orchard, farm, juice-making and bottling business. After school and university, Will decided a sailor's life was the way to go so he went off yachting for a few years. His family had acquired the farm and orchards surrounding his grandparent's stately home, so he decided to join his father looking after one of the top apple and pear orchards in the country.

Perched on the Hampshire Downs about eight miles from Winchester, the orchard had been providing fruit to local company, *Hill Farm Juice* for apple juice since the 70's. When the owner decided to retire, Will acquired *Hill Farm Juice* thus taking ownership of the entire process from tree to table.

Being rather English, Will doesn't like to shout too loudly about his success, but *Hill Farm Juice* has won the odd award including a *Two Star Gold* in the *2010 Taste Awards* for *Hill Farm Cloudy Apple* and has twice been *Hampshire Life Magazine's, 'Drinks Producer of the Year.'*

Will doesn't use any additives except for ascorbic acid, (vitamin C), which is used as an anti-oxidant. It's just him, his family, (with a bit of local help), a whole bunch of apples and his favourite toy; one pretty big juice making mechano set.

naked jam...

Jennifer Williams
Barton-on-Sea

My mom taught me everything I know about cooking and my dad everything about gardening. Fruit in perfect season is like a summer dress on a hot day, it looks beautiful no matter who wears it."

Jennifer grew up in a family where gardens and cooking were a way of life. Dad was a gardener and mom was a cook. They grew everything and as the seventh of eight children, she was part of the garden picking team.

After completing a degree in maritime environmental management, Jennifer worked as a researcher for the European Union focusing on environment issues until family life brought her back to her kitchen and garden. Her children Oliver and Francesca inspired her to get involved with *Baby Organics* where she worked on its research panel developing recipes but one job and raising a family was still too quiet a life for Jen so she started helping friends set up their vegetable gardens and taught them how to cook.

Then a bit of tragedy struck. Jennifer's sister Jackie was diagnosed with cancer. Jen wanted to do anything to help, she started making soups but Jackie wanted jam. In 2010 Jackie lost her battle but Jennifer's obsession with making the perfect jams for her sister was entrenched. A year later she entered her marmalade in *The World Marmalade Awards* and won a bronze medal. In 2014 she won silver.

Her obsession was in full swing, the next logical step was to perfect foraging with the seasons, choosing the perfect moment to pick to get the very best out of each ingredient. It wasn't unusual for Jennifer to catch herself counting blossoms on trees and measuring rainfall.

Jennifer is still making perfect jams in her kitchen, she never tires of it. Her mad passion also keeps the memory of her beloved sister Jackie alive and close to her heart.

Arreton, Isle of Wight
Paul Thomas, director

Specialty tomatoes have been grown on the beautiful Isle of Wight for over 30 years, where the high sunshine levels and maritime climate offer a perfect environment to grow the ripest and tastiest fruit.

A team of highly skilled growers oversees the production of both organic and non-organic tomatoes, and employs a number of sustainable farming methods. Each year all of the plant waste is composted, including the biodegradable string used to train the plants, producing natural fertiliser to enhance the organic soils. A team of UK native bumblebees looks after the pollination of every plant and rainwater is harvested for irrigation. The folks at *The Tomato Stall* take the sustainability of the environment seriously and are proud to have *Conservation Grade Status*, giving 10% of the land back to nature.

Every year, over 200 varieties of tomatoes are grown including an active trials programme constantly searching for the very best. The heirloom varieties offer an astonishing mix of colour and flavour and are increasingly popular with chefs.

The Tomato Stall began taking Isle of Wight tomatoes to farmers' markets over 7 years ago and since has expanded into supplying farm shops, delis and restaurants throughout the UK, as well as producing a range of tomato inspired products including the delicious *Golden Tomato Sunshine Juice* and the unique *Oak Roasted Tomatoes*.

Lyburn Farmhouse Cheesemakers

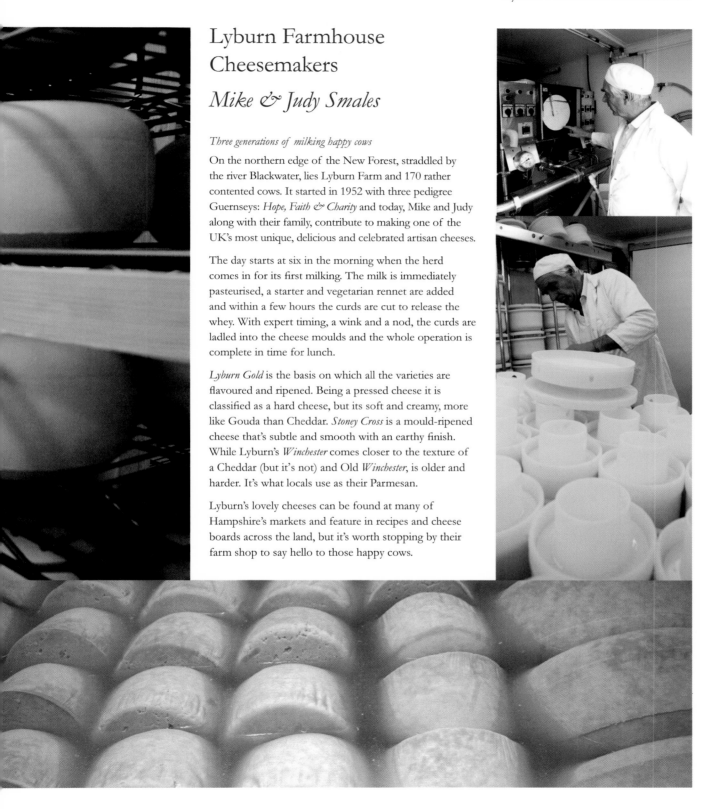

Lyburn Farmhouse Cheesemakers

Mike & Judy Smales

Three generations of milking happy cows

On the northern edge of the New Forest, straddled by the river Blackwater, lies Lyburn Farm and 170 rather contented cows. It started in 1952 with three pedigree Guernseys: *Hope, Faith & Charity* and today, Mike and Judy along with their family, contribute to making one of the UK's most unique, delicious and celebrated artisan cheeses.

The day starts at six in the morning when the herd comes in for its first milking. The milk is immediately pasteurised, a starter and vegetarian rennet are added and within a few hours the curds are cut to release the whey. With expert timing, a wink and a nod, the curds are ladled into the cheese moulds and the whole operation is complete in time for lunch.

Lyburn Gold is the basis on which all the varieties are flavoured and ripened. Being a pressed cheese it is classified as a hard cheese, but its soft and creamy, more like Gouda than Cheddar. *Stoney Cross* is a mould-ripened cheese that's subtle and smooth with an earthy finish. While Lyburn's *Winchester* comes closer to the texture of a Cheddar (but it's not) and Old *Winchester*, is older and harder. It's what locals use as their Parmesan.

Lyburn's lovely cheeses can be found at many of Hampshire's markets and feature in recipes and cheese boards across the land, but it's worth stopping by their farm shop to say hello to those happy cows.

Hampshire wine

Peter Gentilli

To quote Monty Python's, *The Life of Brian*, 'What did the Roman's ever do for us…?' One thing they failed to mention was they brought vines to Hampshire about 1900 years ago, roughly around 100 AD and that's where the story begins. The Romans, of course, loved their wine and planted vineyards across the extensive chalklands of southern England including Hampshire. Though their stay was reasonably short-lived, those that took their place inherited their love of wine, the vineyards thrived and wine continued to be made and slurped in vast quantities.

The middle ages saw a drastic decline in local production. The King's endless skirmishes in France required funding and his army needed uniforms. The local climate was well suited to sheep and wool manufacturing, so most of the vines were replaced with sheep and most of the vintners by wool fullers and merchants. What was left belonged mainly to the church so local wine manufacturing was now in the 'hands of God' so to speak, but as we know, the monks knew a thing or two about producing some pretty decent plonk. (Dom Perignon springs to mind!)

Henry VIII's abolition of the monasteries was the last straw. Without the monks' expertise and the land re-distributed, (mostly to Henry's cronies who supported his rather abysmal attempts to control France – oh how history repeats itself!), the wine industry collapsed. Besides, soldiers and wool farmers were thirsty lads. They wanted beer, so ale and mead became the alcoholic drinks of the day and remained so right up to modern times.

In the second half of the 20thC winemaking returned to Hampshire. Britain was recovering from WW2. The rationing programme had just been lifted and goods previously considered unobtainable to all but the wealthy began to appear. Luxury was the name of the game and it became socially acceptable to indulge in food and drink. This encouraged wealthy landowners to plant vines and start producing wine and Hampshire led the way!

In 1951, in the small village of Hambledon, Major General Sir Guy Salisbury-Jones sat gazing across his

fields and pondered what crops to plant. Perhaps he was sipping a glass of wine when he had the inspiration to plant vines. The result was the country's first modern commercial vineyard. Just over 60 years later the UK now boasts around 600 vineyards, 50 of which are in Hampshire, ranging from the large and successful *Leckford Estate* to much smaller select vineyards such as nearby *Danebury Vineyards*.

Of course, wine tastes have changed dramatically since the 50's when the tall tapering bottles of German Hock such as *Blue Nun* and *Black Tower* began to grace the tables of most dining rooms. Our tastes have evolved since then and the vineyards with them, switching to traditional Bordeaux and Burgundy-style bottles with grape varieties such as Chardonnay and Pinot Noir leading the way.

Sparkling wine in particular is the new local focus and rightly so. The south coast of England shares the same chalky soil and latitude as the famous Champagne region and produces wines of similar style and equal, if not greater, quality. English sparkling wine has rapidly created a name for itself, at home and internationally, and Hampshire boasts top-class sparkling wine producers such as *Jenkyn Place* and the *Danebury Vineyards* both featured here. They are two of a number of vineyards producing wonderfully quaffable fizz using the traditional Méthode Champenoise. But it's not just in production that Hampshire plays a key role in the local industry. Hampshire is home to a wide array of wine merchants such as *Berry Brothers & Rudd*, the UK's oldest wine merchant. *Berry's* moved its centre of operations from central London to Basingstoke in the 60's and from its bonded warehouse ships some of the world's finest wine around the globe. The county also boasts younger, innovative wine importers like *Caviste* that specialises in unique producers, including natural wines (organic & biodynamic) from around the world and supplies many of the UK finest restaurants.

This book is about the bounty of Hampshire and the Isle of Wight. It showcases some of their many fabulous chefs and establishments dotted around the region whose talent draws food lovers from around the world. So it goes without saying that where there's excellent food, there's always excellent wine!

Hampshire beer

Peter Gentilli

Beer is without doubt the traditional, alcoholic drink of England. We've been guzzling the stuff for centuries; long before the Romans got us into wine. In fact, archaeologists have confirmed that we've been brewing the stuff in one shape or form since prehistoric times. Throughout history, from the Romans up to the industrial revolution, beer consumption has been on the up.

In the early 1800's, we were even incentivised to brew beer and sell it to wean people off the dreaded 'gin epidemic' that was costing lives. The beer continued to flow freely right up until WW1 when there was a substantial decline in consumption thanks to a number of new laws designed to reduce public drunkenness. Pubs were forced to reduce their opening times to no more than six hours a day, duty on beer was increased hugely and alcohol levels were restricted. It even became illegal to buy 'a round' in order to discourage over indulgence!

Post-WW1 the picture began to get much rosier for beer lovers and pubs became a vital morale-booster during WW2. Then, in the 1960's, restrictions on home-brewed beer were lifted and microbreweries began to pop up around the nation. It was great news for Hampshire hop growers and of course, the county's beer drinkers.

Hampshire has historically been one of Britain's key hop growing counties. Until the 1960's they were extensively grown from Alton to Southampton and Portsmouth and the demand to feed a growing industry was such that people would flock from as far as London to enjoy the country air and extra earnings a 'hop picking holiday' provided. But there was a huge cloud gathering on the horizon for Hampshire's traditional breweries. While mechanised picking saw a potential increase in hop production, the lager revolution had begun. The county's large lager breweries went from strength-to-strength but others struggled because the revolution didn't stop with lager consumption. Real ale producers also found a treacherous and well-funded enemy in keg bitter and the spectre of such household names as *Watney's Red Barrel*, *Whitbread Tankard* loomed large and *Double Diamond* certainly didn't work wonders for the traditional brewers and their die-hard real ale customers.

But the 1970's saw the tide turn with the *Campaign for Real Ale,* now famously known by all and revered as, *CAMRA.* Traditionalists threw their efforts into saving the traditional British pint, *CAMRA* thrived and as a result, Hampshire now boasts a plethora of breweries both large and small producing wonderful ale.

Hampshire was not to be left behind in the real ale revival. There have been some singular heroes in both the recent past and working today that have played a hand in shaping our modern breweries, hostelries and drink. One man who deserves credit is Peter Austen, who led the charge in 1978 brewing his first pint at the *Ringwood Brewery* in the New Forest. Thirty years later, now owned by brewing giant, *Marston's,* the *Ringwood Brewery's* success is legendary as a model of good brewing and excellent beer.

More recently, there has been a trend to go 'back to tradition.' Popular microbreweries abound and all inspired by the love of a good pint. Many of these artisans craft interesting, characterful beers but have not come from a brewing background. They have honed their skills through self-interest.

Kevin Robinson is one of these adventurous men. He started because he wanted to make beer that tasted interesting. *Vibrant Forest Brewery* (p344-345) was born in his garage near Lymington while Kevin was still working in IT. He's moved out of the garage now but he's still making very interesting beers.

Kevin's not alone, Phil Robins, founder of the *Longdog Brewery,* in Basingstoke came from a background in telecoms. Whereas Graham Trott, founder of the *Triple fff Brewery* in Alton, was a cabinetmaker by trade.

Meanwhile *Upham Brewery (these pages),* under the stewardship of David Butcher and Chris Phillips, offers the other side of the coin with a progressive business plan for growth backed by strong investment. They too started small and through a process of trial and error developed beers that were consistent and a perfect pint every time. Through careful planning they are in the process of recreating family-style pubs. Tied houses run by great partners. They credit their partners for the quality that they keep and serve the beer. After all they are responsible for the customer.

The Hampshire branch of *CAMRA* currently has 25 registered breweries and undoubtedly there are more on the way and all power to their elbows.

The Hampshire pint is in very safe hands!

Garnishes & extras

The Plough

Tartar sauce
1 large shallot, finely diced
1 tbsp Lilliput capers
4 to 5 gherkins, finely diced
1 tbsp fresh dill, parsley, tarragon, finely chopped
juice of ½ lemon

Skin and trim the other half of the trout fillet then dice into very fine cubes. Mix the rest of the ingredients in a bowl then stir in the trout. Season to taste with salt and lemon juice and serve immediately.

Avocado purée
2 avocados, peeled & stone removed (Hass preferred)
1 tbsp crème fraiche
juice of 1 lemon

Cream all ingredients until smooth. Season to taste. Spoon into a piping bag and chill until ready to serve.

Cucumber ribbons
½ cucumber, peeled & seeds removed
75 ml Moscatel vinegar
50 ml white wine vinegar
50 g sugar
½ tsp mustard seeds
2 cloves
1 star anise
½ cinnamon stick

Using a vegetable peeler, slice the cucumber to make fine ribbons then cut them into 1x4 cm pieces then make pickling liquor by boiling together the rest of the ingredients then cool. Just before serving soak the cucumber ribbons for 5 minutes maximum. Place on kitchen paper to drain.

The Little Gloster

Scandinavian rye bread
175 ml whole milk
175 ml water
2 tbsp brown sugar
1 sachet instant yeast
250 g rye flour
200 g strong white flour, plus extra for dusting
1 tbsp sea salt
2 tsp caraway seeds
a splash of sunflower oil for greasing

Butter
600 ml whipping cream, warmed to room temperature
ice
a pinch of salt

For the butter, fill a jar half way with cream, seal tightly and shake vigorously for 10 to 15 minutes. (It's a good workout.) Release the contents into a bowl and reserve the buttermilk for further baking if you like. Mash the butter with a fork to release excess whey. Drop the butter into ice water and knead it to release the final buttermilk. Continue to rinse in fresh ice water until the water runs clear. Mash in salt or other seasoning to taste, roll in cling film and refrigerate until ready to use.

For the rye bread, pour the milk, water and sugar in a saucepan and heat gently, stirring constantly until the liquid is lukewarm and the sugar has dissolved. Remove the pan from the heat and pour the mixture into a bowl. Stir in the yeast and leave for 10 minutes until froth forms on the surface. Sift together the flours and caraway and make a well in the centre then pour the warm yeast mixture in and mix with a wooden spoon to pull the dough together. Turn the dough out onto a floured surface and knead for 10 minutes until it is smooth and elastic. (Don't cheat on the time and put your heart into it!)

Put the dough in a large, lightly oiled bowl and cover loosely with oiled cling film. Leave to rise in a warm place for 1½ hours until doubled in size. Knock the dough back on a floured surface and knead for another minute.

Preheat the oven to 180°C. Shape the dough into a fat oval or round loaf, pulling the dough from the top and sides and tucking it underneath to make a neat shape. Place the loaf on a baking tray lined with parchment and score the surface 4 times with a sharp knife. Cover it loosely with the oiled cling film and leave to prove for a further 40 to 50 minutes until it has doubled in size once more. Bake the loaf in the centre of the oven for 40 minutes until it is well risen and the base sounds hollow when tapped sharply. Cool for at least 20 minutes before serving.

TerraVina

Braised red cabbage
1 red cabbage, finely sliced
250 ml red wine
150 ml red wine vinegar
200 g muscavado sugar
knob of butter

In a heavy-based saucepan sweat the cabbage in the butter until just soft. Add the red wine and reduce by ²/₃ until dark and rich, add the vinegar and reduce again by ²/₃ then add the sugar and cook down to a nice sticky glaze.

Parsnip purée
3 parsnips, peeled
200 ml whole milk
2 knobs of butter

In a heavy-based saucepan sweat the parsnips in butter without colour until they start to soften then add the milk and boil until soft all the way through. Place in a blender and blend until very smooth. Season to taste and serve warm.

Parsnip crisps
2 parsnips, peeled & very finely sliced (use a mandolin)
1½ pomace oil for frying

Preheat a deep fryer to 140°C and fry the parsnip slices until lightly golden brown and crisp. Allow to drain on kitchen roll and season to taste.

Pain d'epices
125 g strong flour
125 g plain flour
20 g baking powder
50 g caster sugar
1 tsp each, ground cinnamon, nutmeg & star anise
30 g candied citrus peel
1 vanilla pod, seeds only
zest of 1 lemon
zest of 1 orange
250 g honey
125 ml milk
6 medium eggs

Preheat oven to 150°C and butter and flour a 1 kg loaf tin. Sift together the dry ingredients then stir in the citrus peel, vanilla seeds and zest. Using a mixer with a paddle attachment add the honey, milk and eggs and mix for 5 minutes. Turn onto a floured surface and knead for another 5 minutes until smooth and elastic. Bake for 40 minutes until a bamboo skewer comes out clean. Allow to cool in the tin for 10 minutes then remove to finish cooling on a wire rack.

Preheat oven to 110°C and place 1 cm slices on the oven rack and leave to dry for about 2 hours. Don't allow to brown. Break into pieces and whizz in a blender to a very fine crumb. Store in an airtight container.

Vinaigrette
100 ml sherry vinegar
300 ml olive oil
1 banana shallot, chopped
salt & pepper

Whisk all together.

The Globe

Flowerpot brioche Serves 4
Equipment: 6" red clay flower pots

500 g granary, strong, whole meal or white bread flour
7 g sachet fast-action dried yeast

1 tsp salt

300 ml warm water

2 tbsp olive oil, plus extra for the flowerpots

1 tbsp clear honey

a splash of olive oil

1 tbsp chopped rosemary, thyme, oregano, chives or basil

Tip the flour, yeast and salt into a large bowl. Pour in the warm water, the olive oil and honey. Mix with a wooden spoon until the mixture clumps together, then tip out onto a floured work surface. Knead the dough for 10 minutes until smooth and elastic. Continue to dust the surface as you work the dough.

Brush the flowerpots with oil and line the sides with baking parchment. Divide the dough into 6 pieces and shape into smooth balls. Place one ball of dough into each flowerpot and cover with lightly oiled cling film. Leave in a warm place for 1 hour.

Preheat oven oven to 200°C. When the dough has doubled in size, remove the cling film and lightly brush with a oil, sprinkle with herbs and a pinch of salt. Place the pots on a baking tray in the oven and bake for about 20 minutes until risen and golden. Allow the pots to cool before serving.

Lainston House

Bacon vinaigrette

460 g pancetta, rind on, trimmed & diced

350 ml vegetable oil

3 sprigs of thyme

3 garlic cloves, peeled & whole

100 ml chardonnay vinegar

In a saucepan cook the pancetta in a little oil until golden, add the garlic and thyme and sweat for 3 minutes then add the oil, bring to a simmer and set aside to infuse for 4 hours. Deglaze the pan with the vinegar and add this to the oil. Pass through a chinois and season to taste. Store in a bottle at room temperature.

Bacon jus

250 g smoked streaky bacon

1 onion, peeled & finely diced

1 carrot, peeled, halved & cut into
    2 cm pieces

½ garlic head

10 white peppercorns

10 black peppercorns

5 juniper berries

150 g Cabernet Sauvignon vinegar

250 ml Madeira

1 litre lamb stock

Roast the bacon until quite dark then add the vegetables and continue to roast until they are golden. Deglaze the pan with vinegar until it is completely evaporated then add the Madeira and reduce to a glaze. Add the stock and spices and simmer for 15 minutes, pass through a chinois and reduce to a rich sauce consistency.

Apple & vanilla purée

400 g Granny Smith apples, peeled & finely sliced

20 g sugar

a pinch of salt

¼ vanilla pod

Place all the ingredients in a vacuum bag and cook in a steamer for 45 minutes. Transfer to a bowl, remove the vanilla and blitz with a hand blender until very smooth. Pass through a fine sieve and check seasoning adding a bit of sugar if too tart or salt if sweet. Place into a squeeze bottle until ready to use.

Parsley purée

100 g curly parsley, leaves only

ice

salt & pepper

1 tsp instant food thickener (see page 355)

Boil the parsley in salted boiling water for 3 minutes in a large pan of water. Strain and without refreshing, blitz in a food processor for 3 minutes with the ice until smooth. Season to taste then add the instant food thickener to gain a nice consistency and place in a squeeze bottle until ready to use.

Hummus purée

600 g tinned chickpeas (drained weight)

7 g salt

10 g garlic

50 g olive oil

35 g lemon juice

a few splashes of water

Blitz all the ingredients together in a food processor until smooth adding small amounts of water until you reach a thick creamy consistency then pass through a fine sieve, season to taste. Spoon into a piping bag and set aside until ready to use.

Tomatoes & lemon verbena

30 vine cherry tomatoes

2 sprigs of lemon verbena

200 ml olive oil

50 ml sherry vinegar

20 g sugar

10 g honey

5 g salt

Blanch for 5 seconds until the skins just begin to blister then peel and vacpac with the rest of the ingredients and marinate in the refrigerator for 24 hours. If using a conventional ziplock bag, double the marinating time. Before serving, heat in a little of the liquor.

Mint & spinach emulsion

50 g garden mint

200 g baby spinach

ice

For the mint and spinach emulsion, blanch the mint in salted boiling water for one and a half minutes, refresh in ice, squeeze out and place into a thermomix jug. Blanch the spinach for ten seconds in salted boiling water, refresh in ice and squeeze out moisture. Place in the jug with the mint. Blitz with enough water to make a smooth wet purée, season with a bit of salt and pour into a squeeze bottle.

Lemon cake

140 g caster sugar

250 g butter

4 eggs

125 g soft flour

125 g ground almonds

5 g baking powder

1 vanilla pod, split & seeds removed

60 ml milk

zest of 4 lemons

a pinch of salt

Preheat oven to 180°C. Cream the butter, sugar and vanilla seeds in a bowl until light and creamy then gradually add the eggs. Sift together the flour and baking powder then using a metal spoon fold the dry into the wet. Pour into a 22 cm greaseproof tin and bake for twelve minutes then turn down the oven to 140°C for a further 50 minutes until the cake is just cooked and a toothpick comes out clean.

Basil chocolate

This component is in the 'too difficult box'. The author's recommendation is to go to Lainston House and enjoy Olly's creation.

1 kg white chocolate

100 ml basil oil

Chill a vacpac machine for one hour in the freeze. Melt the chocolate to 50°C. Add the basil oil and while still warm add to an espuma canister. Charge with one gas capsule and squirt into a plastic container. Vacpac until the mix rises in the container then turn the machine off before the pressure is released. Leave to set then turn the machine back on and release the pressure. The chocolate should be fully aerated.

Lemon curd

1 litre lemon juice

600 g egg yolks

15 eggs

750 g sugar

600 g butter

75 g cornflour

Boil together the lemon and butter. In a bowl, mix the sugar and cornflour. Place the egg yolks in a separate bowl, whisk in the lemon mixture then pour the mixture back into the pan and cook until it thickens and pour into a squeeze bottle.

Exclusive Chefs Academy

Butter sauce

100 ml white wine

small shallot, finely chopped

3 tbsp double cream

200 g butter, cut into 2.5 cm cubes

salt & pepper

To make the butter sauce, place the white wine and chopped shallots in a pan over medium heat. When the wine has reduced to almost nothing add the cream and reduce again until it starts to become sticky. Keeping the pan over the heat start adding the diced butter whisking constantly to form a smooth sauce. Season to taste and pass through the fine sieve and keep warm until ready to serve. Do not let it get cold or it will split.

Fondant potatoes

4 potatoes (King Edward)

1 garlic clove, whole

a sprig of thyme

Preheat oven to 170°C. Peel the potatoes and cut them to the size you want the fondant to be with a pastry cutter. Trim ideally 6 to 7 cm in diameter and 2 cm thick. Put a frying pan on the heat, add a little oil and fry each side for 3 to 4 minutes until lightly coloured. Add the garlic, thyme sprig and stock until the bottom of the fondant is just covered, and pop in the oven for 10 minutes until cooked.

Carrot purée

250 g carrots, chopped (home grown, soil-covered ones if possible)

12 g butter

100 ml milk (less if you prefer a thicker purée)

25 ml double cream

salt & pepper

Melt the butter in a pan and add the carrots. Cover the pan and cook slowly for 10 minutes. Add the milk and cream and bring to a simmer until the carrots are very soft then strain the carrots reserving the liquid. Purée with a hand blender adding some milk and cream back to the mixture until silky. Season with pepper and just a tiny pinch of salt.

Red onion marmalade

2 kg red onions, thinly sliced

4 garlic cloves, thinly sliced

140 g butter

4 tbsp olive oil

140 g golden caster sugar

1 tbsp fresh thyme

a pinch of chilli flakes

750 ml (1 bottle) good red wine

350 ml red wine vinegar

200 ml port

Melt the butter and oil in a large, heavy-based saucepan over a high heat. Add the onions and garlic and cook without colour. Sprinkle over the sugar, thyme and check seasoning. Cook over low heat uncovered for 40 to 50 minutes, stirring occasionally until the onions are very soft and sticky and starting to caramelise so they break with a wooden spoon.

Pour in the wine, vinegar and port and simmer uncovered for 30 minutes, stirring occasionally until the onions are a deep rich colour and the liquid has reduced by $^2/_3$. It's done when drawing a spoon across the bottom of the pan clears a path that fills rapidly with syrupy juice. Leave to cool in the pan then scoop into sterilised jars and seal. Can be used immediately, but keeps in the fridge for up to 3 months.

Watercress purée

140 g watercress leaves, washed & roughly chopped

a few ice cubes

2 tbsp water

salt & freshly ground black pepper

Bring a saucepan of salted water up to a rolling boil, add the watercress, cover and return to the boil. Drain the watercress and refresh under cold water. Blend the drained watercress in a food processor with 3 to 4 ice cubes and just enough water to make a smooth purée. Season to taste.

Pebble Beach

Lobster butter
shells, legs and creamy parts of a cooked lobster
125 g butter

Blitz the lobster shells in a food processor and transfer to a small saucepan. Add the butter and heat.

When butter is toasted slightly pass through a fine chinois. The butter can be used immediately in sauces or chilled and whipped.

Glossary

Chef's equipment

Dariole moulds: dariole is a French word that refers to a small, cylindrical mould. They are typically made from aluminium as this offers the best overall distribution of heat and used for both sweet and savoury dishes.

Gastrotrays: are stackable stainless steel trays. They are made in standard sizes:
GN2/1: 650 × 530 mm
GN1/1: 530 × 325 mm
GN2/3: 354 × 325 mm
GN2/4: 163 × 325 mm
GN1/2: 325 × 265 mm
GN1/3: 325 × 176 mm
GN1/4: 265 × 163 mm
GN1/ : 176 × 162 mm
GN1/9: 108 × 176 mm

Griddle screens: are a heavy-duty abrasive scouring pad originally designed to clean difficult surfaces. Chefs often use them in place of a vegetable peeler to scour away the outer skin of vegetables such as carrots, giving them a consistent and lightly textures surface.

Mandolin or Japanese mandolin: started out as an efficient radish slicer. It's a plane with a sharp blade that slices vegetables from thin to micro-thin depending on the grade of the plane.

Micro-plane graters: are used for the ultra-fine grating of various food items, such as nutmeg, hard cheese and citrus zest.

Mouli: is a traditional French, hand-operated utensil used to grate small quantities of food. It has a metal drum with holes that grate the food and a handle for turning the drum.

Pacojet: 'pacotising' is a 'micro-puree' for fresh, deep-frozen foods that instantly creates ultra-light mousses, naturally fresh ice creams and sorbets, aromatic soups, sauces or fillings without thawing. Intensive flavours, natural colours and vital nutrients are captured in individual, ready-to-serve portions.

Silpat mat: is the brand name of a silicone mat used in baking and in the production of candy to provide a non-stick surface without the use of fat or greaseproof paper.

Smokers:
Cold smoking: is typically used as a flavor enhancer. The item is hung then cold smoked for just long enough to infuse flavour. Smokehouse temperatures for cold smoking are typically done between 20 to 30°C.
Hot smoking: exposes foods to smoke and heat in a controlled environment. Like cold smoking, the item is hung first, then smoked. Although foods that have been hot smoked are often reheated or cooked, they are typically safe to eat without further cooking. Hot smoking occurs within the range of 52 to 80°C.

Sterlising jars: Jars should be made from glass and free of any chips or cracks. Preserving or canning jars are topped with a glass, plastic or metal lid, which has a rubber seal. Two-piece lids are best for canning, as they vacuum-seal when processed. To sterilise, wash jars, lids and a pair of tongs with hot, soapy water then boil the jars and lids in a large saucepan, covered with water for 15 minutes. Use tongs when handling the sterilised jars and lids. As a rule, hot preserves go into hot jars and cold preserves go into cold jars. All items used in the process of making jams, jellies and preserves must be clean. This includes any towels used, and especially your hands.

Terrine mould: is a fairly deep dish with straight sides, grips or handles, and a tightly fitting lid that rests on an inner lip. Terrines are manufactured in a wide range of sizes; they can be made of glazed earthenware (with the lid sometimes shaped like an animal) or of porcelain, ovenproof glass or even enameled cast iron. The food cooked or served in such a container is also known as a terrine.

Thermometers:
Meat thermometer: is used to accurately measure the internal temperature of meat and the degree of 'doneness' that correlates closely with the temperature will cooking.

Sugar (or candy) thermometer: measures the temperature at the stage of cooking a sugar solution. It is also used for accuracy in deep frying.

Thermomix: is a highly diverse tool that can control precise temperatures, constant movement, even distribution and heat for extremely efficient cooking. Time, temperature, speed, and weight are the four controllable functions. Though it sits on the worktop, it costs about the same or more than most domestic ovens.

Specialist ingredients

Agar agar: is a natural vegetable gelatine alternative. It is used to make jellies, puddings and custards.

Burrata: is a traditional cheese from the Puglia region of Southern Italy consisting of a solid mozzarella shell and soft combination of mozzarella, rennet and cream in the centre.

Court bouillon: traditionally, court bouillon is water, salt, white wine, vegetable aromatics (mirpoix of carrot, onion and celery) seasoned with bouquet garni and black pepper. It lacks the acids of complex stocks and required little cooking time.

Instant food thickener: was originally designed to ease digestion for individuals with digestive disorders. It can be added to both hot and cold foods or liquids to obtain any level of consistency.

Isomalt: is a sugar substitute that does not crystalise in the same way that sucrose-based sugars do. Understanding the full properties of this ingredient is advised.

Kappa carrageenan: is available online or from chef's supply shops. It creates a firm gel with a brittle texture that is suitable for both hot and cold preparations and works particularly well with dairy. Its a gelling agent extracted from a type of red seaweed that grows off the Irish coast and has been used to make a traditional Irish pudding for centuries and is now used by some of the world's top chefs as an alternative to gelatine and pectin. It is vegetarian and vegan friendly.

Kiffir: is an ancient technique of culturing milk at room temperature. The 'grains' must be acquired from someone who is making kiffir. To make lardo, a trimmed piece of lard is placed immediately in marble basins that have been rubbed with garlic.

Kombu: an edible kelp widely used in East Asian cooking.

Lardo di Colonnata: is meat cured in salt, black pepper, rosemary, and garlic between layers of lard. Seasoning varies by producer. Aging occurs naturally in warm caves over a minimum of 6 month period, during which the amount of liquid released by the salt-covered lard is measured regularly. It is an extremely effective curing and aging practice because it does not require any additives or preservatives.

Maldon salt: flaked sea salt from east of England. When seasoning raw meats and fish use course salt as fine table salt will leech into the meat.

Maltodextrin: is used as a white powdered food additive. It is made primarily from corn starch in North America and wheat starch in Europe. It is virtually flavourless and commonly used for making soft drinks and beer. It can also be found as an ingredient in a variety of other processed foods.

Pomace: is olive oil extracted from pulp after the first press. It is used as a neutral oil in the same way rapeseed and sunflower oil are used.

Simple syrup: is a mixture of 50% water and 50% sugar boiled until the sugar is completely dissolved and slightly thickened.

Sorbet syrup: is the same as simple syrup but typically uses 65% sugar and 35% water.

Verjus: is made from unripe grapes and is a classic French alternative to vinegar.

Whey: is the liquid remaining after milk has been curdled and strained as in the case of making cheese or butter. Sweet whey comes from rennet-based processes such as making hard cheese and sour whey is the by-product of making products such as cottage cheese or set yoghurt.

Xanthan gum: is an additive commonly used as a thickening agent and stabiliser to prevent dressings and sauces from splitting. It is commonly made by fermenting lactose in whey.

Yoghurt powder: is used in a variety of yogurt-based foods. It has a longer shelf life than fresh yogurt, with good solubility. It can be mixed in both hot and cold liquids, and, in both cases, it enhances the texture and flavor of the food products. It also has binding properties that makes it an appropriate replacement for starches, stabilisers and gums.

The basics

Blood temperature: is 37°C or the temperature of the body.

Cleaning and shelling scallops: turn the shell so the dark side faces upward. Insert a sharp knife between the top and bottom halves and pry open. Find where the muscle meets the top half of the shell and separate the two and discard the top half of the shell. Clean the inside of the scallop shell of everything but the white muscle by starting at the hinge and swiping along the muscle. Detach the muscle from the shell, rinse under cold water gently rubbing to remove all impurities, trim and pat dry.

Cook without colour: sauté until softened but not browning.

Crème Anglaise for ice cream:
150 ml milk
4 egg yolks
1 vanilla pod, seeds scraped
50 g caster sugar

Place the milk, vanilla seeds and pod in a saucepan and bring just to the boil, then simmer for 5 minutes. In a bowl over a bain marie, whisk together the egg yolks and sugar. Transfer the yolk mixture to a clean bowl. Pass the hot milk through a fine sieve then add the yolk mixture in a steady stream, whisking constantly until the mixture thickens into a crème Anglaise. This can be used as is for a topping or the basis for ice cream.

French trim: used for refined rib cuts, the bones are exposed by cutting off the fat and meat covering them. Typically, three inches of bone beyond the main muscle (the ribeye) are left on the rack, with the top two inches exposed.

Filleting mackerel & sardines: remove the head by prying it gently back and with a small sharp knife slice the length of its underside and remove the innards. Gently pry open the sardine's cavity to butterfly the fish. Run your fingers along the fish's backbone to loosen it from the meat. Starting from the top to the tail, gently lift out the backbone and ribs and remove any stray bones. The tail should pull off with the bones.

Italian meringue: is made by beating egg whites to soft peaks then slowly streaming in boiling sugar and beating the mixture until it is thick and glossy. A basic meringue, also known as a French meringue, is made by beating granulated sugar into egg whites until the mixture reaches soft peaks. The hot sugar syrup used to make Italian meringue cooks the egg whites as it is incorporated. This means that you don't need to cook or bake the meringue before using it. It also means that the meringue is going to be a lot more stable and less likely to deflate or weep.

Pane: to pass parcels of food through seasoned flour, beaten egg and breadcrumbs.

Pastry
yield: 2, 200 g pastry shells
300 g unsalted butter
110 g icing sugar, sifted
2 eggs at room temperature
500 g plain flour, plus extra for dusting

In a large bowl beat together the butter and sugar until light and fluffy. Beat in the eggs one at a time until smooth. Tip in the flour and mix to a smooth paste that comes away cleanly from the side of the bowl. Turn the dough out onto a lightly floured surface and form into a ball. Wrap in cling film and refrigerate for at least 2 hours.

Ribbon stage: The purpose of reaching this stage in beating is both to ensure that enough air has been incorporated into the mixture, and to ensure that the sugar is thoroughly dissolved in the egg yolk so that the egg mixture, when heated, won't become granular.

Rocher: a single, perfect scoop done with one hand

Short pastry:
125 g plain flour
a pinch of salt
55 g butter, cubed
2 tbsp cold water

Put the flour and salt in a large bowl and add the cubes of butter. Use your fingertips to rub the butter into the flour until you have a mixture that resembles coarse breadcrumbs with no large lumps of butter remaining. Try to work quickly so that it does not become greasy. Using a knife, stir in just enough of the cold water to bind the dough together. Wrap the dough in cling film and chill for 10 minutes before using.

Vegetable stock
120 g leeks
60 g carrots
60 g celery
1 g coriander seeds
5 g garlic
4 g thyme
5 g curly parsley
45 ml white wine
125 g plum tomatoes
1 litre water
5 g salt
15 ml olive oil

Peel all the vegetables and cut into a 1 cm dice. Heat the olive oil in a thick-bottomed pan, add the carrots and leeks and cook very slowly for one hour, until caramelised. Add the celery and cook for another 30 minutes. Crush the coriander seeds using a pestle and mortar and add to the vegetables with the garlic, thyme, parsley and wine and boil for 30 seconds. Add the chopped plum tomatoes and continue to cook slowly for a further 30 minutes. Add water and salt, and simmer for a further 45 minutes, skimming frequently and strain through a fine sieve.

Vinaigrette:
½ litre olive oil
1 tbsp dry mustard
splash of balsamic vinegar
1 garlic clove, crushed
1 shallot, finely chopped
1/4 cup fresh herbs
1 egg yolk
salt & pepper

Conversion table

Liquid measures		Solid measures		Linear measures	
15ml	½ fl oz	5g	⅛ oz	3mm	⅛ inch
20ml	¾ fl oz	10g	¼ oz	5mm	¼ inch
25ml	1 fl oz	15g	½ oz	1cm	½ inch
35ml	1¼ fl oz	20g	¾ oz	2cm	¾ inch
40ml	1½ fl oz	25g	1 oz	2.5cm	1 inch
50ml	2 fl oz	40g	1½ oz	3cm	1⅛ inch
60ml	2¼ fl oz	50g	2 oz	4cm	1½ inch
65ml	2½ fl oz	65g	2 ½ oz	4.5cm	1¼ inch
85ml	3 fl oz	75g	3 oz	5cm	2 inches
100ml	3½ fl oz	90g	3½ oz	6cm	2½ inches
120ml	4 fl oz	100g	4 oz (¼ lb)	7.5cm	3 inches
150ml	5 fl oz (¼ pint)	120g	4½ oz	9cm	3½ inches
175ml	6 fl oz	135g	4¾ oz	10cm	4 inches
200ml	7 fl oz	150g	5 oz	13cm	5 inches
250ml	8 fl oz	165g	5½ oz	15cm	6 inches
275ml	9 fl oz	175g	6 oz	18cm	7 inches
300ml	10 fl oz (½ pint)	185g	6½ oz	20cm	8 inches
325ml	11 fl oz	200g	7 oz	23cm	9 inches
350ml	12 fl oz	215g	7½ oz	25cm	10 inches
375ml	13 fl oz	225g	8 oz (½ lb)	28cm	11 inches
400ml	14 fl oz	250g	9 oz	30cm	12 inches (1 ft)
450ml	15 fl oz (¾ pint)	275g	10 oz		
475ml	16 fl oz	300g	11 oz		
500ml	17 fl oz	350g	12 oz (¾ lb)		
550ml	18 fl oz	375g	13 oz		
575ml	19 fl oz	400g	14 oz		
600ml	20 fl oz (1 pint)	425g	15 oz		
750ml	1¼ pints	450g	16 oz (1 lb)		
900ml	1½ pints	550g	1¼ lb		
1 ltr	1¾ pints	750g	1½ lb		
1.2 ltr	2 pints	1kg	2¼ lb		
1.25 ltr	2¼ pints	1.25kg	2½ lb		
1.5 ltr	2½ pints	1.5kg	3½ lb		
1.6 ltr	2¾ pints	1.75kg	4 lb		
1.75 ltr	3 pints	2kg	4½ lb		
2 ltr	3½ pints	2.25 g	5 lb		

Liquid measures

2.25 ltr	4 pints
2.5 ltr	4½ pints
2.75 ltr	5 pints
3.4 ltr	6 pints
3.9 ltr	7 pints
4.5 ltr	8 pints
5 ltr	9 pints

Solid measures

2.5 kg	5½ lb
2.75 kg	6 lb
3 kg	7 lb
3.5 kg	8 lb
4 kg	9 lb
4.5 kg	10 lb
5 kg	11 lb
5.5 kg	12 lb

Oven temperatures

Gas	C	C fan	F	Oven Temp
¼	110	90	225	very cool
½	120	100	250	very cool
1	140	120	275	cool or slow
2	150	130	300	cool or slow
3	160	140	325	warm
4	180	160	350	moderate
5	190	170	375	medium hot
6	200	180	400	fairly hot
7	220	200	425	hot
8	230	210	450	very hot
9	240	220	275	very hot

Index

Index